‖‖‖ ‖‖ ‖‖‖‖‖‖‖‖‖‖‖‖‖‖‖‖‖ ‖‖ ‖‖‖
✔ KT-198-610

Television, Ethnicity and Cultural Change

The Sou··· ··st Essex
Colle·· ··· ·· ·········· ··ıe
Carnarv·· ·· ···· ·· ········ ··
Tel: Soutl·eno (0·· ·· 220400 ·ax···· ·· ····

Fusing audience research and ethnography, this book highlights the ways in which cultural identities are being formed and transformed through the interplay of local and global communications. It explores how television is implicated in the emergence of 'new ethnicities' and broader patterns of cultural change among families in Southall, west London – a major centre of the Indian diaspora.

Based upon in-depth fieldwork, this study analyses how young Punjabi Londoners negotiate their identities in everyday 'TV talk'. It examines their reception of a wide range of TV and video programmes and films – including news about the 1991 Gulf War, ads for global products, *Neighbours* and the 'sacred soap' the *Mahabharata*. As a form of self-narration, their TV talk shows how identities are constituted and deployed strategically in local culture.

The book vividly portrays young people both reaffirming and challenging the cultural traditions of their parents, and expressing their aspirations towards cultural change through their recreative reception of television. It contributes rich and much needed empirical data to contemporary debates about globalization, culture and identity.

Marie Gillespie lectures at the centre for Journalism and Mass Communications Studies, University of Wales, Cardiff. For over a decade she taught and carried out ethnographic research in Southall. She has published several articles in the field of media and cultural studies.

30130503954474

CIR
UNIV
STL
791.23/45089
GIL

Comedia
Series editor: David Morley

Television, Ethnicity and Cultural Change

Marie Gillespie

A Comedia book
published by Routledge
London and New York

E0000487538 9 001

First published 1995
by Routledge
11 New Fetter Lane, London EC4P 4EE

Simultaneously published in the USA and Canada
by Routledge
29 West 35th Street, New York, NY 10001

© 1995 Marie Gillespie

Typeset in Times Ten by Florencetype Ltd, Stoodleigh, Devon
Printed and bound in Great Britain by
Clays Ltd, St Ives PLC

All rights reserved. No part of this book may be reprinted or
reproduced or utilised in any form or by any electronic, mechanical,
or other means, now known or hereafter invented, including
photocopying and recording, or in any information storage or
retrieval system, without permission in writing from the publishers.

British Library Cataloguing in Publication Data
Gillespie, Marie
    Television, Ethnicity and Cultural Change (Comedia Series)
    I. Title   II. Series
    302.2345089

Library of Congress Cataloguing in Publication Data
Gillespie, Marie
    Television, Ethnicity and Cultural Change / Marie Gillespie.
    p.   cm. – (Comedia)
    'A Comedia book.'
    Includes bibliographical references and index.
    1. Television broadcasting – Great Britain.
    2. Minority television viewers – Great Britain.
    3. East Indians – Great Britain – Social life and customs.
     I. Title.   II. Series.
    PN 1992.3.G7G46   1994
    302.23'0941 – dc20   94-22627

ISBN 0–415–09674–X (hbk)
      0–415–09675–8 (pbk)

To
my Mother and Father,
Tom,
Margaret and Rosa

Contents

Figures

Acknowledgements

This book could not have been written, nor my fieldwork carried out, without the generous help and support of many people. First and foremost I thank all the young people in Southall who participated in this study, for their willingness to share their thoughts and experiences and for all that they have taught me. The hospitality, kindness and friendship which they and their families have shown me is much appreciated. It would be impossible to mention all who contributed to this study and all those whom I grew to respect and love; I have many precious memories of my years in Southall and many dear friendships remain. But I would like to thank the Dhani family especially, who took me into their home and gave me such a warm welcome, and continue to treat me like a member of the family.

It was my good fortune that my fieldwork in Southall coincided with that of Dr Gerhard Baumann, to whom I owe very special thanks as both friend and fellow ethnographer. His intellectual inspiration, encouraging advice and unfailing support guided me throughout the trials and tribulations of fieldwork. My fondest thanks to him for everything.

This book is based upon research carried out in the Department of Human Sciences at Brunel University. My supervisor, Professor Roger Silverstone, devoted much time to helping me clarify my ideas and I greatly value his assistance and encouragement. Professor Adam Kuper, Dr Ann Phoenix and Dr Eric Hirsch made very helpful comments on early drafts of my work. My external examiner, Dr Graham Murdock, provided excellent feedback on my thesis.

Kindest thanks are due to Dr David Morley, who encouraged me to develop my research in the first place. His work on TV audiences has been a formative influence on my own, and his editorial advice on turning the thesis into this book has been of immense value. I am also grateful to my tutors and later friends and colleagues on the MA in Film and TV Studies at the University of London Institute of Education – especially Dr David Buckingham, Philip Drummond and Bob Ferguson – for their continued support, encouragement and guidance.

I am indebted to all those who assisted with the Southall Youth Survey, especially Mozzi Hajian, without whom we would never have managed to analyse the returns. His technical advice and assistance, and the many hours he put into helping us, are warmly appreciated. I have benefited greatly from the advice of Dr Eleanor Nesbitt and Dr Darshan Tatla, of the Punjab Research Group, who have generously shared their knowledge of Punjabi language and culture with me.

I thank my parents and brothers for standing by me through my many years as a student, for their love and support and their faith and confidence in me. Special thanks to my brother Brendan, who proofread much of my thesis.

Last but not least I thank my husband Tom Cheesman, without whom this book would probably never have been delivered before our twin daughters, Margaret and Rosa. His practical support has been invaluable; and the book has gained immeasurably from his intellectual companionship. Needless to say, the failings of the book are mine alone.

Introduction

This book is about the role of television in the formation and transformation of identity among young Punjabi Londoners. It addresses issues at the intersection of two fields of great interest in contemporary social and cultural studies, bringing them together for the first time: the cultures of migrant and diasporic communities; and the cultures of media consumption. In doing so, it uses the methods of ethnography.

Hitherto the preserve of social anthropologists, ethnography is the empirical description and analysis of cultures based on intensive and extensive fieldwork in a selected local setting. It has much to contribute to the study of both diaspora and media cultures, and thereby to key theoretical debates in social, cultural and media studies, especially those concerning ethnicity and identity in the context of recent trends towards the simultaneous 'globalisation' and 'localisation' of culture. Ethnography highlights the small-scale processes, rather than the large-scale products, of people's perceptions, thoughts and action. The ethnographer reads the world, as she reads mediated messages, through the eyes of her informants themselves; she focuses on the microprocesses of daily uses, interpretations and identifications, rather than macrohistorical logics of 'longue durée'. But ethnography can also make manifold connections between micro- and macroprocesses; between the public and private, the domestic, local, national and international spheres in contemporary societies; and between 'micro' issues of power in everyday life and 'macro', structural social features (cf. Marcus and Fisher, 1986; Morley, 1991). Ethnography greets cultural theory with empirical questions. This ethnography sets media consumption and reception, and issues of ethnicity and identity, in the context of its subjects' cultures and everyday lives.

The subjects of this study are young people of Punjabi family background, mainly in the 14–18 age group, living in Southall, west London, the largest 'Asian community' outside the Indian subcontinent. Though Southall's families are predominantly of Punjabi Sikh background, this is by no means a homogeneous 'Asian community'. Cross-cutting religious, caste, linguistic and regional differences, variations in patterns of migration and socio-economic status, as well as co-residence with smaller numbers of mainly London Caribbean and Irish families, all mean that there is no neat equation here between culture, community and geography. The youth of Southall describe themselves in various ways according to context. However, to describe them as 'Punjabi Londoners' is to frame them in terms of two significant and related, but by no means comprehensive, aspects of their identity: their cosmopolitanism, and their involvement in the particular media experiences and cultural practices of the Punjabi, or more broadly Indian, diaspora.

The experience of migrant or diasporic people is central to contemporary societies (Appadurai, 1990; Hall, 1987; Hannerz, 1990); and so too is the globalisation of capitalism, particularly as manifest in transnational TV and film industries and their attendant cultures of consumption. In focusing on both these phenomena together, this study contributes much-needed empirical evidence to theoretical debates about the nature, scale and pace of cultural change today. As members of a cultural minority in Britain, and as members too of the majority youth culture, London Punjabi teenagers in many ways constitute ideal subjects. Not only does their testimony reveal much about the local impact of global youth advertising and marketing, and other media products, both entertainment (e.g. soaps) and information (e.g. news). But they are also, as adolescents, at a crucial, interstitial point in their lives, when questions of identity are subject to particularly intense negotiation – and this allows the emergence of 'new ethnicities' (Hall, 1988) and the dynamics of cultural change to be studied with exceptional clarity and detail. These young people's identities are both formed and transformed by their location in history and politics, language and culture. But through their material and cultural consumption and production, they are also constructing new forms of identity, shaped by but at the same time reshaping the images and meanings circulated in the media and in the market.

My fieldwork was conducted in 1988–1991: a time of profound, often revolutionary, political and social change in various parts of the world. The collapse of communism in the USSR and Eastern Europe; the fall of the Berlin Wall; the release of Nelson Mandela; the massacre at Tiananmen Square; the Romanian revolution; the Gulf War of 1991; the fatwa pronounced on Salman Rushdie – these and other world-historical events form the wider backdrop of this study. They impacted upon the local world of people in Southall in varied ways. In young people's perceptions, mediated largely by TV, they heightened a sense of risk, uncertainty and global interconnectedness; they reinforced a recognition of common humanity, yet at the same time intensified an awareness of deep differences; and they emphasised the tensions between global, diasporic, national and local perceptions of 'shared identity'. In Britain at this time, a decade of Thatcher's rule as Prime Minister was coming to an end. The social and economic crisis manifest in high rates of often long-term unemployment, and in the consequences of the progressive dismantling of the public sector, was making itself felt acutely among many families in Southall.

My study focuses on the re-creative consumption of TV among Southall youth during this period. By highlighting the ways in which this locally specific youth culture is shaped by both cosmopolitan and diasporic experiences, my study sheds light upon broader issues of media, ethnicity and cultural change as we approach the year 2000. The increasing globalisation of economic, political and cultural relations is matched by a massive rise in the flow of migrants, both voluntary and involuntary, and an equally enormous rise in the flow of images, narratives and information which cut across and challenge established national and cultural boundaries and identities. Yet any tendencies towards cultural homogenisation accompanying these processes are matched by simultaneous tendencies towards the fragmentation, pluralisation and diversification of markets, cultures and peoples.

In the decades since the Second World War, the flow of migrants has been mainly towards 'the west' or 'the north': the centres of former colonial power (Balibar, 1991). Relations between global 'centre[s]' and 'margin[s]' have shifted radically (Julien and Mercer, 1988). The resulting encounters – collisions and collusions – between colonisers and colonised, between tradition and modernity, between 'the east' and 'the west', 'the south' and 'the north', have precipitated enormous social and cultural changes. In Britain in particular, established notions of 'national culture' and 'national belonging' – of what it means to be British and of who belongs – have been challenged and transformed. At the same time, in Britain and elsewhere, national cultural boundaries have also been challenged by globalising tendencies in the media, and by accompanying changes in patterns of cultural production, distribution and consumption.

CULTURAL CHANGE: BRITISH, ASIAN AND BLACK IDENTITIES

Social interaction and relations are no longer dependent on simultaneous spatial co-presence. Instantaneous communication through a variety of media fosters intense relations between 'absent others' (Giddens, 1990: 18–21). As this happens, our experiences of time and space become 'distantiated' – we experience distant events unfolding instantaneously on screen in our homes (Giddens, 1990; Williams, 1989: 13–21) – or 'compressed' – spatial and temporal differences are radically undermined (Harvey, 1989). This speeding up, or growing intensity, of time–space compression, has profound effects on social, economic and cultural processes. We have become used to a constantly accelerating pace of change (Harvey, 1989: 284). Yet the dynamics of globalisation are dialectical and unevenly experienced across time and space. McGrew cites several mutually opposed but simultaneous tendencies at play in contemporary culture: universalisation versus particularisation; homogenisation versus differentiation; integration versus fragmentation; centralisation versus decentralisation; and juxtaposition versus syncretisation (McGrew, 1992: 74–75). This last pair is of particular relevance to my study. By compressing time and space, globalisation catalyses the juxtaposition of very distinct cultural and social practices, different ways of life, which both reinforces social and cultural boundaries and creates shared cultural spaces in which ideas, values, knowledge and institutions undergo processes of 'hybridisation' (McGrew, 1992: 75; cf. Jameson, 1991; Perlmutter, 1991). But how adequate is this term? Many commentators voice a conviction that our vocabulary is ill-suited to describing the kinds of cultural change now in process (e.g. Gilroy, 1993a: 15).

Cultural change is, in a sense, a tautological term in any case. All cultures are lived and therefore always in flux. In fact all cultures are 'hybrid', 'syncretic', 'creolised' or 'impure'. Culture, by its very nature, is changing in encounters with 'others', although it is also commonly reified as shared possession (Baumann, forthcoming), as purportedly objective 'heritage' (Gilroy, 1987). None the less, ethnographic methods in particular enable us to track and identify the pace and nature of change in specific settings. But in British cultural studies, the processes of 'hybridisation' or 'syncretisation' have mainly been studied in relation to the expressive cultures of Britain's black settlers – in relation to popular music, dance, fashion and style, though also in relation to experimental film (Gilroy, 1993a, 1993b; Hall, 1988; Hebdige, 1988; Julien and Mercer, 1988; Mercer, 1988). These cultural critics have at the same time made important interventions in the growing debate about issues of 'race' and ethnicity in film and TV representations, which have become sites of contestation over what it means to be British today, over what Britishness itself means as a national or cultural identity.

While my study is indebted to these works in many respects, it differs from them not only in its methods, but also in that it examines cultures of consumption rather than expressive culture, as well as in highlighting the experience of Britain's 'Asian' settlers. British Asian youth culture, in contrast with black expressive cultures, has been for the most part silent and invisible until very recently. Writers such as Hanif Kureishi (*My Beautiful Laundrette*, *The Buddha of Suburbia*) and, notoriously, Salman Rushdie began to emerge as figures of national and international repute in the 1980s. But the presence of a broad-based Asian youth culture in Britain is only now beginning to be felt, as new forms of cultural expression in music and film make themselves heard and seen. Bhangra was just starting to join the 'mainstream' of popular music while I was conducting my fieldwork. When the Birmingham-born Sikh singer Apache Indian recently (1994) became a disc jockey on BBC Radio One, British Asian youth culture achieved a level of public, national visibility which could not have been envisaged when I was researching in Southall. The feature film *Wild West* (Channel 4 Films), shot on location in Southall, went on general release a couple of months after I left. It, too, is an index of the coming of age of the 'hybrid' culture which was in the making while I was there. *Wild West* follows the story of a country-and-western band consisting of three Muslim brothers and a couple of Sikh and Hindu friends, as they try to find fame and fortune. It portrays Southall as a derelict multi-ethnic suburb, riven by gang wars and family feuds. The hero's mother's only wish is to return home to the Punjab, while his – realised in the final shots – is to fly to the USA, in the hope that an 'Indian' country-and-western band will have more chance of getting a recording contract in the States than in Britain – a hope which the film leaves ambiguously open. With little or no attachment to either the Punjab or Southall, with 'no country but country music', America is the focus of the heroes' dreams – as indeed it is of the dreams of many young people in Southall.

The names 'Wild West' and 'Apache Indian' represent playful puns on 'Indian' and 'west' and 'east'. At once affirming their 'Indian' (sub-continental) identity and redefining it in terms of the (doubly) 'western' popular cultural stereotype of 'cowboys and indians', the protagonists of these British Asian cultural expressions are inventing names for their identity which announce them as 'familiar others'. Eastern 'Indianness' connotes, in Britain, an uncomfortable political, imperial history of strife and hatred, as well as a culture of absolute 'oriental' difference (Said, 1978). But western Indianness – American or 'red' Indianness – connotes, through the tradition of 'western' genre films and TV shows (as well as by association with country-and-western music), an altogether more benign antagonism grounded in mutual respect. Impossible, no doubt, in the USA itself, this appropriation of native American style, cross-cut with country style, by public avatars of Asian youth culture in Britain, is indicative of a bid to assimilate to the 'west' on terms at least partly of one's own making. The (eastern) Indian heritage is celebrated as a resource, only punningly renamed so that it fits into a ready-made place on the cultural map of 'western' youth. As Indians of the Wild West, these young performers remain true to the culture of their parents, and also maximise their chances of acceptance in the cosmopolitan youth culture of their non-'Indian' British peers, black and white.

This strategy of familiarising one's 'otherness' in terms of other 'others' may be viewed as typical of a 'subaltern' culture seeking a public platform in a national and transnational context (Spivak, 1988). It highlights a dual concern voiced by many of Southall's youth in particular: to achieve equality and recognition in British society without affronting their parental values. The dynamic and complex process of negotiation between these two key concerns forms the matrix of this book. Its aim is to bring into focus the way that these concerns interlock, conflict and coalesce in young people's everyday experience. Thus this study is not concerned with the few high-profile exemplars of the cultural production of British Asian youth, but rather with the many private lives of Punjabis in Southall – whose trans-cultural experiences and aspirations constitute the material out of which new pluralist, hybrid cultural forms of expression are being wrought.

There is now a voluminous and insightful literature on 'black' identities in Britain. Debates about 'Black Britishness' have been among the most important in cultural studies in the late 1980s and 1990s and indeed, in many ways, constitute the most theoretically advanced area within the whole field in relation to postmodern debates about cultural identity. However, much of this debate has been couched at a relatively abstract level, offering a theoretically privileged view from above that seeks to theorise macrohistorical cultural shifts among black Britons. And it is far from clear, at this stage of research, whether the dynamics of 'black' culture might be comparable, and on what criteria, to the dynamics of 'Asian' culture in Britain. The literature to which this book attempts to provide a counterpoint has little to say about the distinctiveness of the Afro-Caribbean and 'Asian' post-migration experiences. However, there are many points of conceptual and theoretical relevance in this work for the present study. In particular, my study acknowledges the need to study British Asian cultures in the broader framework of the Indian, and more specifically the Punjabi, diaspora, rather than as an 'ethnic commu-nity' set in local boundaries.

The work of Gilroy (1987, 1993a, 1993b) has opened up especially fruitful intercultural and transnational perspectives on the study of black British cul-ture. In *The Black Atlantic* (1993a) he argues that a transnational formation linking America, the Caribbean, Africa and Europe – the black Atlantic diaspora – is the appropriate unit of analysis for any study of black culture. The term 'diaspora' is useful as an intermediate concept between the local and the global that nevertheless transcends the national perspectives which often limit cultural studies; it is also useful for its ability to encompass what Gilroy calls 'the changing same of culture', or the paradox of ethnic same-ness and heterogeneity. This is the paradox that the recognition of a shared culture and history (rather than biological or 'racial' essence) combines with a sense of the deep divergences and differences encompassed by the term 'black' (Hall, 1990: 223). In this respect, the term 'Asian' functions in similar ways to 'black'. It is no accident that both terms have been re-invented in post-colonial societies, by diaspora intellectuals, to convey the sense of a shared culture encompassing deep differences.

A diasporic perspective situates Punjabi families in relation to the web of connections between Punjabis in the Indian subcontinent, in various parts of Britain (Southall, Birmingham and Leeds being the main centres of settlement), in Germany, Canada and the USA. Many in Southall are also 'twice migrants', having formerly lived in East Africa (Bhachu, 1985).

The connections and relations of 'absence' between these places are greatly strengthened by modern communications systems, which have augmented a sense of diasporic awareness among the Punjabi families in Southall. The connections may be simply symbolic links between viewers of the same blockbuster Bombay movies; or they may be more concrete links between kin and friends in the form of 'video letters' and home videos of weddings and other rites of passage, especially coming-of-age celebrations. Such videos serve a range of social, cultural and political functions. They enable families to maintain contact with distant kin; they may be used to introduce eligible marriage partners and their families to each other; they may familiarise Punjabi families in, say, Yuca Valley, California with the lives of their kin in Southall and vice versa, which amounts to a form of video tourism as well as a cultural exchange; or they may serve to disseminate propaganda for the Khalistan ('Land of the Pure') movement, the campaign for the creation of a separate, sovereign Sikh nation in the Punjab; or videos of the lives and works of a Sikh *sant* (holy man) may be circulated across the globe, to be used in religious worship and instruction.

Thus a diasporic perspective acknowledges the ways in which identities have been and continue to be transformed through relocation, cross-cultural exchange and interaction. The globalisation of culture is deeply implicated in this process. Ever more sophisticated international communications technologies and the products of transnational media corporations dissolve distance and suspend time, and in doing so create new and unpredictable forms of connection, identification and cultural affinity, but also dislocation and disjuncture between people, places and cultures. Cultural historians and theorists, say Gilroy, face an immense task in tracking these very complex connections, crossovers and intersections. In this sense his key interest is in the cultural *routes* of the diaspora, rather than in the search for cultural roots.

Gilroy also recognises how youth culture plays 'a special role in mediating both the racial identities that are freely chosen and the oppressive effects of racism' (1993b: 61), and highlights the significance of recent fusions of Asian and black popular music:

> Bhangra has fused traditional Punjabi and Bengali music with hip hop, soul and house. Extraordinary new forms have been produced and much of their power resides in their capacity to circulate a new sense of what it means to be British. (Ibid.: 61f.)

These hybrid forms, Gilroy argues, contribute culturally to a youth social movement with a 'distinct political ideology'. Rather than being merely defensive, they 'contribute directly to an alternative public sphere, a transfigured public realm to which multinational communicative networks contribute':

> The seemingly trivial forms of youth sub-culture point to the opening up of a self-consciously post-colonial space in which the affirmation of

difference points forward to a more pluralistic conception of nationality and perhaps beyond that to its transcendence. (Ibid.: 62)

What Gilroy discusses at the level of expressive culture reaching a national and transnational public, this book shows to apply to the everyday culture of Punjabi youth in Southall, as they engage in the microprocesses of 'reinventing their own ethnicity' (Gilroy, 1993a: 82) in their collective reception of media. 'The popularity of Apache Indian and Bally Sagoo's attempts to fuse Punjabi music and language with reggae music and ragamuffin style raised debates about the authenticity of these hybrid cultural forms to an unprecedented pitch' (ibid.). But not only these kinds of high-profile 'examples of complex cultural exchange and of the ways in which a self-consciously synthetic culture can support some equally novel political identities' need to be studied. For a clearer understanding of what the 'reinvention of ethnicity' means in practice, we need to see the 'infinite process of identity construction' (Gilroy, 1993a: 223) as it is negotiated in everyday discourse among young people, in the various private and public contexts in which they live their lives. But first, we need to examine the concept of ethnicity more closely and situate it in relation to the concepts of 'race' and nationality, and to two other concepts which are much debated in media and cultural studies: postmodernism and globalisation.

REMAKING ETHNICITY

Ethnicity is a contradictory term of contested meanings, ever sliding to encompass new meanings and variously articulated in relation to different political interests. It derives its meanings from its relationship to other discursive formations – particularly those of culture and nature, and 'race' and nation. Ethnicity presents itself both as a natural given and as an accident of history and contingency. It may be contrasted with, but is often confused with, or used euphemistically to replace, the term 'race'. Despite its paradoxes, contradictions and slippages, it is indispensable to our understanding of modern societies and contemporary cultural trends and transformations. It has the power to mobilise and to destroy; it bears many important historical traces and encodes key cultural and political contradictions. It is a term which we cannot abandon, but which needs to be deconstructed, in order to prise open questions of cultural, historical and political difference, and to challenge biological definitions of 'race' and assumptions about the ethnic homogeneity of nations (Hall, 1993).

The term 'ethnicity' now evokes associations which are mainly negative: the revival of cultural forms of racism in Europe directed at particular 'ethnic' groups; the rise of 'ethnic' nationalisms in Eastern Europe; most notoriously, 'ethnic cleansing' in the former Yugoslavia. Such negative connotations are in line with the word's etymological origins. Derived from the Greek *ethnikos*, the term 'ethnic' was originally applied to heathens, cultural strangers, 'others' and 'outsiders'; it excluded the dominant group. Such definitions of peoples as 'outsiders' in contrast to the assumed 'insiders' gave way in the mid-nineteenth century to the now more familiar, ostensibly neutral or objective meaning, of 'peculiar to a race or a nation' (Fitzgerald, 1992: 115). The noun 'ethnicity', though relatively new (it was coined in the 1940s), retains connotations of 'migrancy, minority status, lower class' and an implication of 'hardness of boundaries' (Sollors, 1986: 39, 84); but it now also incorporates some more positive connotations. For example, in some uses ethnicity is linked with a 'building' metaphor which suggests that ethnic identity is something self-constructed, achieved, the product of a collective transformation (Sollors, 1986: 221); or it may be defined as 'something reinvented and reinterpreted in each generation [. . .] something dynamic [. . .] something new [. . .] a matter of finding a voice or a style that does not violate one's several components of identity' (Fischer, 1986: 195); or again, ethnicity may be regarded as a symbolic force with the power to affirm identities and mobilise populations positively, for example in forms of defiant cultural revivalism, renewal and re-creation (Fitzgerald, 1992; Gans, 1979; Hall, 1992).

In the conventional discourse of social science 'ethnic groups' are defined as sharing some combination of common descent (real or supposed); cultural or physical characteristics; and sets of attitudes and behaviours (Smooha, 1989). By this definition people are born into an ethnic group, tend to remain in it through the practices of endogamy, and use cultural and physical markers (language, nationality, religion and 'racial' characteristics such as skin pigmentation and body shape) as a basis for differentiating themselves collectively from others. But as Brass points out, ethnicity is a compound of objective markers, subjective definitions and explicit codes of cultural behaviour:

> Ethnicity or ethnic identity [. . .] involves, in addition to subjective self-consciousness, a claim to status and recognition, either as a superior group or as a group at least equal to other groups. Ethnicity is to ethnic category what class consciousness is to class [. . .]. [It is] a contingent and changeable status that, like class, may or may not be articulated in particular contexts and at particular times. (1991: 19)

Discourses of ethnicity in the social sciences have typically served to conflate the concepts of 'race' and 'nation' with 'culture', and then in turn with 'nature': the term lends itself to an all-too-easy slippage across these concepts. The biological discourse of 'race', where such slippage invariably arrives, has, however, proved itself to be misleading and spurious as a would-be scientific means of differentiating between people(s) (Donald and Rattansi, 1992). Yet 'racial' traits are still popularly seen as given by nature, as fixed and unchanging, in a discourse which makes 'common-sense' semantic links between nature, biology, genetics and blood. This gives rise to various forms of racial essentialism, reductionism, absolutism and determinism: to the notion that people behave as they do because it is 'in their blood'; or, in more recent forms of 'cultural racism', because it is 'in their culture' (for critiques, see Gilroy, 1993a, 1993b; Donald and Rattansi, 1992).

The term 'ethnicity' bears the traces of the great historical forces which continue to shape the world's ethnic mosaic today – colonialism and imperialism, annexation, involuntary and voluntary migration, and nationalism. Nationalism, or the claim of ethnic groups to self-determination, has stimulated the crystallisation of ethnicity and the widespread conflation of ethnic and national identity (Smith, 1981). Indeed, ethnicity as consciousness of shared ethnic identity tends to crystallise in situations where people of different backgrounds come into contact or share the same institutions or political systems (Smooha, 1989: 267; Brass, 1991). Modern nations typically try to constitute themselves as an ethnos, or ethnic unit, in order to exclude others; but at the same time, the dominant ethnic group often adopts the strategy of concealing its own ethnic status and attributing ethnicity only to 'others'. The English have done this for centuries, and the 'heritage industry' in contemporary Britain continues the tradition of affirming Englishness as a 'natural' cultural identity taken to be normative (Gilroy, 1987; Hebdige, 1992). Such forms of cultural racism reaffirm the semantic chain which links and equates one nation, one culture, one 'race' and one ethnicity.

As Hall argues, there is a need to detach 'ethnicity' from this equation and therefore from its associations with nationalism, imperialism, racism and the state – precisely the 'points of attachment around which a distinctive British, or more particularly English, ethnicity have been constructed' (1988: 29). The aim expressed by Hall, and which this book also hopes to serve, is to appropriate the term and construct a more positive conception of ethnicity, departing from an awareness that 'we are all ethnically located and our ethnic identities are crucial to our subjective sense of who we are':

> The term ethnicity acknowledges the place of history, language and culture in the construction of subjectivity and identity, as well as the fact that all discourse is placed, positioned, situated, and all knowledge is contextual [. . .]. The fact that this grounding of ethnicity in difference was deployed, in the discourse of racism, as a means of disavowing the realities of racism and repression does not mean that we can permit the term to be permanently colonized. That appropriation will have to be contested [. . .] just as we had to recuperate the term 'black', from its place in a system of negative equivalences. (Ibid.)

Hall looks forward to a new cultural politics – the seeds of which he sees in black avant-garde film-making in the 1980s, and which Gilroy examines in the context of popular musical developments: 'The new politics of representation [. . .] also sets in motion an ideological contestation around the term "ethnicity". But in order to pursue that movement further we have to retheorise the concept of difference.' This politics of representation is one which 'engages rather then suppresses *difference* and which depends, in part, on the cultural construction of new ethnic identities.' It conceives of representation as not merely expressive but formative of identities; and it conceives of difference not as unbridgeable separation but as 'positional, conditional and conjunctural' (ibid.).

Ethnicity is central to all forms of cultural identity, but it does not constitute identity as a whole. Several other 'axes of difference' are important – axes of difference which refuse to produce singular positions. Differences are gendered and sexual, classed and regional, as well as ethnic and 'racial'. As Hall (1993) argues, these tend to 'locate only to dislocate one another', and such failure to correspond on all axes of difference means that identities are better viewed as a 'field of anatagonisms' in which the pluralisation of differences makes a nonsense out of all forms of cultural and ethnic determinism and essentialism. Identity is 'not an essence but a *positioning*. Hence there is always a politics of identity, a politics of position [. . .]' (Hall, 1990: 226). Identity should be seen as a ' "production" which is never complete, always in process, and always constituted within, not outside, representation' (ibid.: 222).

The media and cultural consumption – the production, 'reading' and use of representations – play a key role in constructing and defining, contesting and reconstituting national, 'ethnic' and other cultural identities. Arguments about the role of media in the construction of national identities are well rehearsed in media studies (see e.g. Morley and Robins, 1989; Schlesinger, 1987). Anderson (1983) argues from a historical perspective that 'print capitalism' was instrumental in forging the 'imagined community' of the nation. In his analysis the changed relations of time and space brought about by the Industrial Revolution, especially by print media and most particularly by the newspaper, led to a heightened awareness of the 'steady, anonymous, simultaneous experience' of communities of readers (1983: 31). The notion of simultaneity was crucial to the construction of national consciousness in its early modern forms as it is today. The earliest newspapers connected people to an idea of the nation, and the mass ritual and ceremony of reading the newspaper continues to contribute to the construction of an idea of the national community (Bausinger, 1984). The fact of engaging, in private isolation, in a joint public ritual with significant though absent others, may be as important culturally as any information conveyed. If this is true of the newspaper, then it is yet more true of the contemporary regulation of simultaneous experience through broadcast media schedules (Cardiff and Scannel, 1987; Scannel, 1989), perhaps especially as regards the evening broadcast news on TV (Morley and Robins, 1989: 33).

A certain technological determinism is inherent in Anderson's account, however. Taking issue with the tendency to attribute powers to form and transform identities to media in themselves, Schlesinger (1987) reminds us of the need to turn the question conventionally asked upon its head:

> we should not start with communications and its supposed effects on national identity and culture, but rather begin by posing the question of national identity itself, to ask how it might be analysed and what importance communications practices might have in its constitution. (1987: 234)

Many critics draw upon post-Saussurean linguistic theory in arguing that identities are constructed through the articulation of difference, through relations of alliance or opposition, domination or subordination (Hall, 1988; Schlesinger, 1987; Morley and Robins, 1989). Thus Said (1978) has shown, for example, how the discourse of orientalism constructed a superior European cultural identity in opposition to a subaltern, non-European, oriental other. By articulating new kinds of spatial and temporal relationships, communications technologies can thus transform the modes of identification available within societies. In the contemporary context, new developments in media are arguably lessening the importance of geopolitical borders and spatial and temporal boundaries, and so threatening the vitality and significance, even the viability of national cultures. The implications of these developments are currently much discussed in terms of postmodernism and globalisation.

POSTMODERNISM AND IDENTITY POLITICS

Postmodernist commentators (Baudrillard, 1988; Hebdige, 1989; Jameson, 1991) emphasise the pluralisation of sources of identity and of 'imagined communities' which owes much to mass media representations, or 'simulations'. Harvey (1989) argues that the acceleration of communications, and the associated time–space compression, have radically affected the transmission of social values, meanings and identities. If we are indeed entering a postmodern era, one of its characteristics is said to be that social identities are increasingly marked by 'fragmentation, multiplicity, plurality and indeterminacy' (Thompson, 1992: 223). Identity politics has assumed a major significance in the discourse of postmodernism, effectively supplanting the focus on class politics in left cultural criticism. This eagerness to talk about identity is, in Mercer's view, symptomatic of the 'postmodern predicament of contemporary politics', the key motifs of which are:

> displacement, decentering and disenchantment [. . .], the fragmentation of traditional sources of authority and identity, the displacement of collective sources of membership and belonging such as 'class' and

'community' that help to construct political loyalties, affinities and identifications [. . .]. Identity only becomes an issue when it is in crisis, when something assumed to be fixed, coherent and stable is displaced by the experience of doubt and uncertainty. (Mercer, 1990: 43)

Baudrillard (1988) argues that the postmodern can be distinguished from earlier eras by the proliferation of communications through mass media, particularly TV, coupled with the full emergence of the consumer culture dominated by simulations, or signs detached from referents. He argues that activities of consumption now play a larger role in defining people's identities and consciousness than class. Our perceptions of self and other have been changed by the consumer lifestyle, by the constant stream of TV images, by the media's power to seduce us into a 'hyper-reality'. Baudrillard's conclusions are much disputed, though his analysis is widely accepted. Yet several questions need to be raised. Does the fragmentation and pluralisation of social groups allow creative potential to be released? Is it, as some commentators argue (e.g. Gott, 1988), a form of liberation? Several studies have produced evidence indicating that working-class youths in the UK use fashion to construct a sense of public identity, showing how underprivileged groups actively shape their own identities in the face of powerfully organised commercialism (Chambers, 1986), developing distinctive subcultures through 'bricolage', the creative use of recontextualising combinations of the products of consumer culture (Hebdige, 1988, 1989; Nava and Nava, 1992).

This book does not set out to celebrate consumer creativity any more than consumer culture itself. But following de Certeau (1984), it does take the view that consumption, despite its overdetermination by the market and the unequal distribution of access to economic and cultural capital (Bourdieu, 1984), is not a passive process but an expressive and productive activity. In de Certeau's terms, the 'powerless' as consumers of representations take some control over their lives by employing 'tactics': through 'the silent, transgressive, ironic or poetic activity of the readers', the 'strategies' of the powerful are resisted. Thus, in order to understand the effectivity of TV we need to study not only its images and narratives but what the consumer 'makes' or 'does' with them:

> The 'making' in question is a production [. . .] but a hidden one [. . .]. To a rationalised, expansionist and at the same time glamorous and spectacular production corresponds another production called consumption. The latter is devious, it is dispersed, but it insinuates itself everywhere, silently and almost invisibly, because it does not manifest itself through its own products, but rather through its ways of using the products imposed by a dominant economic order. (De Certeau, 1984: xii–xiii)

De Certeau's themes have been much elaborated (e.g. Fiske, 1987, 1989b; Silverstone, 1989). Hebdige (1989) argues that consumer culture encourages people to articulate what they would like to become, creating new 'communities of consumers'. Chapter 6, on the reception of advertising, will show that there is much truth in this account, but the problem remains that the role models and style images set up by the media are limited within the discourse of consumerism. The cultural aspirations of young people in Southall are frequently expressed through the tropes of advertising, notably in terms of the American/global teenage dream of freedom, fun, beauty and love represented most forcefully perhaps by Coca Cola ads. Hebdige's emphasis is on people's capacity to actively use the media to construct identities and new communities, and he sees the traditional collectivities of nation and class breaking down while 'new narratives of emancipation' are being written. He argues that the new transnational media possess a power to bind disparate, dispersed groups into 'communities of affect' that are explicitly utopian, citing the examples of the 1980s pop charity spectaculars – Band Aid, Live Aid, the Free Mandela concerts – as countering the general postmodernist stress on fragmentation. Events such as these express and stimulate a desire to feel connected to others, constructing alliances which, as Hebdige himself points out, may be transitory and superficial; none the less they may signal new forms of collective identification in a global youth culture.

The discussion of these issues, when framed by the debate on postmodernism, is frequently frustratingly lacking in substantial evidence, and often vitiated by an overt or covert assumption that identities are somehow self-selected, freely chosen through consumption activities. This view falls prey to the New Right's discourse of consumer freedom and choice. While consumption activities are undoubtedly important, and increasingly so, in constituting identities, there is no significant empirical evidence that the market and the media now shape identities more powerfully than categories of class and ethnicity, religion and 'race', nation and region – at least not for many social groups. Certainly among the youth of Southall, the continuing power of social structures and political power relations is manifest in the range and kind of identities which are ascribed to them and by them to one another, or which are assumed and contested by them. Young people seek to contest, subvert and transform what they experience as imposed, 'racialised' or 'ethnicised' identities, and consumption practices are one key means of doing so. But class position, which determines differential and unequal access to material and cultural resources, continues to shape consumption practices, and ethnicity and gender also continue to frame the limits of their creative freedom. And more important still, it remains the nation state which, in the first instance, constructs its internal ethnic 'others', its 'racial minorities', as such.

Though postmodern cultural criticism usefully highlights issues which are important to this study, its often inflated claims tend to be based on anecdotal evidence coupled with an epistemological relativism of dubious political value. With Habermas (1989), I would want to hold on to the possibility of constructing an enlightened public sphere of communications (cf. Murdock, 1989; Scannel, 1988). The debate in contemporary social science on the process of 'globalisation' has more substantial relevance to this study.

GLOBALISATION/LOCALISATION

It is now commonplace to argue that the interconnectedness of cultures brought about by the transnational flow of images, commodities and peoples is leading to the formation of a global culture, dominated by transnational corporations, and increasingly Americanised and commercialised (Mattelart, *et al.* 1984; Schiller, 1969, 1973). The acceleration of global flow by communications technologies means that cultural forms (for example the Indian 'sacred soap' the *Mahabharata*, discussed in Chapter 3, and the Australian soap *Neighbours*, discussed in Chapter 5) are available for worldwide consumption on a mass scale. Anthropologists and cultural historians, in response to the development of cultural studies in advanced capitalist societies, are now beginning to analyse how consumers in all sorts of settings create or conform to personal and social identities through acts of consumption, and how commodities provide a resource for developing shared, collective frames of reference (Appadurai, 1986; Douglas and Isherwood, 1979; Miller, 1987, 1992). (Indeed Miller only came to study the reception of the American soap *Young and Restless* in Trinidad [1992] because no one would talk to him while it was on, and so he was forced to watch with his informants.)

The local reception of globally networked news, ads and soaps discussed in this study highlights the dialectical processes of globalisation, which is defined by Giddens as:

> the intensification of world-wide social relations which link distant localities in such a way that local happenings are shaped by events occurring miles away and vice versa. This is a dialectical process because such local happenings may move in an obverse direction from the very distantiated relations that shape them. *Local* transformation is as much a part of globalisation as the lateral extension of social connections across time and space. (1990: 64)

Giddens identifies 'time–space distantiation' as a characteristic trait of globalisation. This involves the disengagement of certain dimensions of experience from presence and place:

The sense of the familiar is often mediated by time–space distantiation [. . .]. [This is] less a phenomenon of estrangement from the *local* than one of integration within globalised 'communities' of shared experience [. . .]. The newspaper and the sequence of TV programmes over the day are the most obvious concrete examples of this pheno- menon. (1990: 140)

Similarly, Hall suggests that, as relations of time and space are 'basic co-ordinates of all systems of representation' and narrative, 'changes in time–space relationships within different systems of representation have profound effects on how identities are located and represented' (1992: 301–302). All identities are located in symbolic space and time: they draw on what Said (1990) has termed 'imaginary geographies' and are bound up with 'invented traditions' (Hobsbawm and Ranger, 1983) which mythically link past and present and connect individual experiences to larger – e.g. national – historical events. The new transnational communications and media networks, arguably, are undermining these particular, local and national co-ordinates of identification, with the result, some say, that a homogeneous global consumer culture is in the making.

One proponent of the cultural homogenisation thesis is Meyrowitz (1986). He argues that the electronic media, particularly TV, have led to a radical restructuring of social life by disrupting the traditional link between culture and geography, allowing people to escape from forms of identity forged by the relation between person and the 'symbolic place' identical with geographical locality. In his view, the media are destroying our sense of locality; the popular search for 'roots' and the resurgence of concern with ethnic identity, he says, are signs of the decay of group identity rather than of its regeneration.

This argument has some truth but it is overblown. It is overly deterministic; and Meyrowitz produces no substantial empirical evidence to support his claims about the extent of homogenisation. He assumes the media have uniform effects, but overlooks the extent to which the media continue to be produced in and directed at a variety of distinct places, as well as the fact that there is no uniformity of access to the media, or to the cultural and educational resources which are likely to make profound differences to the ways in which people respond to them. But the question he raises is important for this study: how is the sense of place affected by the media? What implications does media consumption have for the variously local, national, diasporic and global senses of place relevant in Southall? It turns out – as I will show in detail later – that young people in Southall have a very strong sense of place, as members of spatially defined communities at all these levels, even if they may not feel that they 'belong' equally in all of them, all the time. The tensions between them necessitate a reflexive attitude among young people, producing a very acute awareness of cultural differences – what Gilroy (following Du Bois, 1986) refers to as 'double consciousness', the sense of dual identity which comes from being 'in but not of the west' and from the 'unhappy symbiosis' between 'racial', nationalistic and diasporic modes of thinking, being and seeing (Gilroy, 1993a: 127). This awareness catalyses and intensifies processes of identity negotiation. So local identities are indeed being redefined under the impact of global media, in being recontextualised; but that is not to say that they are being weakened (see Miller, 1992, for a similar argument).

Hall (1992) suggests three possible consequences of globalisation on cultural identities: erosion, strengthening and the emergence of new identities or 'new ethnicities'. Hall has coined the term 'global-postmodern' to refer to a perceived breakdown of all established cultural identities, the fragmentation of cultural codes, pluralisation of styles, and emphasis on the ephemeral, fleeting, aspects of contemporary culture, coupled with the global ubiquity of such features of youth culture as the jeans and trainers uniform: 'the more social life becomes mediated by the global marketing of styles, images and places by globally networked media, the more identities become detached – disembedded – from specific times, places, histories and traditions and appear free-floating' (Hall, 1992: 303). Yet, as I have already argued, there are in fact limits to the extent to which identities can become entirely free-floating and self-selected. Not only must it be emphasised that the process of cultural globalisation is highly uneven, as the distribution of globalisation around the globe reflects the unequal relations of power between 'the west and the rest', or more accurately between the most developed consumer societies and the rest (Hall, 1992; Sreberny-Mohammedi, 1991). The tendency towards homogenisation is also countered by opposing tendencies towards differentiation and pluralisation.

The powerful revival of ethnicity and the growth of the politics of identity – drawing both on 'hybrid' and 'symbolic', and on exclusive and essentialist models of ethnicity – is seen by Bauman (1990) as calling into question the homogenisation thesis:

> Ethnicity has become one of the main categories or tokens, or tribal poles around which flexible and sanction-free communities are formed and in reference to which individual identities are constructed and asserted. There are now fewer of the centrifugal forces that weakened ethnic integrity. There is instead a powerful demand for more pronounced, though symbolic, rather than institutionalized ethnic distinctiveness. (1990: 167)

Indeed transnational media and marketing corporations have become very aware of ethnicity as a form of difference and increasingly both target 'local' versions of products at specific ethnic as well as national markets ('multi-local' niche marketing on a global scale) and exploit ethnic difference as a marketing tool. Thus one aspect of globalisation is actually the corporate exploitation of local differentiation (Robins, 1991; Wilson and Gutierrez, 1985: 216; Levitt, 1983: 30f.). This tendency seems likely to encourage the emergence of new global *and* new local and ethnic identities, without necessarily displacing national identities. It is perhaps a strategic response on the part of marketing corporations to the wide-spread expression of anxiety about global homogenisation, which above all is seen to threaten national identities.

TRADITION/TRANSLATION

It is possible to observe both a proliferation and a polarisation of identities, both a strengthening of existing local identities and a formation of new identities. As Robins argues:

> The continuity and historicity of identity are challenged by the immediacy and intensity of global cultural confrontations. The comforts of Tradition are fundamentally challenged by the imperative to forge a new self-interpretation based upon the responsibilities of cultural Translation. (Robins, 1991: 41)

These challenges are felt most powerfully by diasporic groups, such as black Britons and British Asians, some of whom have made a 'strategic retreat to more defensive identities [. . .] in response to the experience of cultural racism' (Hall, 1992: 308) – in response, for example, to the rise of a 'morbid celebration of Englishness' (Gilroy, quoted in Morley and Robins, 1989: 16) in the 1980s. Hall claims that this strategy has been developed in a variety of ways, including re-identification with: 'cultures of origin'; the construction of strong 'counter-ethnicities' as forms of symbolic identification (e.g. cultural rastafarianism); revivals of cultural traditionalism, religious orthodoxy and political separatism; and the formation of 'new identities' around terms (such as 'black' or 'Asian') chosen and inflected to encompass differences (1992: 308). Hall concludes that globalisation does have the power to contest and dislocate national identities, in that it has a pluralizing impact, opening up new possibilities and positions of identification. But its general impact is ˙ highly contradictory, as different groups, let alone individuals, respond in a range of different ways to the diversification and concomitant politicisation of identity.

Robins (1991) provides a scheme for thinking about these responses. Some gravitate to what he calls 'Tradition', in the attempt to restore their former 'purity' and certainty. Others gravitate to what he calls 'Transla-tion', (following Bhabha, 1990; cf. Rushdie, 1991) exploring their identities as transformative processes in the interplay of history and politics, representation and difference. And yet others oscillate between tradition and translation (cf. Bhabha, 1990). It is this oscillation that is becoming evident on a global scale today. Identities are in transition, involved in a multiplicity of crossovers and mixes. Thus globalisation may mean neither universal assimilation into one homogeneous culture, nor a universal search for roots and revival of singular identities, but a complex, highly uneven process of many-sided translation.

The term 'translated' has been adopted by cultural critics to describe:

> those identity formations which cut across and intersect natural frontiers, and which are composed of people who have been dispersed forever from their homelands. Such people retain strong links with their places of origin and their traditions, but they are without the illusion of a return to the past [. . .]. They bear upon them the traces of the particular cultures, traditions, languages and histories by which they were shaped. The difference is that they are not and never will be unified in the old sense, because they are irrevocably the product of several interlocking histories and cultures. (Hall, 1992: 310)

Members of such ' "cultures of hybridity" ' are 'irrevocably translated': as 'the products of the new diasporas created by the post-colonial migrations', translated men and women 'must learn to inhabit at least two identities, to speak two cultural languages, to translate and negotiate between them. Cultures of hybridity are one of the distinctly novel types of identity produced in the era of late-modernity' (ibid.).

Translated, or hybrid or syncretic cultures, emerging out of the fusion of different cultural traditions, may constitute a powerful creative force. But they can also encounter fierce, often violent, opposition where they are perceived as threatening fundamentalist projects of cultural 'purification' (as in the case of Salman Rushdie, and as in the case of the new ethnic nationalisms in Europe). And there is perhaps little reason to hope that 'new ethnicities' have any less destructive potential than 'old' ones. But translated cultural identities are the inevitable consequence of the simultaneous globalisation of media communications and growth of migration and transnational diasporic 'communities'. Two researchers, Appadurai and Hannerz, have recently advanced the analysis of this new type of formation in important ways.

Appadurai (1990) addresses the cultural politics of 'deterritorialisation' and the sociology of displacement that it expresses. The tension between homogenisation and heterogenisation, in his analysis, is the central problem of today's global interactions, and the key to its analysis lies not in homogenisation but in 'indigenisation'. Inasmuch as 'one man's imagined community is another man's political prison' (1990: 295), Appadurai diagnoses a widespread and increasing fear of 'cultural absorption' by larger polities and cultures. It is thus the 'central paradox of ethnic politics' today that 'primordia (whether of language or skin colour or neighborhood or of kinship) have become globalised' such that sentiments of intimacy and localised identity may ignite as political sentiments across 'vast and irregular spaces, as groups move, yet stay linked to one another through sophisticated media capabilities' (1990: 306). Such 'primordia' may well be the 'product of invented traditions' (Hobsbawn and Ranger, 1983) or 'retrospective affiliations'. But 'because of the disjunctive and unstable interplay of commerce, media, national policies and consumer fantasies, ethnicity, once a genie contained in the bottle of some sort of locality (however large) has now become a global force, forever slipping in and through the cracks between states and borders' (Appadurai, 1990).

Appadurai describes a global process of 'disjunctures and conjunctures' between 'ethnoscapes' (the landscapes of living persons) and 'mediascapes' – 'image-centred, narrative based accounts of strips of reality' which:

> offer to those who experience and transform them [...] a series of elements (such as characters, plots and textual forms) out of which scripts can be formed of imagined lives, their own as well as those of others living in other places. These scripts can and do get disaggregated into complex sets of metaphors by which people live (Lakoff and Johnson, 1980) as they help to constitute narratives of the 'other' and proto-narratives of possible lives, fantasies which could become prologemena to the desire for acquisition and movement. (ibid.: 299)

Appadurai therefore asks us to examine empirically which sets of communicative genres are valued in which ways, and 'what sorts of pragmatic genre conventions govern the collective "readings" of different kinds of text' (ibid.: 300). This is the task which this book undertakes; it is one which is all the more urgent because of the major political implications of these cultural processes.

'Deterritorialisation [...] is one of the central forces of the modern world, since it brings labouring populations into the lower-class sectors and spaces of relatively wealthy societies' (ibid.: 301), and one of its results has often been to create an intensified sense of critical attachment to the politics of the home state. 'Deterritorialisation [...] is now at the core of a variety of global fundamentalisms including Hindu and Islamic fundamentalism'. The Hindu example is most pertinent here. Appadurai argues that the Hindu diaspora has been exploited by various 'interests both within and outside India to create a complicated network of finances and religious identifications, in which the problem of cultural reproduction for Hindus abroad has become tied to the politics of Hindu fundamentalism at home' (ibid.: 302). Such links are explored in Chapter 3, where I focus on Southall's local video culture and its role in the 'reinvention of traditions', and where I provide a case study of the 'devotional viewing' of Doordarshan's (Indian national TV) serial version of the *Mahabharata* in a

Southall family. As Appadurai puts it: 'Deterritorialisation creates new markets for film companies, art impresarios and travel agents, who thrive on the need of the deterritorialised population for contact with its homeland' (ibid.: 302). Both through media representations and through experiences of touristic travel as 'return to the homeland', ethnically specific 'mediascapes' of 'invented homelands' are constructed. These mediascapes then often, through the processes described above, become the site of desires for change which are transferred to the living 'ethnoscape'. Thus Appadurai argues that: 'The creation of "Khalistan", an invented homeland of the deterritorialised Sikh population of England, Canada and the United States is one example of the bloody potential in such mediascapes, as they interact with the "internal colonialisms" [. . .] of the nation-state' (ibid.).

As we shall see, however, most young people in Southall tend to reject these forms of cultural politics, associating them with their parents. Some young men appropriate the symbols of Sikh fundamentalism as a style, in order to present a 'hard' (macho) image; but their Sikh peers often regard this as posturing, with little if any real political significance (see Chapter 6). The great majority aspire not to reterritorialise their ethnic group, but rather to transcend it in a mode of being described by Hannerz (1990) as 'cosmopolitan'.

Hannerz explores cosmopolitanism as 'a state of mind' and 'a mode of managing meaning' (1990: 238) in the context of globalisation. It involves both a certain 'orientation' which he describes as 'a willingness to engage with the Other' and an 'openness toward divergent cultural experiences, a search for contrasts rather than uniformity'; and also a set of competences (ibid.: 239). These general and specific competences include the ability to adapt flexibly to other cultures, and skill in manoeuvring in and between particular cultures. The acquisition of such competences is, in fact, a central concern for young people in Southall. Chapter 4 shows in detail how the learning and testing of these competences shapes talk among peers and in families about news on TV.

The growth and proliferation of transnational communications and social networks 'generates more cosmopolitans now than there have been at any other time' (ibid.: 241). Cosmopolitans experience transnational and territorial cultures as 'entangled' in a variety of ways: 'the real significance of the growth of the transnational cultures [. . .] is often not the new cultural experience that they themselves can offer people – for it is frequently rather restricted in scope and depth – but their mediating possibilities' (ibid.: 245). Transnational media play an increasing role in providing people with experiences of other cultures, helping to make cosmopolitans of them. Media mediate cultures; and as cosmopolitans read media, they translate between territorial, local, diasporic, national and global cultures and identities.

The transnational cultures are bridgeheads for entry into other territorial cultures. Instead of remaining within them, one can use the mobility connected with them to make contact with the meanings of other rounds of life, and gradually incorporate this experience into one's personal perspective. (Hannerz, 1990 : 245)

Cosmopolitans are, Hannerz suggests, perhaps 'never quite at home again' (ibid.: 248), as their plural cultural experience makes them unable to enjoy the 'untranslated' local's sense of the 'natural' necessity of specific cultural forms. But he suggests, citing McLuhan, that 'the implosive power of the media may now make just about everybody a little more cosmopolitan. And one may in the end ask whether it is now even possible to become a cosmopolitan without going away at all' (ibid.: 249). In this sense too, the experience of migrants and diasporas is far from being marginal: it may well represent an imminent global/universal future. Yet as Hannerz observes, there can be no cosmopolitans without locals since, for the former, the experience of diversity depends on access to varied cultures, just as locals increasingly feel the need to carve out special niches for their cultures and preserve them from the threat of assimilation and homogenisation (ibid.: 250). In negotiating ethnic and cultural identity, locals and cosmopolitans may thus have a common interest, one which is potentially at odds with that of nation states.

ABOUT THIS BOOK

This study examines the issues broached here at a theoretical level – issues of the translation/transnationalisation of cultures and identities – from the local and domestic point of view. In accordance with the generic conventions of ethnography, my opening chapter introduces readers to the place of fieldwork. It outlines Southall's social history and geography and describes the diversity of cultures which coexist in the town. In presenting a social profile of Southall, I have drawn upon 1981 Census data (data from the 1991 Census were unavailable at the time of writing) and selected data from an extensive survey of some 300 Southall youths, conducted by Dr Gerhard Baumann and myself. Further details of the survey are given in Chapter 2, and selected results are given in the Appendix. The first part of Chapter 1 thus situates the subjects of this study in a firm sociological context. The combination of quantitative and qualitative data is a characteristic feature of this ethnography; it enables concrete empirical details to be analysed alongside the more subjective perceptions of individual informants.

In the second half of Chapter 1, key aspects of Southall's youth culture(s) are highlighted, particularly those themes which are most likely to be familiar to outsiders, since they figure prominently – indeed almost exclusively – in national media coverage of Southall and British Asian youth more generally: the themes of arranged marriages, gangs and bhangra. They are discussed here in terms of local young people's views, rejecting the commonplace thesis of 'culture clash' between monolithic entities, in favour of a more dynamic account of diasporic cultural change.

The second chapter explains the genesis and methodology of the study, setting it in the twin contexts of my own personal and intellectual history and the history of academic research on TV audiences. Here I argue for the unique advantages, for such research, of the fully anthropological ethnographic approach, incorporating the use of survey methods. I detail the formal and informal strategies I used to gain access to young people's 'TV talk', and reflect on the practical and ethical problems such work entailed. Finally I address some theoretical issues in current anthropological debate concerning ethnographic authority and responsibility, and the writing of ethnography 'in the field' as part of the reflexive practice of anthropology in modern urban settings.

'TV talk' – the embedding of TV experiences in conversational forms and flows – becomes a feasible object of study only when fully ethnographic methods are used in audience research. While the TV talk analysed in this book includes statements elicited in interview situations, my approach goes well beyond the kinds of 'semi-structured' or 'unstructured interview' which other researchers have employed (and in some cases misleadingly dubbed 'ethnographic'). My data includes forms of spontaneous, but often ritualistic, talk which could only be documented by intensive and extended fieldwork methods. Significantly, my focus on TV talk in Southall arose out of the ethnographic enquiry: it was not the planned object of research, but proved to be a crucial form of self-narration among the young people I was studying and a collective resource through which they negotiate their cultural and ethnic identities. Southall TV talk is also, naturally, a rich source of data on local appropriations of national and transnational media products. Both dimensions are important to this study: TV talk as a source of ethnographic data and ethnography as a strategy in audience research.

Chapter 3 then explores the general characteristics of audio-visual culture in Southall, especially in the domestic sphere, in terms of the role of media use in catalysing and negotiating cultural change. It first highlights the ways in which TV and video are used in diasporic families, both to maintain and remake and to challenge and revise cultural traditions. I analyse young people's readings of, and attitudes towards, the representations of India current in both Hindi and 'western' film and TV; and I explore the special place of 'sacred soaps' and 'devotional viewing' in many families' audio-visual culture. Here I introduce a case-study of one Hindu family's reception of two TV versions of the *Mahabharata* – the ninety-one-part serial produced by the Indian network Doordarshan, and Peter Brook's stage version, which were both broadcast on British TV during the time of the fieldwork. This case-study affords important insights into the elaboration of domestic religious culture through media use: it demonstrates how audio-visual texts come to be viewed as sacred, integrated into traditional patterns of domestic worship, and also serve as didactic resources, used by parents to foster religious and cultural traditions and by young people to explore the philosophy of their cultural heritage. The following sections on the place of 'western' soaps in family viewing, and on the range of news media available locally, serve to prepare the reader for the more detailed analyses in subsequent chapters. They highlight the themes of generational and gender difference in viewing preferences, and the complex ways in which viewing practices and debate about competing and culturally distinctive systems of representation, are woven into the fabric of family life.

The final sections of Chapter 3 address the role of media use and appropriation in transforming cultural traditions, focusing concretely on the interlinking of festive rituals and rituals of media reception and appropriation. A section on Christmas and TV highlights the ways in which, to varying extents, the key festive ritual of the dominant British 'white', Christian/secular culture, which is experienced almost exclusively through TV, is integrated into Southall family life. It is followed by a case-study of one group of teenagers' performance of the climactic dance scene from the American hit film *Dirty Dancing*, at a high-school Diwali concert. This event exemplifies how, conversely, the key festive ritual of Hindu and Sikh culture in Southall may be transformed – and in this instance, very deliberately subverted – by the creative appropriation of media products aimed at a global youth market. Such an affirmative celebration of American teenage culture is subversive, in terms of the views of local elders: as my closing chapter will show in more detail, it must be seen as a strategic identification with an alternative ideal since they find few images in British or Indian media in which they see themselves 'reflected' or with which they can identify.

Chapters 4 to 6 explore in depth the themes of cultural diversity and re-invention, negotiation and transformation. They document and analyse the important role of the 'recreative reception' (Cheesman, 1994) of TV in mediating processes of cultural change among young people. TV talk is not only a form of social interaction integral to the peer group's sense of common identity. It furnishes and refines shared cultural resources which young people collectively harness, for purposes of comparison and critique, as they negotiate relations within the peer group, with parents and other elders, and with the 'significant others' of the wider world, in Britain, in the Punjabi diaspora, and beyond. TV talk is a major forum for contest and debate over 'old' and 'new' identities, and for the formulation of cosmopolitan aspirations.

The young people who are the subjects of this study talk mainly about a set of interlinked concerns, which in part are shared with youth anywhere and in part shaped by the specific local, diasporic and national contexts they inhabit. Their talk centres on becoming adult and what that involves; on family relationships and social relations in the local neighbourhood; on courtship – 'going out', 'dating' – and marriage (which is quite imminent for many 16-year-old girls in Southall); and on style and fashion. Their TV talk closely reflects these concerns: it is, in a sense, a metonymic microcosm of their talk in general, which in turn reveals the central preoccupations of their lives, often more candidly than the talk of adults would.

Becoming adult always means acquiring a certain desirable status and a certain set of competences. In Southall it means being able to situate one-self in, and move appropriately across, a range of different frames of reference: in relation to global and local, diasporic and national contexts, as well as in relation to the politics of class, 'community', 'race' and gender. That is, adulthood in Southall is inescapably cosmopolitan in Hannerz's (1990) sense. And, as it does for most adolescents, becoming adult also involves intense negotiations in the family context; but again they take culturally specific forms here. Family relationships and duties, under the code of *izzat* (roughly translatable as 'family honour'), involve maintaining the family's status in the local community. Gender relations in particular are subject to intense social control, exercised largely through networks of gossip and rumour, which aim to protect the chastity of girls in order to achieve 'proper' marriage arrangements. So 'going out' is regarded as subversive of the norms of the parental culture; but it is a central feature of the peer culture none the less. And similarly, young people's preoccupation with style and fashion, which largely involves endorsing 'western' products and images, is viewed with suspicion by most parents: it is in styles of speech, dress and consumption generally that cultural change is most manifest.

In developing – in talk as much as in other social interaction – patterns of gender relationship which are 'new' (they neither exactly follow parental norms nor amount to wholesale adoption of 'western' norms) and similarly in characteristic patterns of material consumption young people (again) situate themselves simultaneously in various frames of reference. The ways in which they do so exemplify the contextual and contractual character of identities; and they make evident the pragmatism which enables them to 'switch codes' both culturally and linguistically with ease and speed. But insofar as talk is the medium of such negotiations within and between peer and parental cultures, one of its essential elements is talk about TV, occasioned by TV or informed by the experience of it. TV talk is a crucial forum for experimentation with identities. It is possible to say things in TV talk which would be otherwise difficult or embarrassing if not unsayable. Common experiences of TV supply referents and contexts for talk which is explictly or implicitly about identities and identity positions. The sustained analyses in

Chapters 4 to 6, therefore, address the significance, in Southall youth culture, of talk about three important TV genres: news, soaps and ads.

There is, of course, no absolute correlation between conversational themes and media genres. Indeed, it is often argued that the experience of TV as 'flow' reduces the importance of generic distinctions in the analysis of its reception (see Williams, 1975, 1989). Yet in all the cases I discuss in these chapters, TV talk (typically initiated by the phrases 'Did you see ... ?' or 'Have you seen ... ?') reveals close links between the reception, evaluation and appropriation of the genre in question, and specific social and cultural concerns of the peer group. As I have indicated, young people's concerns form a densely interrelated whole, in which any one theme implies a set of others. None the less, particular concerns are implicated in the consumption of the TV genres in question, which can be isolated for purposes of analysis; and, furthermore, these concerns are often expressed and debated most fully in the context of discussions of particular genres.

News addresses young people as citizens, soaps address them as social actors, ads address them as consumers. They collectively respond to these genres in distinctive ways as participants in a peer group culture in the process of redefining itself with and against its significant others. Talk about news among teenagers reveals a preoccupation with their ambiguous status between childhood and adulthood, with what is involved in becoming adult. It often leads on to explicit consideration of the themes of citizenship, class and 'race', and religious, cultural and national difference and identity. These themes are variously inflected in relation to local, national and international news (the local repercussions of the latter are usually foregrounded). Proficiency in news talk is understood to be one of the competences which must be acquired if one is to become adult. Many bilingual young people mediate British TV news – including information on citizens' rights and duties – to their parents as translators, and this activity itself confers status, as well as encouraging a cosmopolitan orientation in Hannerz's (1990) sense. And acquiring such proficiency also involves learning about, and at the same time redefining, local, national and diasporic news histories and current agendas.

Talk about soaps – in particular *Neighbours*, much the most popular TV programme at the time of fieldwork – reveals critical views of the social and cultural characteristics of Southall as a 'neighbourhood' and a 'community'. It often leads on to comparative and contrastive reflections about the place of 'gossip' in local life, about patterns of kinship and gender relations, about courtship and marriage and about intergenerational conflict about these subjects. Soap talk often functions as a surrogate for talk about personal and family concerns which cannot be directly voiced. It also often concerns what are perceived as positive aspects of the social life represented in *Neighbours* – in particular the freedoms enjoyed by young people in the soap, notably in the field of gender relations and in the unconstrained communication between people of all generations. Young people contrast these representations with their experience of local and domestic life. But the deeper reasons for the enormous popularity of *Neighbours* lie elsewhere. It is due to a homology which young people perceive, between a feature of the social relations depicted in *Neighbours* and a feature of social relations in the adult world of Southall, which they intensely resent: the centrality of gossip as a medium of information and control, especially the social control of gender relations. As my analysis shows, this homology can be extended: in important respects, the form of narration which characterises soaps, and the form of their collaborative reception in talk, both resemble gossip and rumour as processes of collective narration. And gossip – especially about gender relations – is of course also an essential feature of young people's everyday communication, as they freely admit. The term 'gossip' is, then, the linchpin which articulates the relationship between soap, soap talk, social experience and social interaction in the peer group and in the social environment which they inhabit.

Though the social life represented in *Neighbours* is sometimes talked about as an ideal of 'teenage freedom', it is in talk about ads that teenagers articulate a fully utopian vision of cultural change. Ad talk generally serves as a forum for the discussion of issues of the body: style and dress codes, body care and norms of beauty, and food and drink consumption. Both the bodily preoccupations common to most adolescents and the specific politics of body style imposed by the racism of the dominant 'white' culture emerge in these discussions. And in them, hierarchies of youth taste are elaborated, sometimes very explicitly, in contrast with hierarchies of parental taste. As they define themselves as individual bodies, identifying themselves as consumers, young people generally define themselves in opposition to their parents. And the appropriation in ad talk of two key symbols of 'global/American teenage culture' – Coca Cola and McDonald's – points to a widespread perception of a utopian alternative to the identities which are otherwise locally available, whether in social practice or in audio-visual representations. The images and music of Coca Cola ads evoke a 'feeling' of liberty, equality and sociability, which is concretely associated with the consumption of fast foods in franchise outlets *outside* Southall, where young people socialise beyond the gaze of parents and elders, free from the threat of adult gossip. This 'new' form of sociability is identified as proper to their own generational culture, and as the common cultural property of global teenagerdom.

Thus news, soaps and ads serve as cues and as resources for the reflexive exploration of cultural differences and for the articulation of both real and imaginary options. Young people respond to these genres by collectively and individually positioning themselves as citizens, social actors and consumers in various relations to parental diasporic cultures, British national 'white' culture and the global culture of teenage consumerism. In view of the plurality of identities – ethnic and cultural, religious, national and 'racial', and not least gendered – which are ascribed to them, it is perhaps no wonder that the cosmopolitan, global identity suggested by Coca Cola and McDonald's 'multi-local' advertising has such strong appeal. But that vision of free-and-easy sociability is utopian and meanwhile, London Punjabi youth are engaged in constructing a viable culture through negotiations around the diverse resources available to them both in 'real life' and on screen.

Chapter 1

Southall: *Chota Punjab*, west London

Southall is a densely populated, multi-ethnic suburb of west London situated near Heathrow Airport. The majority of its inhabitants are of Punjabi origin – some having come to Britain from East Africa – and predominantly of Sikh religion, complemented by sizeable numbers of Punjabi Hindus and Muslims from both sides of the Indo-Pakistan border. This diverse Punjabi majority lives alongside minorities of English, Irish and Afro-Caribbean backgrounds. Southall has attracted migrants since the beginning of this century when local manufacturing industries began to develop. In the 1930s they came from the depressed coal-mining areas of South Wales and Durham as well as from the poorer rural regions of Southern Ireland. West Indian migration to Southall began in the late 1940s and continued until the 1960s, mainly from Antigua, St Lucia, Grenada and Dominica. Punjabi migration began in the 1950s. With the partition of India in 1947, the Punjab was split between India and Pakistan and there was a massive relocation of its inhabitants. Large numbers of Sikhs and Hindus migrated into the Indian part of Punjab, intensifying economic competition and the demand for land. Males from the rural villages of the Punjab, predominantly farmers and landowners of the Jat caste of Sikhs, in fear of becoming landless and in search of better prospects, took up the offer of jobs at Woolfe's Rubber Company, Nestlé and Lyons food-processing plants and other local industries (Bains, 1988). Paradoxically, the tightening of British immigration laws in the 1960s led to a surge of migration, this time of the wives and children of earlier migrants who, fearing the imposition of further immigration restrictions, came to join their husbands and to reunite their families (Brah, 1982).

During the 1970s Jat Sikh migrants were joined by Sikh families from Kenya and later Uganda, forced to abandon their businesses and clerical jobs by 'Africanization' policies. Most of the Sikhs were of the castes of Tarkhan and Lohar, carpenters and blacksmiths, who had been shipped to East Africa to build railways and towns earlier this century. A number of factors distinguished East African emigrants from their Jat predecessors. Their shared urban background and professional skills gave them an economic advantage and a greater facility to adapt to life in Southall (Bhachu, 1985). They emigrated in close-knit family units, often with established social and economic networks, and were used to living in cohesive communities. In contrast, Jat Sikh migrants more resembled 'new frontiersmen' who, at least before the arrival of wives and children, had attempted to adapt to British working-class expectations and lifestyles (Aurora, 1967). The East African cohort of migrants was characterised by religious diversity. There were sizeable numbers of Muslims and Hindus alongside the Sikh settlers who were bound together by shared experiences in East Africa. Upon arrival in Southall, East African emigrants were greeted with a rather ambiguous welcome by their Jat predecessors, who felt threatened by their presence in such large numbers and the inevitable increased competition for jobs (Bhachu, 1985).

This brief history of migration to Southall gives an indication of the cultural and religious diversity, as well as the diversity of histories – and stories – of migration, within what is often assumed to be a homogeneous 'community' of 'Asian' immigrants (and a problem rather than an asset) by the media and public opinion alike. These internal cleavages give life in Southall its distinctive quality and it is worth elaborating upon them in further detail. The balance of religions in Southall in the 1990s reflects its history of migration. According to our survey data (see Appendix 1b; details of the administration of the survey are given in Chapter 2), Sikhs comprise just over half the local population (51 per cent) whilst Hindus (16 per cent) and Muslims (15 per cent) are represented in similar numbers. Eight per cent of respondents were Christians, 5 per cent 'other' and 5 per cent had parents of two different religions.

Indeed religion is by far the most significant marker of cultural distinction among young people in Southall (see Appendix 3). In a remarkable consensus three-quarters (75 per cent) of all respondents to our survey, when asked to 'write down some cultures' they were aware of in Southall, defined the word 'culture' in terms of religion. This figure is increased further by those responses which named a religious festival or ritual as a marker of cultural distinction (8 per cent). Religion is the cornerstone of ethnic identity and the distinction between cultures by religion is characteristic of life in Southall, at least among young people. Terms of 'racial' identity are comparatively rarely cited: 'Asian' (14 per cent), 'black' (7 per cent), 'white' (5 per cent). Terms of national identity (e.g. 'Indian', 'British' [31 per cent]), regional/linguistic terms (e.g. 'Punjab', 'Gujarati' [11 per cent]) and subcultural markers (e.g. 'Rasta' [9 per cent]) are also far less common than distinctions based upon religion. Furthermore, each religion has its own internal cleavages.

The main cleavage among Sikhs, all of whom speak Punjabi, is caste, even though, in principle, Sikhism refuses caste differences. Among Sikhs in Southall, caste differences have come to assume a significance comparable with that which they have in Hinduism, a religion based upon caste distinctions. Caste normally dictates at which of the six gurdwaras, or temples, in Southall a family will worship (though a few assume a 'higher' caste identity by, among other things, worshipping in the appropriate gurdwara). The gurdwara is more than a place of worship: it is a focal point of the Sikh congregation where people go to pray, sing, eat and socialise together, within the limits of gender segregation. Worship takes place mainly on Sundays although some, especially older, women attend every day to pray. Before entering the room where the *Guru Granth Sahib* (or 'holy book') is installed, shoes must be removed. Women wearing traditional Punjabi dress – *salwar kameez* – will draw their *chunni* or scarf over their heads. Any men not wearing a turban will cover their heads with a handkerchief. Young people are encouraged to attend regularly and many do so not only for religious reasons but also because it is an opportunity for socialising. The gurdwara is a good place to 'spot' and 'check out' potential boy- and girlfriends, many young people claim; their parents turn a blind eye to surreptitious, silent flirtation in this context, because it poses no threat to the norm of caste endogamy. Our survey data (Appendix 8) indicates that 37 per cent of boys and 53 per cent of girls had been to their place of worship in the month prior to the survey. Young Muslims do so (52 per cent) more than their Sikh (33 per cent) or Hindu (29 per cent) peers.

Most Sikhs in Southall are of the Jat (farmer/landowner) caste. According to our survey data, approximately 65 per cent of Sikh parents worship in gurdwaras of the Jat caste. Twenty-two per cent worship in gurdwaras of the Ramgharia castes – a general term comprising several castes of skilled craftsmen, such as the Tarkhans and Lohars. The 'twice-migrants' from East Africa are mainly of these castes. Eleven per cent worship in the Ravidas gurdwara. Guru Ravidas is not recognised by orthodox Sikhs as one of the Ten Gurus. This congregation includes the 'low' Chuhre (sweeper) and Chamar (landless labourer) castes, perceived by many as 'untouchables'. The social hierarchy of caste distinction is readily apparent. In fact many 'low-caste' Sikhs gravitate towards worshipping in Hindu mandirs due to their marginalisation within the Sikh 'community'.

The notion of caste is deeply rooted in Indian society and in local consciousness. The following account was written by Kerenpaul, a 15-year-old Sikh girl, for a Sociology A-level essay on caste among Southall Sikhs:

> Caste is based upon two central ideas, purity and occupation. A person's caste is in essence a kind of identity badge [. . .]. How 'pure' a person is considered to be is determined by caste. You often hear people say 'Oh! I'm pure cos I'm a Jat', especially boys who believe they are 'hard' because they are Jat. A person's whole life is based upon what caste they are. It's your social identity. But people who are traditionally considered

to be at the bottom of the caste system i.e. Chuhre, Chamars or Ravidas, they are supposed to be slaves, non-pure, untouchables. They are supposed to work for the higher castes and they are not allowed to eat with people of a higher caste who will not accept food from them. But in Southall they drive around in expensive cars, wear gold jewellery, have huge houses and I know 'pure' Jats who look up to these people [. . .]. Occupations here have confused everything in the traditional caste system. There are Chamars who are electricians and Jats who are cleaners [. . .].

If a Jat girl marries a Tarkhan guy it's regarded as 'bad' because the girl is marrying down the so-called system; this is because the girl joins the husband's family and adopts his name and his caste. If the marriage fails people say it is because they inter-married. People talk – like they'll say 'You know the girl down the street, you know, the one who married the Chamar' [. . .]. You can tell a person's caste by their surname and where they worship but some people change their name and worship in the Jat gurdwara to avoid being seen as 'impure'. [. . .] Some people get sworn at because they have a Ramgharia surname [. . .]. Most young people do not like to discriminate against people on the basis of caste. All Sikhs share the same religion so there shouldn't be a caste system – at least that's what our prophet Guru Nanak preached [. . .].

The caste hierarchy among Sikhs is firmly established and is of the greatest significance when it comes to marriage arrangements, since caste endogamy is the rule. In many respects, the caste system has intensified because in Southall the different castes mix socially and live in close proximity, whereas Punjabi villages are usually organised along caste lines and therefore there is a greater degree of caste segregation in daily life. However, some anomalies have also arisen in the British context. The Ramgharias who migrated from East Africa often have better jobs, more money and more conspicuous styles of consumption than their Jat neighbours. In the eyes of some Ramgharias, this has challenged the established caste hierarchy, as it conflicts with distinctions of class. Caste distinctions are deeply embedded in local consciousness; they are crucial in marriage arrangements, and young people often feel a special affinity with peers of the same caste, tending to cement their closest friendships with those who are 'the same' in caste terms. Yet this is by no means the rule, and many bonds are forged across religious and caste boundaries, as young people progressively develop a common 'Asian' identity in the British context, based on a shared present rather than distinctive heritages. And few people in their everyday lives wish to discriminate, at least openly, on the basis of caste.

The main, interrelated cleavages among Hindus are those of region and language. In responses to our survey, half of all Hindu parents are shown as speakers of Punjabi, just over one third as speakers of Hindi and 15 per cent as speakers of Gujarati. Ironically, and in contrast with the Sikh experience, because Hindus are in a minority and there are few temples, there has been a tendency for caste differences to diminish in importance when it comes to sharing places of public worship – although this is not the case where marriage is concerned.

Among Muslims, although there is a shared sense of belonging to a global 'community' of faith, or *ummah*, cleavages of regional background are important in Southall. The main distinctions are between those from Pakistan, the Indian Punjab, East Africa and Mirpur, on the borders of Kashmir (smaller numbers come from Bangladesh, Somalia, Mauritius, the Seychelles, Malaysia, Trinidad and Fuji). There are also quite significant internal cleavages between those adults who have lived in urban centres such as Lahore and those whose backgrounds are in poorer, more rural districts such as Mirpur. In fact the rural or urban origins of parents is often cited as a further marker of distinction – rural parents being deemed more traditional and 'set in their ways' than their urban counterparts. Survey figures indicate that 50 per cent of parents come from a village; 32 per cent from a town; and 18 per cent from a city – although there are probably wide variations in how these three categories are perceived.

These various cleavages within, as well as between, religions mean that young people may unite or divide along several 'axes of difference'. They may forge strong ties by virtue of shared religion, caste, migration history, region or language. Their sense of ethnic identity is variously composed according to the importance which is attached to any one criterion in a particular context. Despite the centrality of religion as a mark of distinction, a shared East African background, for example, may override this difference. And furthermore, any and all of these distinctions may be, and increasingly are being, transcended in the formation of a broad-based 'British Asian' identity.

SOCIAL PROFILE

The social and cultural life of Southall can only be appreciated in the context of its broader demographic and topographical features (see map, p. 34) The 1981 census gave Southall a population of 66,488. The most densely populated area is Northcote ward: an area of terraced housing built in the 1920s and 1930s, containing the Town Hall, police station, other civic buildings and several gurdwaras, churches and temples. This, the most urbanised part of what is called 'new' Southall, encompasses the Broadway, Southall's main artery: a busy highway lined with locally owned shops selling silk, saris and jewellery, food and music. Shop windows are adorned with huge posters of the latest Bombay stars;

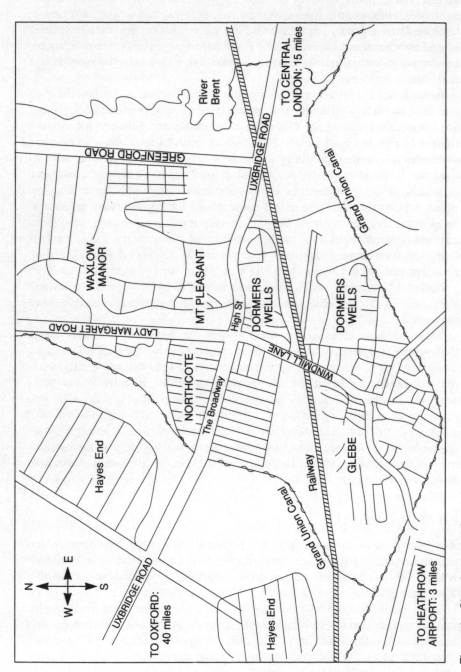

Figure 1 Sketch map of Southall

market stalls protrude on to the broad pavements selling spices, vegetables, clothes and music cassettes.

Southall, or *Chota Punjab* ('little Punjab'), as it is known locally, is divided by what was formerly the Great Western Railway line, a territorial and symbolic boundary separating 'old' and 'new', which is exploited by local youth gangs eager to defend their 'patch'. South of the railway line is Glebe ward, or 'old Southall', which covers a larger area than Northcote. It is less densely populated and contains Edwardian terraced houses, shops, churches, temples, gurdwaras and an impressive mosque with a tall minaret. Glebe and Northcote wards contain the highest number of house-holds with families of South Asian origin – 'white' families having moved to the more 'leafy' and sparsely populated peripheries of Southall. Indeed, Southall has the highest proportion (59 per cent) – and number – of house-holds headed by persons born in the 'New Commonwealth and Pakistan' (NCWP) in the London borough of Ealing, of which it is part. On 1981 census figures, 39 per cent of the population were born in the NCWP while 57 per cent of the population are UK born (including the children of NCPW parentage born in the UK).

Southall also has by far the youngest population profile in the borough of Ealing. Overall, one quarter of its population are of school age. Twenty-seven per cent of its residents are 16 or younger and 44 per cent are under the age of 24. In Northcote ward, around the Broadway, this figure rises to one third. The presence of youth can be felt on the streets, in the cafés and bars, in games arcades and in the parks. Young males can often be seen conspicuously 'cruising' up and down the Broadway in red Ford Capris and white Triumph Stags, sound systems at full volume pumping bhangra or reggae beats, trying to catch the eyes of girls walking by, shouting provocative and flirtatious remarks. As an elderly Sikh cab driver once told me with cheerful sagacity: 'I always made a rule of living at least two miles from the Broadway when my children were growing up – and I advise all my friends to do the same. The Broadway – you see it's like honey to bees – something happens to young people when they live too near the Broadway.'

But at night, after the shops close, usually at around 8 p.m., the Broadway empties and all is quiet – except for large groups of young boys who can be seen on street corners and in the side-streets off the Broadway, huddled around, talking 'men's' talk, smoking, at times drinking and casually enjoying themselves.

However, Southall also has the highest percentage of unemployed people in the borough. School-leavers constitute the largest group of unemployed (22 per cent), followed by the 20–24 age group (15 per cent) (1981 census data). Official figures are of dubious accuracy and probably underestimate the number of unemployed. According to registered unemployed figures appearing in the local newspaper (*Informer*, 12 April 1991), the number of unemployed in Southall had risen threefold, from 3,266 in 1981 to 9,637 in 1991. Of Southall's 66,488 residents, just under half were economically active at the time of the 1981 census. Of these 61 per cent were male and 39 per cent were female. The majority of employed people in Glebe and Northcote wards, where most 'Asian' families live, are employed in semi-skilled and unskilled manual jobs. The main occupations for both men and women are in the manual grouping (38 per cent). In contrast, in Waxlow ward, where more white people live, there is a greater percentage of people employed in professional and managerial jobs. According to our survey data, nearly three-quarters (71 per cent) of young people claim to aspire to better occupations than their parents. This highlights young people's aspirations towards increased mobility – geographical, economic and social – a theme which will recur in this study.

Ethnographic data highlights the ever greater economic role of women in families and their greater likelihood of being exploited. In the youth survey (see Appendix 1c), 69 per cent of mothers were reported as employed outside the home, 28 per cent as housewives and 3 per cent as retired. Of the 69 per cent in employment, 38 per cent fall into the manual, 10 per cent into the semi-skilled and 17 per cent into the skilled job categories. The decline of local manufacturing industries has caused a sharp rise in male unemployment, while the expansion of the service sector has improved employment opportunities for women especially. One of the key local employers of both women and men is Heathrow Airport and the service industries that have arisen around it. Though many parents work long hours and do several shifts, such jobs are eagerly sought after: they are relatively secure and, moreover, they offer the perk of reduced airfares to the subcontinent (as low as 20 per cent of the normal fare), allowing many families to visit relatives annually or at least much more frequently than they could afford to otherwise.

Increased economic independence has brought some women greater autonomy, and this is probably one of the most significant factors affecting changes in gender roles and relations in the family. However for others, employment means being doubly exploited – on the work front and in the home. Many women are employed in low-paid, part-time jobs in local catering firms, factories and 'sweat shops' for manufacturing clothes. Others work from home and are paid on a piecework basis. Often they are paid in cash and deprived of their statutory employment rights. At the same time most mothers and daughters are still expected to take full responsibility for cooking and cleaning and other domestic duties.

Southall has the highest proportion of owner-occupied housing (approximately two thirds of families are owner-occupiers) in the borough (1981 census data). This can be explained partly by discrimination in access to council housing in the early stages of settlement, and partly by the cultural preference, widespread among Punjabi families, for buying rather than renting their homes – in many cases facilitated by the pooling of economic resources in the family and living in larger groupings. Southall is further distinguished by larger households compared with the rest of the borough. The survey and census data concur in this respect, even though the data was elicited in quite different ways. Census data indicates that households of six or more are three times more common in Southall than in other parts of the borough. In the youth survey, data about household size were elicited through questions about the number and composition of eating groups, and about the presence of grandparents or other kin in households. Eating groups of between four and six were prevalent among 68 per cent of respondents; groups of between six and eight among over one third (35 per cent). One in five respondents had either an aunt or an uncle in their daily eating groups; just over one in ten a grandparent.

Our survey data certainly reflects the concentration of relatives living in or near Southall. On average just under a third of Sikh, Muslim and Hindu respondents have grandparents, and 34 per cent have ten or more cousins living in or near Southall. The strength of social networks is not only a result of the density and proximity of kin living locally but also due to strong affinities between families, based on shared regional, religious, caste or linguistic background; shared occupations; family alliances through marriage; same street of residence; children attending the same schools; and shared attendance at social gatherings of various kinds. Southall retains some features of the *pind* or village life, in the sense that kinship and social networks are relatively homogenous in a religious and cultural sense, and are marked by a high degree of face-to-face contact and a low degree of anonymity. The density of the population, particularly in Glebe and Northcote wards, in a relatively small geographic area, generates an intensity of social interaction that is probably quite unique in a London suburb. Young people, in particular, see this as having both positive and negative consequences.

YOUTH CULTURE(S)

Nearly three-quarters (74 per cent) of the young people who took part in our survey agreed that Southall is a close-knit community where 'nothing can be kept a secret' and 'everybody watches what everybody else is doing' (see Appendix 4). The lack of privacy, anonymity and secrecy in Southall is of far greater concern to young people than its isolation from the wider society or the inequalities existing within it. Competitiveness and rivalry between families is the obverse side of the security and other benefits afforded by dense kinship and social networks. Living in such close proximity intensifies local gossip networks which act as a means of social control, particularly of gender relations. A girl's reputation must remain 'high' and 'pure' if she is to be married honourably and respectably. *Izzat* is one of the central motivating principles of local life (its role is enlarged upon further in later chapters). Encompassing a variety of religious, moral and social connotations, *izzat* refers to family honour, pride and respectability. A family's *izzat*, its corporate moral integrity and public standing, must be safeguarded at all costs – and this depends in large part on the conduct of females. Chastity is of paramount importance if daughters are to be married with honour and respect. Gender relations, especially in public, are subject to tight social control by adults. The slightest misdemeanour, such as a boy and girl seen talking in public, can activate the gossip networks and cause family rifts.

Young people find many ways of subtly subverting the tight control of gender relations. Whilst outings 'outside Southall with family' are most frequent, 56 per cent of boys and 48 per cent of girls claimed they had been outside Southall with friends in the last month. Often these outings take place during school-time, unknown to parents, and may involve attending daytime bhangra discos in London, going to the cinema and seeing boyfriends and girlfriends beyond the watchful eyes of relatives and neighbours. However, most girls' lives are centred around the home, family and school, leaving them very little opportunity for socialising beyond these contexts without some kind of surveillance. In contrast, boys have greater freedom of movement and spend much more time on the streets, in games arcades and cafés and at local leisure and sports centres. Not only are public and private spaces gendered, but so is status within the family.

Boys have higher status and tend to be treated preferentially in Punjabi families. Amrita, a 16-year-old Sikh girl, and an A-level Sociology student, characterises gender relations in Punjabi families as follows, expressing views which are very typical among local girls:

Girls have inferior status within Punjabi culture. For instance, when girls are born, parents do not celebrate. Yet when boys are born, Indian sweets are distributed to relations, parties are held by the happy parents and expensive gifts of gold and clothing are given to the mothers and close female relatives. Having daughters is viewed as a burden by parents because of the dowry which has to be given when they get married. Once the girl has been married a great weight is lifted from the parents because she is no longer their responsibility and does not account for family *izzat*. Before a girl gets married everything she does rebounds off her parent's *izzat*. For example if she gains a university degree she boosts family *izzat* [. . .].

Rakhri is a traditional ritual still practised every year in Southall where a sister ties a bracelet to her brother's wrist to show her respect and love. There is no similar ritual for boys to show their love and respect to their sisters, instead boys give their sisters money after they have tied *rakhri* which indicates a girl's dependence upon her brother for material wealth.

If their sisters tie *rakhri* on them it means they are responsible for protecting their sisters' honour. This is a sexist ritual which helps to maintain male dominance over females [. . .]. The more *rakhri* a boy wears the more status he has because these are symbols which indicate he has a number of sisters dependent on him and therefore he has power and authority over them [. . .]. The higher status of boys is also shown in the home where they are not expected to do housework or cook like girls [. . .]. Boys also have more freedom to have girlfriends. They would not let their sisters date a boy but they would conveniently forget that they are also dating someone else's sister.

It is worth noting that the practice of *rakhri* has altered somewhat in the British context, as many girls extend the ceremony to close male friends who are perceived as being 'like brothers'. In one Hindu family I witnessed a daughter ceremoniously tying the *rakhri* bracelet on the wrist of a Muslim boy, a friend of the family. He in turn gave her £20! The parents watched with no sign of disapproval. Hinduism in particular, among the religions in Southall, seems open to the incorporation of others into its rituals.

But gender segregation of young people who are not related to one another remains the norm. Parents are anxious to avoid 'dangerous liaisons' at all costs, and to promote caste endogamy if possible, and certainly religious endogamy. They seek to maintain a taboo on courtship, though there is evidence that attitudes are becoming more relaxed in this respect.

Attitudes to courtship among young people are most certainly influenced by, among other factors, films and TV. As we shall see in Chapter 5, on the negotation of issues of kinship, courtship and community through TV talk about soaps, the widespread popularity of the Australian soap *Neighbours* and other western programmes aimed at teenagers encourages young people to experiment with 'dating'. In many of their favourite American or Australian programmes, dating or 'going out' is the norm, and they find the American teenage lifestyle represented in these programmes and films very appealing. Young people in Southall remark that American teenagers begin dating, with the approval of parents, at a much younger age than their British counterparts; that there are socially acceptable public places and social spaces where young people can go on dates – such as soda bars and graduation balls; and that 'hanging out' in mixed gender groupings publicly is more common. Such opportunities are denied to them in Southall, they feel, but they improvise substitutes: thus they go outside Southall, to fast food outlets such as McDonald's in neighbouring suburbs (see Chapter 6); and at school they organise discos, fashion shows and even, in one year, a very American-style graduation ball.

Popular American TV 'youth' programmes nevertheless heighten their awareness of the gender segregation which many consider as an oppressive feature of local life. As we shall see in Chapter 6, on style and taste, aspirations towards cultural change are frequently expressed with reference to an idealised American teenage lifestyle represented by the media, which encourages the idea that American kids have the freedom and funds to have fun and to date whoever they wish. It is perhaps partly for these reasons that America and Australia are also the countries that most young people (46 per cent) would like to visit, as compared with the various centres of the Punjabi diaspora: Canada (7 per cent), India (5 per cent), Pakistan (2 per cent), continental Europe (5 per cent) and East Africa (4 per cent) (see Appendix 12). These may be 'diaspora kids', but their aspirations for travel and lifestyle are essentially American. Their favourite pop and film stars are also American (37 per cent), or English stars (26 per cent), followed by 'Asian' (18 per cent) and Australian stars (9 per cent). (At the time of the survey Michael Jackson was cited as the favourite star of some 23 per cent of boys and girls, followed by Tom Cruise [14 per cent], Madonna [13 per cent], Kylie Minogue [12 per cent], George Michael [10 per cent] and Jason Donovan [10 per cent]).

ARRANGING MARRIAGES

Most young people express the wish for more tolerant attitudes on the part of parents on the issue of courtship, usually referred to as 'going out (together)' (see Appendix 7a). The majority of respondents to the survey agreed with the statement that 'parents should know more about it [going out] and be more understanding' (67 per cent); that 'going out with a boy or a girl is normal at my age' (58 per cent); and that 'going out does not have to lead to marriage' (57 per cent). Some three-quarters of respondents agreed that 'people should be free to marry whom they like', a statement which can be taken to imply a rejection of the parentally sanctioned rules of religious and caste endogamy (Appendix 7b). It certainly reflects the wish of many young people for greater participation in family decision-making about their marriages. In fact just under half agreed that they would prefer to marry someone of their 'own culture'. But caste, it would seem, is not a very significant factor for most young people in decisions about marital partners. Only one in five considered that 'people should marry in their own caste'. These responses are contradicted by ethnographic data which indicates that, although caste is a taboo topic which is rarely discussed or indeed mentioned in the peer culture, except among close friends, it is of paramount importance, especially, but in fact not only, in the eyes of parents, when it actually comes to the moment of arranging marriages. Young people will affirm the principle of romantic love – free choice of partner – in responding to a questionnaire and indeed often in spontaneous conversation; but in practice marriage arrangements are negotiated between parents and young people, leaving the youngsters widely varying degrees of autonomy, and ultimately most conform 'voluntarily' to parental wishes. Some young people demonstrate considerable ingenuity in orchestrating their own marriage arrangements: after 'going out together' clandestinely for several years, one couple I knew contrived to be 'introduced' to one another by a matchmaker in front of their unwitting parents, and a successful marriage ensued!

However, prior to the moment of settlement of marriage arrangements, many young people appear to experience an almost inexorable drive to become romantically involved with people who are not of the same religion or caste. Many tales of tragic teenage love affairs circulate in Southall – real Romeo and Juliet scenarios involving midnight assignations, brief encounters, furtive meetings and the scaling of high walls to speak through bedroom windows – intensifying the excitement, sense of risk and romance. At least as I heard them, these tales are mostly sexually innocent, and they share melodramatic features with the plots of Hindi movies.

The mere suggestion of a marriage outside one's caste is often enough to provoke a family crisis. Yet when it comes to the moment of marriage, most are reluctant to sacrifice their family for the sake of a 'love marriage' to an 'unsuitable' partner. Among Punjabis marriage is perceived as a union between two families, not just two individuals, and individual desires are deemed subordinate to family duty. The following account of marriage arrangements among Punjabi Sikh families is fairly typical, though increasingly there are variations in customary practices. The so-called 'arranged marriage system' as practised in Southall is rarely as rigid and repressive as its critics imagine, especially when one considers that most marital unions, in all cultures, are subject to the application of fairly standard criteria; they may simply be less explicitly articulated than in the case of Punjabi families. This account was written by Harjinder, a 17-year-old Jat Sikh girl, who was one of my key informants. It was part of a Social Studies project which acquired personal significance as her parents had just begun looking for a 'suitable boy' for her. It gives some insight to the nature of the negotiations involved:

> From about the age of seventeen a girl's parents will start looking for a suitable boy. Some parents tell their friends that they're looking but most ask their relatives if they know a suitable boy. Then when a boy is found for the girl, let's say by the girl's *thaii* [her dad's older brother], a meeting with the boy's parents is arranged by the *bachola* or matchmaker who takes the girl's parents to meet the boy's parents. The girl does not attend this meeting. On the way to the meeting the *bachola* tells the girl's parents the boy's age, whether he works, how big his family is and what qualifications he has. Things have changed a bit since my mum got married in the Punjab. She says that in the Punjab the most important things in deciding on a suitable boy or girl were caste, *izzat* [or family honour], the 4 *got* [clan] rule – which means you cannot marry any

descendants of your 4 grandparents, and land. In England it's a bit different. Caste and *izzat* are still most important but then come education/job, the person's age, personal qualities, attractiveness – all these come into the decision.

When the girl's parents and *bachola* arrive, the boy's mother serves tea and food like Indian sweets. The girl's parents ask questions like what type of girl is the boy looking for and they tell them. Then the girl's parents go home and discuss with the matchmaker whether they like the boy. If they like the boy they tell the girl what he looks like, where he works, how old he is and what qualifications he has. Then it's up to the girl. If she likes him another meeting is arranged for the boy and his parents to come to girl's house. The girl and boy are introduced to each other by the matchmaker. All this meeting is focused on the boy and the girl. A lot of eye contact is made between the boy and the girl when they go into another room to talk to one another. An older person is present – usually the girl's aunt. The boy can ask questions to the girl about her education, hobbies and vice versa. Then after about fifteen minutes they come and join the others. Then the boy's parents go home and say that they will let the matchmaker know their answer in a few days. If the answer is yes and the parents like the girl, and the boy likes the girl, the matchmaker tells the girl's parents the good news. Often this is the one and only time a girl sees her future husband before they get married. Even in Britain Jat Sikh parents disapprove of courtship.

Then another meeting is arranged by the *bachola* known as the *rokha*. This is the 'stopping' of the future groom and the bride. This is when the girl's male kin reserves the boy. This means he can't see any other girl and vice versa. The girl's parents go to the boy's house to *rokh* the boy and the boy's parents go to the girl's house to *rokh* the girl [...]. It's important not to tell friends that you've done a *rokha*. This is to prevent a scandal taking place if things go wrong. Then another meeting is arranged at the girl's house to arrange when the 'court marriage' should be done. At this meeting *daaj* or dowry is also discussed. Sometimes the boy tells his parents that he likes the girl a lot and does not wish his parents to ask for any dowry. This shows that he loves the girl. Yet most families ask for some dowry. Most girls' parents give gold, beds, clothes, washing machines and microwaves. Some boys' parents might only ask for gold. Others might ask for more furniture. Yet not all girls' families can afford expensive items so the *bachola* negotiates with the two families. If the boy's parents don't get the *daaj* they want they may call off the marriage. This is why not a lot of girls like the idea of *daaj*. Love should be important yet greed can overpower love when it comes to gold. The *daaj* causes a lot of problems and friction between people. It can even destroy a marriage [...]. 'Court marriage' is another term for marriage which takes place in a registry office. This has to take place in Britain because the Indian marriage does not involve a certificate and so in the eyes of English law a religious wedding in rural Punjab would not be legal in Britain. After the court marriage the groom goes back home with his family and the bride goes back with hers. The religious wedding takes place maybe three or even six months later. The night before the wedding the girl has a party with all her female kin who put henna in her hands in beautiful patterns and spices to make her skin glow [. . .] they sing and dance [. . .]. On the day of the wedding everyone gets ready and takes a bath. The bride usually wears a red sari with pearls and sequins and lots of gold jewellery that her family give her as part of her dowry. The groom usually wears a suit and a pink turban with a feather in it. When the groom is ready he is taken into the leaving room where all his family are waiting. The mother gives the boy *sagan*. This is usually an Indian sweet. The groom's auntie or sister-in-law puts black eye-liner on the groom. This is also traditional. Then the *bharat* leave. These are the boy's family members and close kin [. . .].

The bride's family hires a hall for the actual wedding [. . .] and they also prepare the food. All the guests arrive at the hall. Then it is time for *milnis* or the exchange of presents, like garlands, turbans and blankets, between the male kin of the bride and groom. Then the *bharat* are given breakfast. Meanwhile the *Guru Granth Sahib* [the Sikh holy book] is brought into the other side of the hall where the ceremony is to take place. The holy bible of Sikhs is set up by the *phatee* or holy-men. These men are very strict vegetarians [. . .]. They begin to sing hymns. The *bharat*, the groom and his family are brought in and sit on white sheets which are laid out on the floor with all the guests. Then the bride is brought in accompanied by an aunt, sisters and other female kin. Now starts the wedding ceremony [. . .]. Then comes the *bhog*. This is the end of praying when a page from the holy bible is read and *prasad* [holy food] is given out to everyone.

Now is the time to wish the couple good luck. Money is given to the couple by all the guests [. . .]. Then it's time to celebrate [. . .]. An Indian bhangra group, like Heera or Alaap if the family are rich, sets up on the stage. Nowadays, sometimes the boy's side pay for the band. The whole wedding can cost the girl's parents anything from £5,000–£15,000. Food is served by the girl's kin. Whisky and meat is served as well as *roti* and *daal* [Indian bread and lentil curry]. Men and women sit separately. Everyone dances to the music and both sides of the family mix. After three hours the groups say goodbye and the bride goes back to her home to prepare for her *doli* or departure. This is a very sad moment for the bride because she has to leave her family and go to live with her husband and parents-in-law. The bride cries a lot and this is only natural [. . .].

Young people and their families are adapting to changed circumstances and finding new ways of negotiating marriage arrangements, though most are maintaining the fundamental aspects of marriage traditions. Nevertheless, marriage arrangements can be a major source of tension, anxiety and even dread for girls especially. Scandalous and tragic stories about failed arrangements and marriages are rife in local folklore. For example, a girl, betrothed to a boy she liked very much, had her hopes shattered when her younger brothers and sisters, and several of her friends, were watching a pop programme called *Club X* on broadcast TV. The boy appeared on screen kissing another girl. The programme was being taped on video because a favourite group was performing. The boy and his family were summoned to the girl's house, given tea, shown the video and then the door. In this case, the boy presumably thought he had escaped the local gossip network only to find that it had been replaced by TV.

Ethnographic evidence suggests that parents from urban areas are more likely to have relaxed attitudes concerning marriage arrangements and to adopt more flexible criteria in selecting suitable partners for their children, whereas among rural-born parents there is a greater tendency towards more strict adherence to the custom of caste endogamy and to traditional practices in marriage arrangements. Yet intercaste and inter-religious marriages, though still relatively infrequent, are on the rise. Young people are tending to marry at a later age and higher education is seen as way of postponing decision making, gaining professional status and a degree of economic independence. But data from school records indicates that, on average, only about 20 per cent of 18-year-olds go on to higher education. The incidence of underachievement in Southall high schools was a source of continued concern throughout my years of teaching there. Disaffection with school, high rates of youth unemployment and minimal future prospects no doubt contributed to a feature of the local youth culture which achieved some national notoriety: the rise of gang subcultures in Southall.

WILD WEST LONDON? SOUTHALL GANGS

At the time of fieldwork there were two main local gangs: the 'Holy Smokes' and the '*Tuti Nangs*' (various meanings are attributed to the latter name, but a prevalent one is 'broken soul'). Stories about the origins of the gangs have taken on mythical dimensions and are as various as the tellers. Some attribute their existence to family feuds rooted in the Punjab and justify their continuance by the duty to defend family honour. These feuds are seen to spiral down across generations and spill into contemporary Southall life. Others see the gangs as part of a larger, international criminal organisation involved in drug dealing, fraud and embezzlement. The boys at street level are seen to deal in petty crime, car theft, robbery and 'soft' drugs. In between, various levels of criminal activities and types of 'protection rackets' are thought to occur. Younger boys often claim membership of a gang by virtue of a putative family tie with a supposed gang member. Most boys claim that one of their family or friends is in one of the gangs.

The gangs are divided along religious and territorial lines. The 'Holy Smokes' are considered to be a gang of primarily Jat Sikhs, many of whom voice support for the Khalistan Movement – the separatist movement in the Punjab. The '*Tuti Nangs*' are seen as a 'mixed' gang, reflecting Southall's cultural diversity. The 'Holies' are seen to dominate 'old' Southall and the 'Toots' the Broadway area, or 'new' Southall. However, there are 'Holies' who live in 'Toots' areas and vice versa, which gives rise to territorial disputes. In 1988 the local press took up the issue of the gangs and made it a staple storyline over several months (*Ealing Gazette*, February–July 1988). Reports of strong-arm recruitment tactics in local schools, involving pupils as young as 11 and 12, and alleged cases of rape, assault, extortion, fraud, drug dealing, stabbings, shootings and murders were invariably attributed to the gangs. In 1988–1989 a national public outcry and 'moral panic' occurred, inflamed by media coverage such as a documentary entitled 'Southall Boys' (broadcast in the *Bandung File* series, Channel 4, 1989). Using only three case studies, and highly selective, stereotypical images of 'Southall boys', this programme proceeded to paint a picture of Southall as being torn apart by gangs; of families and lives being destroyed by them; and of a 'community in the grip of fear'. Interestingly enough, informants who one can readily believe to be gang members report that 'the worst of the gang warfare was well over by the time the media got their hands on it'. The place of the gangs in local youth culture at the time of fieldwork is discussed further in Chapter 4, in the context of Southall's specific 'news history', and Chapter 6, in the context of the 'hard' style adopted by 'Holy' gang members who appropriate the symbols of militant Sikhism.

BHANGRA

Both the myth and the reality of this polarised gang subculture appear to have subsided in recent years as more varied youth subcultural groupings have emerged, primarily based upon taste in music and dance, fashion and style. These distinctions are discussed further in Chapter 6. However, one form of traditional Punjabi folk music and dance, bhangra, is embraced by young British Asians of every ethnic origin. It has become a focal point for the public emergence of a British Asian youth culture which transcends traditional divisions and aspires to a sense of ethnic unity. It provides one of the most tangible manifestations of the way in which traditional aesthetic forms are re-created when opened up to alternative cultural influences and new technologies of production in changed social contexts.

In rural Punjab, bhangra was performed at harvest festivals, usually by males. The music is characterised by an energetic beat and the use of the double-sided drum or *dhol*. The songs celebrate the beauty of the harvest season and a range of sentiments from friendship to love. Over the past decade this musical tradition has undergone rapid change as new styles have emerged: from 'bhangra beat', 'rock bhangra' and 'house bhangra' to the more recent fusion with reggae, 'ragga bhangra'. Baumann (1990) argues that the emergence and development of these different styles demonstrates with remarkable clarity the articulation of social changes and aesthetic shifts. His research shows how the genesis of 'bhangra beat' in Southall in the 1970s was contingent on the co-operation of musicians from the Punjab versed in traditional bhangra songs and music, and producers from East Africa who contributed their technical skills and business acumen – a product of diaspora culture (Gilroy, 1993a). In contrast, the more recent emergence of 'rock bhangra' and 'house bhangra' in Birmingham, where more heterogenous patterns of settlement among Sikhs occurred, was brought about by the interaction with Afro-Caribbean and Anglo-American styles of popular music.

Bhangra in its various forms in now commonly performed at weddings, engagement and 'coming-of-age' parties among South Asian families across Britain. In London, daytime bhangra discos are regularly held at prestigious venues like the Empire in Leicester Square or the Hammersmith Palais, where they attract audiences of 2,000–4,000. Young people stress the fact that the songs are sung in Punjabi and this is valued for perpetuating the heritage of Punjabi song and poetry. Girls wear traditional *salwar kameez* and dance alongside the boys with hands in the air, shrugging their shoulders to the beat of the music. It is a form and style that British Asian youth can claim as their own and be proud of: neither *gori* (white) nor *kala* (black), it has made British Asian youth both audible and visible for the first time on the British musical scene. In 1993, a Birmingham band fronted by a singer called Apache Indian – who soon went on to become a DJ on BBC Radio 1 – was the first 'Asian crossover' band to hit the mainstream charts. The music fuses bhangra and reggae styles, and Apache Indian's songs, like many new bhangra songs, are subversive, presenting forceful social critiques of issues from drugs and AIDS to the dowry system. This does not lessen local pride in the form; instead it allows for an assimilation of the values of urban British youth culture in combination with a continued attachment to the values shared with parents and rooted in the subcontinent. The cultures of Southall youth bear witness to some remarkable cultural crossovers, 'borrowings' and convergences – the fruits of living with cultural difference – and serve as powerful testimony to the essentially dynamic nature of culture, not as a static, determinate and transmittable entity, but as inherently changeable, permeable and responsive to the social world. We shall now turn to questions of ethnographic fieldwork and the potential it offers for capturing such processes of cultural change as they unfold in everyday life.

Chapter 2

Living fieldwork – writing ethnography

This chapter explains how my research evolved out of an interrelated set of professional, personal and academic interests, accounts for the choice of ethnography as a methodological approach in the study of TV audiences, and highlights the key practical and theoretical importance of 'TV talk'. It outlines the progression of the fieldwork in its main phases – groundwork, immersion, focusing – and addresses some of the problematic issues associated with researcher–informant relationships in 'living fieldwork' – disparities of power, the difficulty of disengagement, and questions of gender and ethnic difference. Finally I discuss problems associated with the act of 'writing ethnography': both the particular problems associated with writing, as I did, 'in the field', and more general problems of 'ethnographic authority' and responsibility.

This study is based on data collected during two years of fieldwork carried out from 1988–1991. During the period of the fieldwork I lived in Southall, sharing a house with young adults of Punjabi family background. However, my involvement with young people in Southall dates back to the autumn of 1981 when, as a probationary secondary school teacher, I was sent on teaching practice to a local high school. This was in the aftermath of the disturbances, or 'race riots' as they were termed by the media, which took place in Southall, Brixton (south London) and Toxteth (Liverpool) in the summer of 1981. Black and 'Asian' youth in these areas took to the streets in a spectacular manner in revolt against heavy-handed policing and racist attacks (CCCS, 1982: 1–36). This was the 'moment' when I entered the field and the period in which my interest in research in Southall began. As part of my teaching degree, I undertook a small-scale research project on young people's perceptions of their relations with parents, school, police and the wider society, highlighting their wish to 'pick the best of both worlds' (Gillespie, 1981).

From 1982–1986 I worked in another local high school as a teacher of English as a second language (ESL) to young emigrés from the Indian subcontinent. Here I learned enough Punjabi to conduct everyday casual conversations. I also began to understand the difficulties faced by teenage immigrants in the British school system, where they were multiply marginalised: physically, from the mainstream of the school (we worked in a hut); educationally, from the curriculum (they were withdrawn from mainstream lessons); and socially, from their British-born Punjabi peers, who tended to reject them as *pendus* (peasants). During this time I was engaged in a number of small-scale 'Action Research' projects (Stenhouse, 1980) aimed at integrating 'ESL students', as they were labelled, into the mainstream of the school and rendering the curriculum accessible to them.

My interest in local TV and video culture grew as I became both aware of the high levels of TV and video consumption and concerned about the relatively low levels of literacy among my students. I became interested in education about and through the media and in what appeared to be 'new' forms of media literacy. In 1986, as part of an MA in Film and Television Studies for Education at the University of London Institute of Education, I undertook a study of video use among families in Southall. The research highlighted how the VCR enables families to maintain strong cultural ties with their countries of origin through the consumption of popular film and television, exported from the Indian subcontinent. It pointed to the ways in which a 'new' communications technology is being mobilised for the purposes of maintaining and re-inventing traditions, showing how it is implicated in the construction of 'ethnic' identities in the Indian diaspora (Gillespie, 1989).

The reasons for my interest in how young people in Southall negotiate generational and cultural differences are personal as well as professional. I shall outline some of these since they have influenced the way in which I have dealt with questions of reflexivity – for the observer is also part of the observational field, and therefore a subject of the research (Woolgar, 1988). My parents emigrated from the Republic of Ireland in the 1940s to London and, though I grew up in London, my family's social network mainly consisted of other Irish immigrant families. Whilst there are obvious differences between Punjabi Sikh and Irish Catholic families in their experiences of migration and settlement, not least in the fact that colour prejudice makes Punjabis an easier target for racism, the similarities between the parental cultures struck me quite forcefully. I was surprised to find my experiences of growing up resonated with those of Punjabi Sikh youth in several ways.

The centrality of religion in the parental culture as a mode of cognition and as a cultural system means that the existence of God is, for most, self-evident. The strength of kinship ties, in many ways influenced by religious beliefs, encourages an emphasis upon family duty and loyalty, honour and obedience. The prevalence of close-knit, relatively large families living in close proximity provides strong support networks but also heightens status competition between families. Parents originate predominantly from rural villages where farming is the main occupation, so that adaptation to urban living is a necessary part of the process of settlement. The experience of being uprooted, displaced and discriminated against tends to produce feelings of insecurity, nostalgia for an idealised past and longing for an idealised 'homeland'. This often encourages attempts to maintain, strengthen and even re-invent cultural traditions which are seen to be under threat or attack. But migration and settlement also inevitably lead to an acceleration of the processes of cultural change – processes in which the media are implicated.

These commonalities between Punjabi Sikh and Irish Catholic families in London have influenced the research process and analysis both positively and negatively. They have helped me in dealing with some of the problems inherent in learning from and studying a culture different to one's own, reducing the risk of my 'exoticising' or 'tribalising' the 'other'. In particular, they have helped one to understand how questions of religious belief and practice, kinship duties and marriage patterns are being negotiated in emigrant families. For example, patterns of 'double-sibling' marriage (i.e. two brothers marrying two sisters), aimed at consolidating the union of families and property, were part of my own family history, and were identified as common in drawing up family genealogies with informants in Southall. Disputes about the inheritance of land in the home country and the financial support given to, and expected by, relatives 'back home' were also much discussed both in my own background and in Southall. Such commonalities have greatly facilitated the rapport between students, informants and myself, helping me – and them – to recognise self in other and vice-versa.

However, at times I have assumed similarities which subsequently proved to be misleading. For example, I tended to underestimate the pressures upon young people in Southall to renounce their individual desires and ambitions in response to family demands. I was also disabused of several preconceptions concerning the nature of religious beliefs and practices, which I supposed to be more homogeneous than they were. The process of identifying and refining similarities and differences has enabled a progressive critical distancing from both my own and my subjects' experiences. This is crucial if one is to overcome the problem of so closely identifying with one's subjects that one runs the risk of projecting one's own concerns on to them and defending their values, beliefs and practices rather than studying them (Woods, 1979).

My academic interests were, therefore, stimulated by my professional experiences as teacher and researcher and by my family's experiences of migration and settlement in Britain. Questions about young Punjabis' uses of the media in negotiating the relations between parental and peer cultures, and issues of cultural identity and difference, maintenance of tradition and change, became a central focus of my academic concern.

Having examined the uses of popular Hindi films in the family context, it seemed logical to extend these interests to an examination of the uses and interpretations of British broadcast TV both in families and in the peer culture. I moved to Southall to embark on the Ph.D. research which would lead to this book, while teaching on a part-time basis in a local high school. As I describe in more detail later in this chapter, I developed a variety of strategies for gaining access to the peer culture, in order to discover how young people express themselves and interact in the absence of parental constraint.

THE SOUTHALL YOUTH SURVEY (1989–1990)

Dissatisfied with the limited scale of my study of VCR use, I decided to investigate the typicality of the responses derived from the interviews. A questionnaire-based survey was carried out among 333 young people (aged 12–18) in Southall from June to August 1989 (see Appendix), in collaboration with Dr Gerhard Baumann. The survey's aims were to collect data on how young people perceive themselves in the many cultures of Southall, in their own youth culture and in relation to their parental cultures; and to establish patterns of media consumption within the broader context of their local life, leisure activities, schooling and education. The survey involved direct questions, open-ended questions, and questions asking respondents to agree or disagree with statements culled from ethnographic data in the idiolect of the peer culture. It produced data about many aspects of young people's lives: family backgrounds, parental employment, kinship and social networks, perceptions of local cultures, leisure pursuits, musical tastes and patterns of media consumption. The results allowed me to correlate details of the social and cultural backgrounds of respondents with the data on TV consumption and other media use; to identify patterns of TV use and consumption linked to age and gender; and to identify correlations with other factors, such as class, religion and parental background, which could then be investigated further in fieldwork.

Dr Baumann and I combined our interests and made our inputs to the questionnaire both separately and jointly. Such a large-scale survey also required the assistance of university students who, as part of Brunel University's work placement scheme, helped mainly in inputting and cross-tabulating the data, using the Statistical Package for Social Sciences. The process of designing the questionnaire, piloting and refining it, and then collecting, inputting and analysing the data took place over an eighteen-month period, alongside fieldwork.

Above all we wanted to avoid the problem of ethnic determinism which reduces all behaviour to ethnic or cultural factors. We started from the premise that questionnaire design is itself a form of data construction and manipulation, rather than a means of gathering facts in some 'neutral' and 'value-free', quasi-ritualistic procedure which might be supposed to produce definitive factual accuracy. The questionnaire-based survey method has many advantages. It permits the relatively rapid and systematic collection of large amounts of data, which can be correlated with selected variables and analysed. Patterns of variation and co-variation form a basis which allows inferences to be made and suggests relationships, sometimes confirming ethnographic data, and sometimes pointing to new lines of enquiry. The survey was designed to enhance the representativeness, reliability and validity of our research overall, as well as to allow for greater precision in testing certain propositions emerging from qualititative data previously gathered.

In conducting this survey in the course of my ethnographic research, I particularly hoped to overcome some of the problems associated with recent small-scale empirical studies of TV audiences, especially in terms of their validity and viability (Feuer, 1986; Hartley, 1987; Clifford and Marcus, 1986). Quantitative survey methods are ideally suited to the purposes of establishing broad patterns of media consumption and taste, if used in conjunction with more qualitative methods (Bourdieu, 1984). For both Gerhard Baumann and myself, the methodological aim was to attempt to overcome the polarity between qualitative and quantitative methods and to assess their compatibility. The survey would, thus, provide a skeleton or framework which would be fleshed out with the detailed data collected in fieldwork.

Although surveys are by no means a defining feature of anthropological fieldwork, Malinowski for one was convinced of their value:

> In survey work we are given an excellent skeleton, so to speak, of tribal constitution, but it lacks flesh and blood. We learn much about the framework of their society, but within it we cannot imagine or perceive the realities of everyday human life, the even flow of everyday events, the occasional ripples of excitement over a feast or a ceremony, or some singular occurrence. (1964 [1922]: 17)

The social survey counts people as units, while social anthropology seeks to understand people, not as units but as integral parts of and agents in systems and relationships. These cannot be counted. Nevertheless, the quantitative survey, combined with more qualitative research strategies, can provide dimensions of typicality for case material and will thereby enhance or verify the total ethnographic picture.

In recent years the survey method has been most unfashionable among academic audience researchers, who have generally expressed increasing preference for the use of qualitative methods. It is dismissed as positivist, empiricist and lacking in explanatory power. It is also criticised for being unable to address questions of 'meaning', since the researcher is unable to tap into the subjective meanings held individually or collectively. It is argued that the questionnaire is not understood and answered by everyone in the same way; that it is a rigid and closed method of data collection and so fails to discover the unexpected; and further, that the survey's focus on taxonomic groups (occupational groups, age groups, household types, social class, community types) fails to take account of casual groupings, relationships and alliances (Moser and Kalton, 1971).

However, many complaints which parade as fundamental criticisms of survey methods are only reacting to poorly designed, inadequately conceptualised and theorised, unpiloted or just ill-managed surveys (Marsh, 1982). Although the survey can hardly deal with the complexity of social processes, and is limited in the kind of data it can elicit, many of its inherent weaknesses can be overcome when it is combined with qualitative methods. There are now some signs of a rehabilitation of survey methods in establishing patterns of media consumption (Murdock, 1989); but surveys are unlikely to be useful unless they form part of an ethnographic approach, which alone can bring us closer to finding answers to the more enduring questions of academic audience research.

ETHNOGRAPHY AND TV AUDIENCE RESEARCH

One of the central problems which have plagued academic audience research has concerned the 'effects' of television. Much of the early research overestimated the power of TV; its audiences were invariably misconceived as a mass of atomised individuals vulnerable to its persuasive and potentially harmful effects. Research has since shifted its focus across different points in the communication process and employed very different methods of enquiry: from a concern with TV's effects upon behaviour to its uses and gratifications; from a focus on the political and ideological role of TV to an examination of popular pleasures and audience interpretations in specific social and cultural contexts. Regrettably, a polarisation of positivist and interpretivist perspectives, and of quantitative and qualitative methodologies has ensued, which has been divisive and debilitating, and disciplinary boundaries too have militated against the development of fruitful enquiry. Reception studies, drawing upon literary theory, have tended to be text-led, whilst sociological approaches have tended to presume ideological effects. Meanwhile broadcasting institutions have continued to rely upon the monthly ratings and other number-crunching devices to attract ever greater audiences. More money has been poured into research into the effects of TV, particularly the portrayal of violence and sex, than any other area of social science research (Lodziac, 1986: 7); but the results have continued to be inconclusive, unreliable and highly contradictory.

Traditional models of research have above all failed to approximate the lived experiences of audiences and to deliver the kinds of insights required to understand the complexities of TV and of its audiences embedded in wider social, political and economic contexts. Since 1980, however, significant advances have been made in qualitative audience research and these have contributed much to our understanding of TV reception processes, especially in the domestic context of viewing (Hobson, 1980; Morley, 1986; Buckingham, 1987; Gray, 1992). More recently, especially among those working in field of cultural studies, ethnography has been championed as a research practice capable of overcoming the impasse of many audience studies (Ang, 1985; Lull, 1990; Silverstone, 1990; Morley, 1991). Clearly, the 'embeddedness' of TV in everyday life demands research techniques and procedures which are sensitive to the microprocesses of its recreative reception and appropriation by viewers.

The central methodological argument advanced by this book is that ethnography can deliver empirically grounded knowledge of media audiences in a way that other, less socially encompassing methods cannot. At the same time, this type of research into TV audiences can generate the kind of ethnographic knowledge of local cultures which is usually considered to be the sole preserve of anthropologists – pointing to fruitful possibilities of interdisciplinary cross-fertilisation. However, audience research, notably in the field of British cultural studies, is increasingly frequently referred to as 'ethnographic' in the apparent absence of an awareness of what validates ethnography as a genre, namely fieldwork based upon intensive, long-term participant observation. What have come to be called 'ethnographic methods' in audience studies should often simply be called qualitative methods. Moores, for example, suggests that in order to merit the name 'ethnographic', reception studies need only share the same 'intentions' as anthropological research; he describes ethnography as a 'perspective', characterised by 'situational embeddedness', and remarks that it need not be based on fieldwork 'in distant lands' – indeed, it seems that it need not be based on fieldwork at all, as the 'in-depth interview' will suffice (1993: 4). But ethnography, as the word implies, is a genre of writing, and it is one which is based on a theoretical framework, a methodology grounded in long-term fieldwork, and – as I will argue – an ethos.

Ethnography is a way of understanding social life in relational and holistic terms. Strictly speaking, it is an academic genre which presents highly detailed empirical data for two, often implicit, purposes. One is the holistic ambition of showing, by means of what Geertz (1973, 1979) called 'thick description', that there is a complex whole formed by the interaction of various social relations and processes, which may be described as 'culture'. The other is that of presenting social theory as emerging, quasi-empirically, from simply 'letting the data speak': this is the temptation of positivism, which perhaps besets media researchers as much as it does anthropologists. Broadly speaking, three models of ethnographic practice can be identified (Clifford, 1983: 141–142); the positivist model pioneered by Malinowski (1964 [1922]); the interpretive model practised by Geertz (1973); and the more recent dialogical model represented by, among others, Rabinow (1977) and Rosaldo (1984). Malinowski created an image of the fieldworker as a kind of scientist and of ethnography as the report of an extended experiment. Geertz privileged the perspective of the 'natives' as opposed to that of the 'scientist' (Geertz, 1979). The dialogic model involves a highly self-reflexive approach and has subjected itself to literary theory.

Despite the widespread interest in ethnography among TV researchers and the proliferation of theoretical writings proposing it as a panacea for audience research, very few existing studies actually draw upon any of these models of practice, and so genuinely deserve to be described as ethnographies. Rather, the term ethnography has come to be associated with one method in social research, the in-depth, open-ended, semi-structured interview. The appropriation of the term has not involved a corresponding shift in, or any fundamental re-evaluation of, research practice. Anthropological ethnography requires long-term immersion and investigation: eighteen months is the standard length of fieldwork required to attain the 'emic' or 'native' point of view (Pike, 1966). The 'native' view envisioned by classical ethnographers is hardly to be grasped through a series of one-off 'in-depth' interviews or brief periods of observation.

Media researchers have paid scant attention to this problem – with a few notable exceptions. The 'terminological usurpation' of ethnography by interpretivist media researchers is criticised by Evans (1990), who argues that borrowing labels without their accompanying contents is at best unimaginative, and at worst deceitful and counter-productive for the development of interdisciplinary social theory construction. The use and abuse of the term has also been examined by Nightingale (1989). She argues that the term is used to legitimate research; to denote its cultural, phenomenal and empirical methods; and to link studies to the academic heritage of cultural studies and to the type of social-realist research advocated by Raymond Williams. To be fair, the studies she chooses to substantiate her claims are unlikely to be described as ethnographic by the researchers involved (Morley, 1980; Ang, 1985; Buckingham, 1987; Hobson, 1982). But she is quite right to point out that the term is used as a legitimatory device. This widespread misuse is significant: it signals not only sloppy usage but also a confusion which has inhibited discussion of methodological issues. Much audience and reception research in cultural studies lacks a sufficiently sociological and anthropological approach and pays too little attention to methodological issues. Several recent studies present findings with little or no reference to how data was gathered, in what type of contexts, from what kind of subjects. As a consequence, it is difficult to evaluate the significance of their results. (This is the case in several of the reports of research in *Cultural Studies* 5/2 [1991], for example).

Only a more fully anthropological approach to TV audience research can provide detailed data about a subject which is crucial to our understanding of the 'effects' of TV, of the ways in which TV impinges upon, and becomes integrated into, the lives of viewers. 'TV talk' is the central focus of my study.

TV TALK

Television represents varieties of socially situated speech, and so, like speech itself, it forms a nexus between language and the social world. It represents models of speech, portrays patterns of sociable interaction and provides shared resources for speaking. Scannel (1989, 1991), working from a historical perspective, argues that broadcasting functions as a shared cultural resource among audiences and has played a major role in re-articulating the boundaries between the public and private spheres. Drawing upon Habermas's concept of the 'public sphere', he defends broadcasting as a 'public good' that has contributed, in an unobtrusive manner, to the democratisation of everyday life. Precisely because the public life of broadcasting is accessible to all, he argues, it is there to be talked about by all. Everyone is entitled to have views and opinions about what they see and hear – which is not the case with most other cultural resources (Scannel, 1989).

Broadcasting, in this view, acts as a form of social lubrication, easing social interaction and sustaining it in countless everyday circumstances: 'It is perhaps the one thing in the UK (apart from the weather) that we all have in common as a topical resource' (Scannel, 1989: 155). Certain kinds of programmes, such as soaps, have become ritual social events in which people talk about the programme before, during and after viewing. Outlining an argument which I take further in Chapter 5, Scannel points out that:

> Gossip is the life-blood of soaps as it is of ordinary everyday life, 'the living breath of events' [. . .]. Gossip in broadcasting, about broadcasting and in ordinary conversation is the very stuff of broadcasting's inter-connection with so-called private life or ordinary daily life. (1989: 156)

The communicative ethos of broadcasting has shifted in recent decades from an earlier authoritarian mode to a more populist and democratic style, according to Scannel. He argues that broadcasting, in representing public displays of sociability, provides models of 'appropriate behaviour' and encourages relaxed, enjoyable and non-threatening forms of social interaction:

> Broadcasting, though obviously a bourgeois institution [. . .] has had to learn to communicate with everyone by adjusting its style and manner to

fit in with the situational proprieties of everyday life and the actual con-
ditions of viewing and listening. In doing this broadcasting has brought
the private into the public, re-socialising the public domain, making it
a space in which talk for talk's sake, talk for enjoyment, talk as a sociable
activity has its place alongside talk that is informative, that is getting
its message across, that is trying to persuade [. . .]. [These] sociable forms
of interaction sustain a world that is, if not more rational in a formal and
theoretical sense, altogether more reasonable. (1990: 20–21)

Scannel suggests that the study of broadcast talk can reveal much about
the quality of public life today as mediated through broadcasting and, more
generally, about the structures of identity, performance and social
interaction in today's society. One of his main points is that to conceive
of programmes as 'texts' and audiences as 'readers' is to mistake the
communicative character of most output on radio and TV which speaks
to listeners and viewers. In particular, it fails to recognise their 'liveness',
their 'embeddedness' in the 'here and now', and the cardinal importance
of audiences and contexts. Broadcasting integrates the public and private
through broadcast talk in the domestic and work places of listening and
viewing.

Scannel's arguments are enormously relevant to, and firmly substantiated
by, the data and arguments presented in this book, which will demonstrate
how broadcast talk and TV talk among audiences become articulated
together in everyday communication. It will show how the content and even
the forms of broadcast talk converge with everyday talk; how they are inter-
twined and interact in all sorts of ways, from the most simple and manifest
level of borrowing vocabulary, idioms, expressions and manners of speech,
to the integration of particular forms of speech such as soap gossip and
everyday gossip; and further, how the forms of sociability represented in
various TV genres encourage audiences to engage in critical and comparative
reflection upon their own forms of social life. The approach adopted here,
therefore, enables the links to be explored between mass and interpersonal
communications.

The crucial importance of relating the study of mass communications to
contexts of interpersonal communication has been highlighted by a number
of researchers. Bausinger (1984) makes the point that they are inseparably
linked in that the media provide materials for conversation. Blumler called
for empirical research to fuse interpersonal and mass communications
rather than considering 'each form or channel [. . .] as a distinct influence
that can be kept separate and measured in some parallelogram of forces'
(1969: 187). Hymes (1964), from an anthropological perspective, outlined
the importance of considering the multiple hierarchy of relations among
messages and contexts in communications research. Goffman's (1959, 1967,
1969) qualitative microsociological research on interpersonal and public

communication has influenced several media researchers, for example Lull (1990), who argues that one of the most promising ways to study mass communication processes is to look at the details of interpersonal interaction. Lazarsfeld (1940) was one of the first to document how media-derived content makes up some of the substance of everyday conversation. Boskoff (1970) notes the importance of keeping abreast with the media in modern urban societies in order to participate on an equal basis in informal conversations with relatives, friends and acquaintances. Allen (1982) argues that media content popularises slang, neologisms and ethnic epithets, creates catchwords and buzz-words, introduces new words and provides reference points for simile and metaphor in everyday language. Allen also examines how, if enough people participate in the process, media content, even of the most serious nature, becomes 'play' and often the stuff of subcultures as it enters the personal networks of everyday conversation.

The conversational value of media content is often assumed to be a trivial 'function'. Mendelsohn (1965) sees talking about media as performing a 'simple', 'socially lubricating' function. Allport (1959) perceives media content as serving at its most vacuous level as 'phatic discourse' or 'chatter', a device to avoid silence and signify social solidarity. However, as I shall argue later, TV plays an often striking role in everyday conversations among young people for whom TV is a major leisure activity and shared cultural experience. For them it acts as a catalyst to talk, serves as a shared topical resource, supports congenial social relations which are neither intimate not entirely impersonal, provides palatable topics for such casual sociable interaction and, in sum, contributes to a shared culture among local youth.

Media content can serve to introduce a number of conversational topics, such as social problems, and leads to an airing of social issues. Clearly, the extent to which media talk plays a socially cohesive or divisive role needs to be examined in specific local, interpersonal communication networks. Furthermore, to separate the two deflects attention away from their complementary effects in structuring interaction. But overall, as Allen (1982) argues, shared media experiences which initiate, sustain, extend or deepen interpersonal communication are more likely to contribute to social integration than social conflict. Given that most face-to-face interaction in the peer culture under study is among friends who already have more or less strong bonds, TV and TV talk are more likely to serve an integrative function than a divisive one.

Viewers' conversations about TV offer one of the best forms of empirical evidence about the social and cultural consequences of TV. As Lull puts it:

> TV does not give families something to talk about, it directs their attention toward particular topics [. . .]. Viewer conversations about programme content are, in my view, one of the most powerful forms of empirical evidence to be considered in any revealing appraisal of the

social and cultural aspects of TV. It is through talk about TV that the audience is constituted in certain ways. (1988: 17)

Other researchers have highlighted the importance of family conversations in mediating the reception of TV. Messaris (1983) identifies two types of family conversation: 'information-oriented conversations', where an exchange of information about some aspect of the reality which is portrayed or referred to on TV is sought; and 'behaviour prescription type conversations', where the appropriateness or otherwise of different types of behaviour, as a model for one's own or others' behaviour, is debated and judged. Such conversations, he argues, often act as a supplement to formal education processes, even when the topic is not strictly educational. They may also serve in the regulation of boundaries of authority, protection or competence and can also, on occasion, constitute a source of considerable tension or conflict between participants.

The didactic potential of TV when mediated by parents is emphasised by Bryce and Leichter (1983). They distinguish between 'embedded verbal mediation' of TV, where learning from TV content is enhanced through child–parent interaction, and 'mediation in non-TV contexts'. They point to the need to broaden our understanding of the family's unintentional mediation of TV, as well as to the contribution that ethnography can make in documenting such everyday interactions. As Leichter points out:

> The criticism and appraisal of TV may be so interwoven with other aspects of family discussion that TV programmes may become the basis for common experiences of family members and become part of their repertoire of personal history. (1979: 36–37)

Ethnography is uniquely suited to documenting such interweavings of personal biography and family history with shared TV experiences. The collective memory of a family or peer group may be triggered by shared TV experiences which spark off the recall of incidents, moments and a range of associations from events to emotions.

A more liberating and subversive version of the function of viewers' conversations is proposed by Fiske (1989a). Re-examining Bourdieu's notion of cultural capital as a resource which works only for the 'bourgeois intelligentsia', he argues that 'popular cultural capital' works to enable subordinate groups to become the producers of their own culture, the makers of their own meanings and pleasure. Adapting Barthes' notion of the 'writerly' text, he describes TV as a 'producerly' text which offers provocative spaces within which viewers can use their already developed competences. Although he exaggerates viewers' autonomy in 'producing meanings', it is clear from his account that one of the most powerful ways in which they do so is through TV talk. Drawing upon the work of Katz and Liebes (1985), Fiske emphasises the ways in which TV promotes talk and gossip, and how the soap opera form in particular enables TV to intersect with a variety of oral cultures:

> People's talk about TV is not just in response to it but is read back into it: our friend's gossip about a programme influences our reading of it [. . .]. Oral culture is a product of the immediate social formation, so the way TV is talked about provides us with two sorts of clues – clues about how TV is being assimilated into the social formation and how that social formation is read back into the text, and clues about which meanings offered by the text are being mobilised in this process. This form of inter-textual relations is a bridge between the textual and the social, and is a crucial, if methodologically difficult area, to study. (1989a: 66)

Fiske argues, and much of my data would support his claim, that 'material social experience is made sense of by textualising it, by bringing a culture's discursive resources to bear upon it'; and that 'reading a social experience parallels reading a text' (1989a: 65). The reading relations of the two are obviously not identical, since they operate in different modalities; but it is precisely the pleasure of playing with the boundaries between representation and 'the real' which makes talking about TV so compelling. TV talk necessarily involves a recognition of the differences as well as the similarities between the real world, as viewers understand it, and the social worlds represented on TV. As we shall see in the forthcoming chapters, young people are continually comparing and contrasting TV worlds with their own social worlds according to a range of criteria with which they evaluate the realism of TV representations. According to Fiske, whilst textual and social experience are different, the discursive repertoires and competences involved in making sense of each, overlap and inform one another. He goes on to say that these discursive repertoires are also the ones that determine subjectivity: 'the subject is an inter-discursive potential. The relations between textual experience, social experience, and subjectivity are perhaps the most methodologically inaccessible; but theoretically and politically, they are among the most important of all' (1989a: 67). The most promising way to resolve the methodological difficulties alluded to by Fiske is by means of anthropological fieldwork; and it is the practice of fieldwork which provided this study's insights into the roles played by TV texts and TV talk in the shaping, construction and re-invention of social and cultural identities.

PHASES OF FIELDWORK

Fieldwork is characterised by a multiplicity of data-gathering strategies, in a variety of contexts, drawing upon the experiences of a wide range of people over a long period of time. Whilst it is possible to categorise the different phases of fieldwork broadly in terms of the gradual refinement and specification of the research problem, ethnography does not lend itself to neatly systematic research designs, but rather to *post hoc* reconstructions of what is in practice a messy process of piecemeal inductive analysis based upon continually incoming data. For, despite the best efforts at systematic research design, the very nature of ethnographic research depends on the ethnographer being surprised at certain moments (Willis, 1980). This involves following leads that could not have been predicted, assuming roles that could not have been planned and witnessing events that could not have been foreseen. A strategic plan is certainly necessary, as is systematic and rigorous data collection, but this rigour is achieved through the diligent and painstaking recording of observations in field notes. Here I shall broadly describe the three stages of fieldwork undertaken in terms of their key foci and activities. It should not be assumed that these stages were in any way mutually exclusive – rather, it is the overlap and at times, the simultaneity of roles, influences and phases, that characterises fieldwork, especially in urban settings (Baumann, 1990).

Groundwork

In the earliest stages of the research, my chief aim was to arrive at a more adequate understanding of young people's constructions of the many cultures in Southall. Previous experiences as a teacher afforded some insight into youth cultures, but internal cleavages based on religion, caste, region and urban or rural background in the parental culture required a clearer understanding of key categories and terms, both English and Punjabi, which were in widespread everyday use. For example, the apparently inter- changeable categories such as 'Asian', 'Indian', 'Punjabi' and 'Sikh' became more distinct as I began to document their use in specific contexts. Similarly, 'westernised', *gora/gori* (white man/woman) and *valāitī* (literally 'foreign', 'European', used in the sense of 'westernised' or 'anglicised', often connoting 'rich') are all terms used by young people to refer to those who seem more 'British' than 'Asian', but again, in different contexts, they may be accompanied by positive or negative connotations. The commonsense knowledge gained from seven years' teaching locally needed consolidation and refinement.

I began to become actively involved with young people and to establish relationships of trust and reciprocity. This was facilitated by teaching Sociology and Media Studies in a local high school for several hours per week throughout the fieldwork. I organised excursions and became involved in school projects which provided important background data in helping to situate TV in the broader context of young people's leisure and social lives. These projects (some of which were undertaken collaboratively with Gerhard Baumann) aimed at exploring perceptions of cultural identity and differences in Southall through a variety of means. For example, a video project with 14- and 15-year-old students involved role-playing scenarios which they devised, dealing with conflicts of values and beliefs. With A-level Sociology students, the family, youth cultures and mass media were studied. With one-year vocational students (aged 16–17) in Community Studies, we explored local politics, racism, religion and advertising. In media studies, with one-year vocational students, we examined different film and TV genres, media institutions and industries, and students produced video soap opera episodes, radio shows and video advertisements of their own devising. These were very revealing in themselves, and I hope to publish analyses of their media productions in future work. The Southall Youth Survey was piloted and administered in this phase of the research.

Immersion

The second phase of fieldwork was the most intensive and hectic, socially demanding, emotionally elevating and distressing. At the same time the analysis, tabulation and cross-tabulation of survey results were completed. In the early stages of fieldwork I kept a low profile and acted, as far as possible, as the unobtrusive observer. However, in this phase, through regular outings and trips, visiting homes, participating at birthday parties, discos and weddings, I was able to share in the lives of my informants in a more genuine way.

There were a number of families whose homes I visited on a regular basis and with whom close and reciprocal relations were established. They were hospitable, warm and friendly and gave freely of their time and experiences. In return, I assisted young people with their school work, arranged family outings and helped parents when I could with household administration, civic and occasionally legal matters. A number of young people became (in anthropological terminology) 'key informants' as well as close personal friends and we saw each other on a regular basis over a two-year period. During this period I conducted more structured and focused interviews with a wide range of young people on various aspects of their TV viewing. My informants appreciated that I was conducting research into young people and television and willingly tolerated my variously naïve and probing questions and interest in seemingly irrelevant details. The survey results and subsequent interpretations were discussed in informal conversations and in interviews. The ability of trusted, key informants to recognise themselves, or not, as the case might be, in the accounts, analyses and arguments which were progressively being produced from the data has been one of the most important means of evaluating and checking my interpretations.

My use, over a period of two years, of a notebook and sometimes an audiotape recorder was eventually ignored by certain informants who claimed to enjoy the fact that their ideas, views and lives were being taken seriously. Verbatim transcripts of conversations and interviews were regularly made. But often, in more intimate moments of trouble, self-revelation or gossip, no recording techniques were used. In such cases I had to rely upon, and indeed develop, my memory to complete my fieldnotes. Extensive use was made of the video camera for both teaching and research. I was frequently called upon to video family occasions: birthday parties, weddings, religious celebrations such as Diwali and *rakhri*, as well as to make video 'letters' to families in the Punjab. These recordings are significant as anthropological documents of family life and rites of passage, and contributed important background data – which again I hope to analyse in detail in future work.

The audio and videotape recorder offer easy ways of recording data when young people become accustomed to their presence. However, the most regular means of recording data was through the fieldwork notes and diary. I had to learn how to do these efficiently, effectively and (what proved most difficult in the early stages) regularly. The skills do not simply involve writing a record of a situation or conversation in a straightforward manner. One is involved in a struggle to make sense of the complexity of social interactions and so, inevitably, processes of selection are involved. Learning *how* and *what* to observe is as much a part of writing fieldnotes as the act of writing itself.

In the early stages of fieldwork, I did not keep a clear distinction between field notes, fieldwork diary and personal diary. Later, I realised the importance of separating these different accounts. Field notes aim at an accurate and factual account of specific observations and experiences and follow a thematic or topical categorisation. The fieldwork diary is kept on a daily basis and consists of an account of everyday proceedings and may include personal comments, speculations, working through ideas and themes as well as a lot of seemingly irrelevant observations. The personal diary is important because during intensive bouts of fieldwork one can become so involved, elated, frustrated or annoyed that this allows for an outlet for personal emotions which might otherwise, and indeed on occasions do, interfere with analysis.

Participation in the peer and family cultures of young people encouraged the sharing of feelings and emotions in relaxed gatherings. But alongside the pleasures, inevitably, one also shares in the pain of life. The sudden death of a parent or sibling is deeply disturbing and shocking. Such experiences helped cement strong friendships which I valued as more than an instrument of ethnography. The ethnographer on her first fieldwork experience is involved in a complex and very interactive learning process, not simply in learning the mechanics and techniques of systematic data collection but also in learning how to be an active listener, learning how to exercise tact, discretion and respect with an unprecedented degree of self-consciousness. The self-reflexive processes involved can equally illuminate, depress, excite, disconcert, inspire, challenge and even transform the fieldworker's self-awareness. Maintaining a balance between involvement and detachment is not always easy and has to be learned as a skill and practised with effort.

During the same period of fieldwork I also developed the habit of watching popular TV programmes and films in order to understand what young people were talking about without having to constantly intervene and ask for explanations. To most adult outsiders, teenage TV talk would be unintelligible, since so much is taken for granted in terms of information and knowledge, and it would seem trivial, since it is not often obvious that much is at stake. Whilst some of this talk is indeed trivial and inconsequential from moment to moment, its totality is not. For, as long-term immersion in the peer group culture revealed, it also involves a collective attempt to locate self and others in the world, to understand social and cultural relations and to transform them.

Focusing

This phase was characterised by a dramatic focusing of the research agenda, guided by both survey and qualitative data gathered in the previous year. Since my principal access as a teacher was to sixth-form students, the focus of the study shifted to the 16–18 age category. There was also the added advantage of having known many of these students as a teacher for several years. I began to focus my efforts on collecting data on everyday, casual conversations about TV. It therefore became necessary to pinpoint strategic sites of social interaction (Murdock, 1989: 234).

Morning registration classes had long interested me as a prime site of conversations about TV, triggered by the phrase 'did you see...?' The ritualistic post-mortems of 'last night's telly', and collective reconstructions of its highlights, offered important insights into the ways in which young people mediate their social relationships through a routinised sharing of their interpretations of TV. Such conversations were also conducted during breaks and lunchtime but, from a research point of view, less reliably so.

The Media Studies classroom was a second site of interaction and observation in which the activities of teaching and research were organised to complement each other. I taught Media Studies GCSE over two years to classes of twenty and thirty 16- to 18-year-olds, most of whom were following a one-year vocational course. The school labelled these students as 'low achievers'. They were very aware of their low status and poor literacy skills as compared with the 'high flyers' or A-level students. In this context I made more assertive and incisive methodological interventions based on the principles of 'Action Research' (Stenhouse, 1980). This term refers to a set of research activities in curriculum development aimed at introducing changes and improvements in pedagogic practice. As a language teacher

I had conducted a number of small-scale 'Action Research' projects, which aimed to assist students in meeting the linguistic demands of different subject areas through collaborative learning strategies involving small group discussion. However, there are specific difficulties with teaching and learning in media studies.

Students perceived Media Studies as a 'fun' subject somewhat on the margins of conventional school subjects, because much of the course involved practical and production work using video cameras, photographic equipment, computer art packages and audiocassettes. The course also demanded the analysis of media texts. However, the problem for the media teacher seeking to develop critical skills is to find out what students consume and what they already know and understand about what they consume. Very often they 'know' more about the popular TV texts than the teacher. Yet what constitutes knowledge about the media, and why and how critical skills are to be developed, continue to be controversial.

My approach, influenced by my training as a language teacher, was to encourage students to draw upon and make explicit their existing knowledge of the media through collaborative learning techniques and discussion in small groups, before they undertook any written work. This approach had proved successful with second-language students and its pedagogic value has long been recognised. For example, in an excellent survey of secondary school classrooms, it was found that one of the main impediments to learning is that teachers tend to talk too much and are often insensitive to the effects and significance of the language they use and expect from their students (Barnes, 1975). The problem in secondary school classrooms is that language is frequently seen as an instrument of teaching rather than of learning. The learning which takes place in small group discussions, when young people are left to their own devices, often remains unrecognised and unexploited. Small group discussions that require students to grapple with new experiences or to order old experience in a new way are extremely important in helping students to think through the conceptual problems set for them and are vital as preliminary aids to written work.

These informal group discussions were taped by students and speedily transcribed by me, analysed and fed back into my teaching. Students became more reflexive about their TV consumption and began to realise how media tastes and preferences are socially structured and culturally distinctive. I was able to mobilise the insights of their talk to develop their understanding and use of concepts of narrative, genre, spectatorship, point of view, identification and the political aspects of popular pleasures. However, the gulf between what students were able to express orally and what they were able to put on paper remained a source of concern to me, especially since assessment is based upon written work alone and many students, despite their efforts, still fought shy of committing

themselves to paper. However there is no doubt that the quality of learning that took place was indeed sophisticated, and it was certainly recognised
as such by students. The Sociology A-level classes were also appropriate
and conducive arenas in which to relate the syllabus to students' personal
experience and discuss the family, religion, mass media, deviance, social
stratification, power and politics and education.

These two sites of interaction – morning registration and informal,
small group classroom work – were but two of the contexts in which data
were gathered. The data presented here is based on various forms of talk
observed, elicited or generated in diverse contexts, sometimes in my presence
and at other times, as in the Media Studies classroom, in my absence; talk
of varying degrees of informality, intimacy, seriousness and enthusiasm,
in pairs, small groups and larger groups, among close friends and among
rivals, in the classroom, during breaks, after school, in the home, at
parties, weddings and outings. Thus I was able to document spontaneous,
genuinely unselfconscious talk in naturalistic settings, rather than talk
generated by interview alone. Each of these contexts and the group
dynamics involved in them, including the role of the teacher/researcher,
also require analysis if one is to interpret the talk accurately – fuller analysis,
in some cases, than I can provide in the present study for reasons of space
and style (in order not to keep interrupting the flow). I hope to provide a
separate study of these questions in the future. As my discussion of the
survey data on marriage partners indicated (Chapter 1), one must always,
of course, consider the discrepancies between what people say, what they
think and what they do. The survey or interview researcher cannot, but the
ethnographic researcher has to find ways of distinguishing among these.
Here key informants can help, as they often can in interpreting talk and
behaviour that the researcher finds puzzling, or in alerting one to alternative
explanations of talk that one had no means of knowing about. By cross-
checking data between different informants, the researcher is able to gauge
the seriousness, veracity, accuracy and plausibility of talk. It helps greatly
to have various kinds of informants – and the more of a cross-section they
constitute, the better. As many cross-validating methods as possible were
used in interpreting talk in this study.

Mostly I did as little talking as I could get away with, being intent, as
Cicourel (1973) advises, on elaborating informants' meanings. Informants'
perceptions are seldom reliably or fully delivered by straightforward
questioning, and one cannot seek easy answers to research questions
by directly probing informants. More oblique, subtle and even obtuse
methods are required, and often discussions of seemingly irrelevant topics
reveal more relevant data. One has to pay careful attention to group
dynamics. In some groups certain individuals attempt to dominate or
subvert discussions for their own ends. But misrepresentations, lies
and ironies can be turned to research advantage, as long as they can be

recognised. Some of the discussions were seen as 'a laugh' in their own right, and laughs were certainly often generated in the group talk I observed and participated in. In joking relationships, facts may suffer some distortion – that is a natural concomitant of humour. But, at times, quite piercing insights can be delivered by comic means.

My role in discussions, therefore, involved surrendering the initiative and allowing talk to flow as far as possible without intervention on my part. Similarly, Woods in his study of a school culture emphasises the importance of active listening and of collecting examples of what he calls 'naturalistic' or 'behavioural' talk, in other words, talk heard and noted by the researcher in the 'ordinary' course of events: 'I was keyed into [the students'] experiences via talk and it was talk which led to empathy [. . .]' (1979: 267). Woods found, as I did, that talking in friendship groups puts young people at their ease and allows the bonds between them to surface. It also helps shift the balance of power in their direction. They act as checks, balances and prompts to each other and in the process inaccuracies are corrected, incidents and reactions recalled and analysed, statements elaborated upon and disagreements voiced. Students volunteered information in the company of their friends and to each other, rather than to me, in the context of ongoing exchanges that I would not have been privy to had I not been engaged in this research. Clearly, this raises an ethical dilemma: it may seem to reduce the research process to nothing more than a form of eavesdropping. However, what counts is how one uses the information to which one is privy: ethnographic responsibility entails the exercise of the utmost tact and discretion. Sometimes members of the group prompted each other to tell me things and tried to involve me in their discussions. Such differences were noted and rather than seeking, by one means or another, to eliminate the 'effects of the researcher', these effects were monitored and so brought under control as far as possible. By systematically modifying one's role in the field, different kinds of data can be collected in similar contexts, and similar data may be collected in different contexts. This allows one to cross-check and make comparisons which enhance the interpretation of the communicative and social processes under study.

THE RESEARCHER AND HER INFORMANTS

Unlike most researchers embarking upon fieldwork in a 'strange' place, prior familiarity helped me to overcome initial problems of access. The problem for the present research was rather to make the familiar 'strange' again. Habitual modes of perception, presuppositions and assumptions had built up over a period of years into forms of 'common-sense', 'taken-for-granted' categories, terms and understandings. I had to be mindful not to allow common-sense categories and dichotomies to structure my analysis of data. For example, binary conceptions of 'Asian' and 'western' cultures simply serve to mask ambivalences and reproduce the public, media and race-relations discourses which have secured the legitimation of state racism in postwar Britain. Ideological constructions of south Asian families, particularly their family and marriage systems, often represent them as based on 'archaic' and 'alien' practices which present a threat to the 'British way of life'. 'Culture clash' and 'intergenerational conflict', rather than racism, were commonly identified as the problem and the cause of youth rebellion in inner cities in the late 1970s and early 1980s (Ballard, 1979; Brah, 1987; Parmar, 1981). Such polarised conceptions of culture and of generational differences impede an understanding of their interrelationships and overlap – like cultures, generations are not impermeable or fixed. As Mannheim (1982 [1929]) argued, each generation is the repository of prevailing ideas. Successive generations fight adversaries both within and without, depending upon their personal experiences, which allows for malintegration as well as solidarity across generations.

The specifically local meanings attached to key words such as 'culture', 'community', 'caste' and 'class' required careful exploration and analysis. In this sense, the 'field' of enquiry to which one seeks access is already constituted in certain ways through the categories which structure the thinking both of the researcher and of her informants. It is not enough simply to reproduce informant categories. They need to be identified and analysed in the contexts in which they are used. It is only through rigorous examination of key words and categories that one can hope to overcome some of the difficulties inherent in defining and constituting the field. It was largely through keeping the fieldwork diary and field notes, and through discussions with key informants and dialogue with colleagues, that I was able to refine my understanding of key words and categories, systems of classification, concepts and symbols.

The role of teacher greatly facilitated access to young people in the formal setting of school and classroom, in the informal contexts of the peer culture and also in the family sphere. Through participation in the school context, one assumes a recognized role in the institution, contributes to its function and thus acquires a status according to one's age, gender and social class. This made it easier for young people to situate me in the dual role of teacher and researcher. I made a point of being very open about my research in the school context with both my students and other teachers. Most of the students saw me as a part-time teacher of Sociology and Media Studies who seemed to spend a lot of time 'hanging out', 'chatting' and generally taking a more-than-usual interest in what they had to say. Some young people found it surprising that an interest should be taken in their views; others found it flattering; others again were puzzled as to what purpose the research had; but in general students were extremely co-operative, willing and supportive of my efforts. On the whole most teachers were sympathetic to my research, although some could not see the point of it. I would often discuss my research with other teachers, and my friend and colleague, Balbinder Panesar, alongside others, provided me with many insights into Punjabi families and culture.

It should be pointed out that, whilst prior familiarity posed certain problems, it also brought advantages. Since I had worked in the school prior to undertaking the research, many of the 16-year-olds, who in the later stages of fieldwork contributed much rich data, had already been known to me since they were twelve. Shared past experiences assisted in developing trust and reciprocity and allowed for relaxed, informal and casual social encounters with most young people. Hargreaves (1967) points to the advantages of adopting a formal role in the field under study, especially in reducing the possibilities of the researcher disturbing 'natural' settings:

> it [. . .] permits an easy entrance into the social situation by reducing the resistance of group members; decreases the extent to which the investigation disturbs the 'natural' situation; and permits the investigator to experience and observe the group's norms, values, conflicts and pressures, which (over a long period of time) cannot be hidden from someone playing an in-group role. (1967: 193)

However, in spite of the ease of access which prior familiarity and the adoption of the role of teacher afforded me, a number of problems require consideration. The next four sections consider how issues of power, detachment, gender and ethnicity affected my fieldwork.

Power relations

Teacher–student relations inevitably involve relations of power, raising ethical questions of responsibility. It might be argued that to use students as informants in the pursuit of one's academic goals may lead to the abuse of power, in particular to the relegation of teaching responsibilities in favour of doing research. Throughout the research I had to remain constantly vigilant with regard to my own motivations and conduct in order to fulfil my first and foremost responsibility to students – to create productive learning situations, to teach and to get them through examinations. Action Research, with its aim of effecting improvements in pedagogic practice and learning environments, assisted me in overcoming many potential ethical problems. In fact, in many ways the research, which I was always open about, worked to the benefit of most students, not only because of the attention they received, but also because the analysis of their work and talk was fed back into my teaching and contributed to the improvement of my teaching, and – I hope – to their learning. This was borne out by the examination results of several classes though not, sadly, of all students.

Levels of literacy in Southall schools are, at best, poor. One of the biggest problems I faced as a teacher was to help students to communicate their knowledge and insights, and to demonstrate the extent and depth of their learning, in written form. Many students lack confidence in their writing abilities but, regrettably, the use of oral assessment methods is very limited in most secondary schools and in examinations.

It may also be said that my marginal status in the school, as a part-timer with no administrative or formal pastoral role, enabled me to circumvent some of the deleterious aspects of teacher–student power relations. When students became involved in disputes with authority figures I was often called upon to act as an arbiter, representing or articulating the student's version of an incident. In the eyes of some of the teachers I was seen as a hopelessly naïve defender of recalcitrant rebels (or 'rockveilers', as the more rebellious students were referred to by teachers). This tended to undermine my status with other teachers but to enhance it in the eyes of sixth-form students among whom I became known as a 'safe' teacher. I was certainly duped on several occasions into defending what proved to be the indefensible and was thus labelled a 'soft touch'. However, a reputation for defending the 'underdog', sympathy, empathy or whatever, eventually allowed me free access to the 'privacy' of the sixth-form commonroom during recreations – strictly peer territory – where my presence became accepted and even welcomed (despite my howling lack of success at playing pool).

Detachment

A second set of potential problems concerns questions of involvement and detachment. As Woods puts it:

> Without detachment the researcher runs the risk of 'going native'; that is, identifying so strongly with members that he finds himself defending their values, rather than studying them [. . .]. The diligent recording of field notes and a generally reflective attitude help to guard against being swamped by the experience. (1979: 261)

The researcher therefore tries to combine a judicious measure of personal involvement and professional detachment. Keeping regular, preferably daily, field notes and a field diary is the most helpful and important way of maintaining a critical distance. Furthermore, doing fieldwork in close proximity to one's academic base (Southall is only eight kilometres from Brunel University) enabled me to engage in dialogue with colleagues, which also greatly assisted the processes of distanciation. However, despite this I did experience role conflict at certain moments. Since most of the time when not teaching (I only taught for six hours per week) was spent observing and listening to young people, I sometimes became more personally involved with students than is customary. Sixth-form students assigned to me the role of problem-solver or counsellor since, as one girl put it: 'My friend told me to come and talk to you, she says you understand our culture [. . .].'

Undoubtedly my approach to fieldwork, involving ongoing dialogue with students in which I was continually representing their representations of themselves back to them, led to my being assigned the informal role of student 'agony aunt'. I was often approached as someone in whom one could confide and to whom one could unload emotional, family, boyfriend or girlfriend problems. This was frequently difficult, upsetting and emotionally draining, and at certain moments it was difficult, indeed impossible, to remain the detached researcher. A number of ethical dilemmas were faced when informants confided information which, according to professional codes, should have been reported to school authorities, but which, out of respect for their request for confidentiality, remained upon my troubled conscience. At other times, having 'hung out' and gone 'cruising' with students at the weekend, I was greeted on the following Monday morning in the corridor with backslapping familiarity as 'one of the posse', which caused some embarrassment in front of colleagues and other students. Detachment is not always easy to achieve since, in living, working and researching with friends, students and subjects, one is simultaneously performing different roles, each with its duties and responsibilities.

Gender

No researcher can escape the implications of gender relations. In the context of field research, Roberts (1981), Golde (1970) and Warren and Ramussen (1977) have highlighted their significance with regard to female researchers. Many female anthropologists, working in societies where gender segregation is the norm, have described the problems they faced (cf. Pettigrew, 1981, on studying Sikhs in the Punjab). Diamond (1970) used an assistant to interview all males between 20 and 40 to avoid 'unsavoury sexual overtones'. Often anthropologists recommend the use of 'key informants', and of a local 'field assistant' of the opposite gender, to gather material or to accompany the ethnographer.

In my own fieldwork, generally speaking, it was much more difficult to establish relaxed and informal social relations with groups of boys, and individual boys, than with girls, although I did establish excellent relations with pairs or small groups of boys who were close friends. I found there was often so much competitiveness and rivalry – to be witty, sarcastic or lewd – between younger boys in larger groups, in particular that, unless the purpose was to assess the impact of peer pressure on communicative interactions, much of the data gathered needed to be approached with more than a modicum of scepticism. In fact, over the fieldwork period there were several fairly disastrous social encounters between myself and large groups of boys – they gain strength in numbers – which occurred mainly on residential school trips. The problem usually emanated from the fact that, on residential trips, teacher–student roles and discipline are relaxed, and one spends all day, and the evenings, socialising with students. On a couple of occasions, the desire to score points in machismo, and youthful folly and frivolity, quickly degenerated into crude sexual innuendo and harassment. But such incidents were exceptional and fortunately, I was able to establish close relations with a number of boys who became key informants, and who felt able to communicate with an openness and lack of self-consciousness that transcended conventional gender and age boundaries or constraints. A number of male students also became informal field assistants for short periods, during school, college and university vacations, accompanying me on visits and outings and generally providing access to areas of male experience that would otherwise have been denied to me as a female researcher. However, despite the fact that it became possible to access male domains of experience, the predominance of girls as subjects and informants in this study should be noted.

Ethnicity

My status as a *gori* or 'white woman' is of central importance to the fieldwork and to the ethnography, as regards both how I was perceived and how I perceived my subjects. In Southall, the typical UK minority–majority relations are reversed and one becomes highly conscious of being the only white person at a wedding, birthday party and even in the road where one lives. London Punjabis make the primary distinction between *gora* (white man) or *gori* (white woman) and *upni* (ours; one of us). Whilst on the whole congenial relations exist between the minority of local whites and Punjabis, there also exists a certain suspicion of *gore* (white people), especially among those who have had little social experience outside their immediate kin and friends. This undoubtedly contributed to my status as an outsider in certain contexts where I was treated with polite distance. However, a basic knowledge of Punjabi proved to be an invaluable way of 'breaking the ice'. The ability to speak, and more importantly to joke, in Punjabi is seen as a mark of respect and recognition for 'the culture' which, in turn, tends to make one more acceptable and accepted. Of course, most people assume that one does not understand Punjabi and on several occasions a companion would be asked 'who is that white woman?' Sometimes I would reply in Punjabi, much to their amusement.

The maintenance of *izzat* (family honour) requires privacy, and this limited my access to the intimacies of domestic life in some cases, although teacher status facilitated it in others. Some mothers, in fact, found it easier to confide in me than in their neighbours, because divulging private or family problems among Punjabis might entail gossip and a loss of *izzat* or respect. I rarely felt that being *gori* posed problems for the fieldwork among young people. They have such little experience of white people, apart from their teachers and a very small number of white peers, that they are pleased to engage on a more personal footing and to cross conventional boundaries of teacher–student roles out of curiosity about *gore*. Many young people asked questions about my family background and posed questions which I would never have thought of asking, which encouraged a reciprocity of viewpoints about cultural differences. I also think that the ambivalences surrounding perceptions of me in my various roles as teacher, researcher, friend, *gori* and 'Southalli' with a bit of Punjabi, all added to my liminal insider/outsider status, and encouraged young people to talk more openly and freely than they might otherwise have done.

Yet some 'Asian' colleagues in both the school and academic contexts have expressed a great deal of scepticism about a white person's ability to understand, appreciate and study 'Asian culture'. Of course this scepticism raises questions about the latent assumptions which I, as a white person, may have about 'my' 'subjects'. One can never claim immunity to ethnocentrism or racism, and it is precisely because such assumptions are part of what we take for granted that they are difficult to bring to one's consciousness, let alone eradicate. In dealing with questions of 'race' and ethnicity, cultural similarities and differences, I have tried to avoid exoticising the subjects of my study and imposing identities and categories upon them. It will be for the reader to assess the quality of my relations with my informants, as it is reflected in the qualities of the data and analysis presented in this book.

WRITING ETHNOGRAPHY IN THE FIELD

Ethnographers typically separate fieldwork and writing, withdrawing from the space of their subjects to the seclusion of a 'home base', often far away, in order to write up their notes. I remained living, and for some time teaching, in Southall while I completed the Ph.D. thesis on which this book is based. While fieldworkers may face a variety of problems on their return, one of the greatest difficulties which faces the fieldworker who remains in the field while 'writing up' is that of disengaging socially. It seems that just as social relations have reached a desirable point, with informants dropping in casually and offering irresistible data, and invitations flowing in to all manner of social engagements, the research grant runs out and it is time to cut off. The temptation to collect 'just a bit more' data is great, but disengagement is essential for the critical distance needed for the final stages of data analysis and writing. The shift from the active and socially engaging processes of living fieldwork to the social isolation and domestic confinement of writing required considerable, and at times painful, adjustment. It is not simply a social but an affective disengagement. My prior availability and the reciprocity involved in fieldwork relations meant that I was still called upon and expected to visit, to help out and generally to maintain relations. It was difficult for informants and friends to appreciate the solitude that writing requires. I also faced ethical questions about 'using' people for one's own academic purposes and then 'dropping' them once the data has been obtained. This situation puts considerable pressure upon the researcher and the only way I found to deal with it was to maintain social relations where and when needed.

Some ethnographers (e.g. Bloor, 1983: 548–549) have argued that a crucial test for the value of an ethnography is whether the actors whose beliefs and behaviour they purport to represent recognise the validity of the account. One advantage of writing up while in the field is that informants can be included as part of the 'interpretive community', and become interactive in the process of writing. However, we cannot assume that any actor is a privileged commentator on his or her own actions in the sense that their account of the intentions, motives or beliefs involved comes with a guarantee of its truth. As Schutz (1964) and others have noted, at best we can only grasp the meaning of our actions retrospectively. Such a process of validation, whilst not unproblematic, has been important to this ethnography; it has been treated, alongside other methods of cross-validation, as yet another valuable source of data and insight.

In writing this ethnography I have consistently included the verbatim quotes of informants in order to let young people's voices speak as much as possible, to bear witness to their experiences and perceptions and also to open up the text for further interpretation. (In some, but not all, cases names have been changed to preserve anonymity.) The criteria for selecting informants' quotes and extracts are their typicality, clarity, relevance and veracity in the eyes of other informants. I have attempted to keep description and my own interpretations, as far as possible, separate. Description is often thought of as being the opposite of theory – the project of descriptive ethnographies being to circumvent a priori approaches to society and culture. The Malinowskian model attempts to meld the personal and the scientific. It demands that the fieldworker live among 'natives' and yet be a detached observer of them. This requirement, Clifford insists, represents 'an impossible attempt to fuse subjective and objective practices'. In contrast, he claims:

> The new tendency to name and quote informants more fully and to intro-
> duce personal elements into the text is altering ethnography's discursive
> strategy and model of authority. Much of our knowledge about other
> cultures must now be seen as contingent, the problematic outcome
> of intersubjective dialogue, translation and projection. (1986: 109)

Clifford's ideal of ethnographic writing – 'a utopia of plural authorship' – is a corrective to classical ethnographers' alleged insensitivity to their political relations with those they study (Asad, 1973: 16–17; cf. Maquet, 1964: 54). Polyphony is advocated, not because its epistemological virtues have been established, but because it seems to absolve ethnographers of the sins of their past: the dominance of the author's voice in the ethnographic text is equated with the dominance of colonial rule. The repeated theme in the essays in Clifford and Marcus' *Writing Culture* (1986) is precisely this concern with representations of 'others' as a form of domination. However, as Roth (1989) points out: 'This conception of representation, however laudable as a political goal, confuses hoped for antidotes to colonialism with matters of warrant and proof,' and 'stylized self-reflection no more guarantees authenticity than does a pose of detachment' (1989: 560). This concern with ethnographic authority is typical of the postmodern turn in American anthropology which seems to have abandoned any serious consideration of problems of validation. Instead these problems are subsumed under the rubric of 'authority', which is itself portrayed as a literary rather than as a practical issue. But any attempt at a literary analysis of ethnographic writing is doomed to failure unless it goes beyond the formal analysis and comparison of texts to include a consideration of the contexts and the fieldwork involved in their production. It would seem to me that ethnography is less a prescribed set of methods than an ethos. It is a way of exploring aspects of human, social processes where living in and studying the local world become so intimately linked that fieldwork becomes a 'way of life' in itself. But it is also a cultural practice, essential to anthropology and, as such, an academic discipline which relies on the goodwill of people to reveal themselves and to be revealed. In this sense it becomes too crude to talk about methods or ethnographic authority, and more fruitful to talk of ethnographic responsibility.

Chapter 3

Local uses of the media: Negotiating culture and identity

TV offers powerful representations of both Indian and British culture for the youth of Southall who, though British citizens, do not always feel themselves to be part of the British nation and, though of Indian heritage and Punjabi background, are often less than willing to embrace all aspects of their cultural heritage. One of this book's key arguments is that the juxtaposition of culturally diverse TV programmes and films in Punjabi homes stimulates crosscultural, contrastive analyses of media texts, and that this heightens an awareness of cultural differences, intensifies the negotiation of cultural identities and encourages the expression of aspirations towards cultural change. In short, the consumption of an increasingly transnational range of TV and films is catalysing and accelerating processes of cultural change among London Punjabi families. But it will also be argued that Punjabi cultural 'traditions' are just as likely to be reaffirmed and reinvented as to be challenged and subverted by TV and video viewing experiences.

This chapter offers some general insights into TV and video viewing among Punjabi London families, providing a broad frame in which to examine questions of media, culture and ethnicity, before the more specific analyses of the uses of TV in the peer group culture which are presented in subsequent chapters. Highlighting certain features of the integration of TV use into domestic and local life which are characteristic of Southall, the chapter examines the following areas: the use of the VCR to view popular Hindi films; 'sacred soaps' and devotional viewing (with a case-study of the *Mahabharata*); the viewing of 'western' soaps in the context of 'watching with mother', and the conflicting themes of intimacy and censure involved in that context; the local news culture; TV at Christmas; and finally, by way of introduction to the subversive potential of the peer group culture, an account of *Dirty Dancing* at Diwali.

FAMILY VIEWING PATTERNS

Viewing patterns can be classified broadly as family centred or sibling specific. TV news, Indian films on video and TV comedies tend to bring the family together and generate discussion (see Appendix 10 for survey figures). In contrast, pop programmes and American films on video tend to be viewed among siblings and discussed mainly among peers. Reported viewing figures reveal that comedy, cartoons and pop programmes were the most commonly viewed genres in the week prior to the survey and that, of all genres, young people prefer to view pop programmes without the presence of parents or adults. Clear gender differences emerge in patterns of viewing. Boys watch more science fiction, science programmes, game shows, documentaries and crime series than girls. In contrast, more girls than boys report watching pop and quiz programmes, soaps, cartoons and children's TV. However, when respondents were asked to name the programmes they watched on a regular basis, *Neighbours* was clearly the most popular programme, with 67 per cent citing it as their favourite. Girls are more drawn to programmes targeted at British 'Asians' than boys. Seventy-five per cent of girls but only 48 per cent of boys watch *Network East* – an arts and news magazine programme. Similar differences were also reported for *Movie Mahal*, a programme about Indian cinema, and Channel 4's Indian film season. This is consistent with the general tendency for girls to display a greater liking for, or at least propensity for, viewing Indian TV and Hindi movies than boys.

Most families have large video collections: 72 per cent of families have up to fifty, 17 per cent more than fifty, and 13 per cent more than 100 videos. The majority of these are reported to be Indian films (67 per cent), English and American films (54 per cent) and British TV recordings (53 per cent). Pop videos (35 per cent), family videos (27 per cent) and religious films (19 per cent) also feature in family video collections. Of these, Indian videos are most often watched with the whole family (66 per cent) and most frequently discussed with parents (32 per cent). Yet when specific films were listed it became apparent that young people are just as likely to have seen recent blockbusters from Hollywood as those from Bombay. Approximately 80 per cent of respondents had seen *Police Academy*, *Beverly Hills Cop*, *Rambo* and *Nightmare on Elm Street*, or *Sholay*, *Naseeb*, *Deewar* and *Quayamat se Quayamet*. But only 39 per cent had seen *Jai Santoshi Maa*, a religious Hindi film; while 64 per cent had seen the Indian classic *Mother India*, the same proportion as had seen *Gandhi*. The figures for *My Beautiful Laundrette* (46 per cent) and *Salaam Bombay* (24 per cent), independent productions targeting a popular but more middle-class audience, confirm a tendency to go for contemporary popular hits, whether American or Indian, rather than 'art' or 'classic' films.

Hindi films are viewed by approximately 60 per cent of respondents on a weekly basis, mainly at the weekend. However, 74 per cent of girls watch Indian films several times a week as compared with only 48 per cent of boys. In response to a series of statements about Indian films gleaned from ethnographic data, informants emphasised above all their usefulness for language learning: half the respondents reported that Indian films assist them in learning Hindi, while 43 per cent claimed that they most enjoyed the stars. Approximately one third claim to enjoy the films, especially the songs and dances, and agree that they bring the family together and represent Indian life realistically. About one quarter of respondents find them too slow or too unrealistic in their portrayal of India. However, there are also gender differences in judgements about Indian films. For girls it is the stars, songs and dances (64 per cent) which are most appreciated while for boys, it is the action (31 per cent). One third of boys report that they do not like Indian films at all. The significance of these figures can only be appreciated in the light of local culture and in the context of family interactions around the TV set.

TECHNOLOGY AND TRADITION

The video cassette recorder (VCR) has been appropriated by many parents and grandparents ('elders') in Southall as a means of recreating cultural traditions in Britain; but, as we will see, their efforts are both subverted and 'diverted' by young people. To set these conflictual processes in context, we need first to consider the history of film and the cinema, both in Southall and in India.

The Indian film industry has a reputation for being the most productive in the world – releasing more than 900 films in 1985 – with an extensive export market (Dissanayeke, 1988). Most shops in Southall rent out popular Hindi films on video (although films in Punjabi and Urdu are also available, they lack the broad-based appeal of the Bombay movies), and in the early 1970s videos were also delivered and exchanged by the local milkmen. In fact, Hindi films have achieved a remarkable cultural hegemony both in India and throughout the Indian diaspora. To understand this one has to examine the development of the Indian film industry which, in order to appeal to mass audiences, had to transcend the regional, linguistic and religious diversity that characterises India. Many of the films combine a 'universal' appeal to themes of 'common humanity' and 'true love' with a careful handling of regional and religious differences. Also, a distinctive form of 'Hindi cinema' has evolved, marked by a certain 'linguistic openness' which makes the films accessible to speakers of Punjabi, Urdu and other South Asian languages. The distinctive visual style, often foregrounded over dialogue, combines successive modes of spectacle, action and emotion in a manner which also facilitates cross-cultural understanding (Thomas, 1985; Mishra, 1985). As Dissanayeke argues (1988), Bombay cinema represents a synthesis of 'traditional' 'eastern' and mythologised, exotic and decadent 'western' cultures, drawing both on Hollywood genres and on Indian cultural forms to create a distinctive product which is a powerful instrument of cultural identity. Its appeal is further enhanced by the prominence of music and song. Film music and song form by far the largest category of popular music in South Asia, widely disseminated on audiocassettes and by all mass media, and providing the model for much of the popular music outside the cinema (Arnold, 1988; Manuel, 1988). Film and film music, then, have made a very important contribution to the formation of a 'panAsian' cultural identity, in Britain and elsewhere in the diaspora.

The first films were shown in Southall in 1953 in hired halls and then in three local cinemas. During the 1960s and 1970s, the cinema was the principal weekend leisure activity and represented an occasion for families and friends to get together; the social event of the week. When VCRs came on the market, many families were quick to seize the opportunity to extend their choice and control over viewing in the home. Many families in Southall obtained VCRs as early as 1978, well before most households in Britain. With the arrival of video, the songs and dances, romance and drama of the Bombay film were to be enjoyed in domestic privacy. A small piece of domestic technology brought the cinema into the home. A lot was gained but much was lost. The weekly outing became a thing of the past as the cinemas closed and the big screen image shrank into the TV box and entered the flow of everyday life in the living room.

In Southall, the rapid expansion of the home video market needs to be seen, not only as providing an extension to an already important and dynamic film culture, but also as a response to the social and cultural marginalisation of minorities from the mainstream of British society, which provides few cultural or leisure facilities for them. The development of an important home video culture in Southall, as among other diasporic ethnic groups – such as the Turkish *Gastarbeiter* (guest workers) in Germany, 80 per cent of whom are reported to watch Turkish videos daily (Knight, 1986) – bears witness to the alienation that many experience, as well as to the desire to maintain links with their 'home' cultures. However, the consequences of nearly two decades of video use are viewed with some ambivalence. Many young people feel that it has served to further isolate Southall from mainstream British society. It is also seen to have particular effects on the lives of women who remain 'locked in Indian culture'. Yet others see it as a liberating pleasure for women who spend most of their time at home, claiming that the VCR contributes to vibrant female domestic cultures. Such contradictory evaluations need to be set in the specific contexts in which they originate.

Viewing Hindi films on video is the main, regular, family-centred leisure activity. The weekend family gathering around the set is a social ritual where notions of togetherness take precedence. The weaving of conversation around the film is facilitated by the episodic structure of the narrative which moves the viewer through successive modes of song, dance, action and affect, providing breaks for the discussion of issues raised by a member of the family in response to the film. While fathers are generally seen to control access to the main TV screen when at home, mothers, and females in the family more generally, are seen to exert more influence over the choice of what is watched. This is partly to do with their greater knowledge of film culture, bolstered through their consumption of glossy film magazines, locally available in English and Hindi, which report on the latest movies and gossip about the stars. But it also reflects the characteristic cultural role of women in the domestic sphere. Many of my informants reported that they viewed their mothers, grandmothers and aunts as the prime 'carriers of culture and tradition' within the family, emphasising the significance of women's cultural power. Assigned and assuming prime responsibility for the maintenance of religious traditions and moral values, women's cultural power extends well beyond the context of TV- and video-viewing choices. This picture, which challenges the prevalent stereotype of 'passive Asian women', is also supported by Brah (1987), who found much evidence for the existence of strong female cultures among British Asians, cultures which affirm a powerfully positive sense of female identity, and in many cases effectively combat the formal, social and economic subordination of women both in households and in the wider community. (This issue of gender and power in Punjabi families is discussed further in Chapter 5.)

As gender differences are important to understanding parental control over viewing, they are also a significant factor in understanding young people's viewing preferences and behaviour. Boys experience greater freedom in deciding how to use their leisure time and spend more of it in public leisure pursuits. In contrast, girls are expected to remain at home where strong and supportive female cultures are strengthened by collectively viewing and discussing Hindi films. Female-only viewing sessions which span three or four generations are common. One of the dominant themes of Hindi movies is the 'clash of tradition and modernity' in Indian society, which is normally resolved at the expense of the latter. However, some girls claim that the more recent Hindi films are challenging 'traditional' values. (This was already the case in 1989–1990, in other words well before the 1994 wave of 'anti-traditional' Bombay films.) Films, or young viewers' interpretations of them, which affirm 'modernity' as against 'tradition' provoke discussion with female elders, many of whom, as their children or grandchildren say, 'are living in the India which they left twenty years ago' and are unwilling to embrace change. In fact many elders in Southall are regarded as having retreated into a cultural conservatism and traditionalism from which their relatives in India, especially in urban centres, have liberated themselves: they are 'more Indian than Indians'. Thus the viewing of Hindi films is often accompanied by an airing of views and intense debates on tradition and modernity; indeed there is evidence that the content of Hindi films is discussed far more, by viewers in India and Britain alike, than is the content of western films (Pfleiderer and

Lutze, 1985). The connection between viewing and discussion, since it enlivens social relations in the domestic sphere, helps to explain the greater liking for Hindi movies on the part of most girls interviewed. In the opinion of two boys, on the other hand: 'It doesn't hurt to watch an Indian film with the parents.' 'No, it kills you.'

In spite of this repeatedly expressed reluctance, among boys, to view Indian films, the screen's ability to serve social interaction in the family tends to override individual preferences. One boy commented, to general agreement: 'Well we don't usually stay in another room while they're watching, if you've got something to yourself, you isolate yourself, don't you?' What might be seen as 'enforced' or 'reluctant' viewing can never-theless take on pleasurable connotations where the emphasis is on the family's 'being together'. Parents have little time for leisure, due to long working hours and the prevalence of shift work, so the time when the family is together around the TV set is often much appreciated by all concerned. Conversely, the family is often fragmented by British and American films: 'When it's Indian films it's all of us together but when it's English films it's just me and my brother.' This is partly due to the texts of such films themselves and, given parental reservations about their morality, or lack of it, the values they are seen to endorse, and sexual explic-itness, young people often prefer to view them on their own to escape parental censure.

The avid consumption of VCR films largely conforms to this dichoto-my: Hindi films are viewed in large family gatherings and accompanied by intense social interaction, while the viewing of most British and American films on the part of young people constitutes a more or less assertive circumvention of parental control and rejection of their cultural preferences. But young people's viewing of Hindi films raises further ethnographic questions about perceptions of India and Britain and what it is to 'be Indian' or 'be British'. The following section addresses the ways in which young people in Southall perceive Hindi films in contrast to western media – especially mainstream Hollywood cinema – in terms of generic characteristics such as narrative form, conventions of realism and ascribed social function, as well as in terms of the domestic uses of films on video.

REPRESENTATIONS OF/FROM INDIA

For young people in Southall, Indian films are invariably an important influence on their perceptions of the subcontinent. This is especially true of those with little or no direct experience of India but, even for those who have spent long periods there, the films provide a counterpoint to their lived experience. A series of related binary oppositions structure interviewees' accounts of how India is perceived through the films:

Tradition. . . . . Modernity
Village/rural . . . . City/urban
Poverty. . . . . Wealth
Communality . . . . Individualism
Morality . . . . Vice

This pattern of social, political and moral discourse is indeed prevalent in Hindi films, where a pristine, moral, rural India is conventionally constructed in opposition to its exotic, decadent 'other', signified by symbols of city life and the west (Thomas, 1985). The interviewees often echoed the films' contrast of village and city life: the village is represented as a co-operative community of extended kin where notions of individuality are absent, where life is 'pure': 'People are so honest there, they never look with the Evil Eye, they help each other even though they're poor, they never skank [betray] one another'. City life on the other hand appears as 'polluted': the city is a place where 'prostitutes hang out and where even pundits [priests] try to rape girls'. But the 'unrealistic' portrayal of village life was also much criticised, and the interviewees were well aware of the selective and ideological nature of such representations: 'There's not so much about the landless labourers and the position of women, you know, who spend hours and hours looking for water and fuel [. . .] in the scorching heat'. However, others referred to the common theme of exploitation of the poor by the rich: 'The films show how rich treat poor, how they don't go to school and have to work from very young, they can't read and so rich people trick them and take their land and crops'.

Striking gender differences emerged in the way accounts of the films were framed. Girls often expressed their perceptions of India by drawing out the social and moral values inherent in films through a retelling of the narratives. Boys seemed much more concerned with representational issues, particularly 'negative images', and in many cases rejected Hindi films *per se* on that basis. Several male informants saw the films' emphasis on poverty and corruption as offensive: 'They shouldn't portray India as if it's really poor and backward even though they're Indians themselves, it's degrading'. Others, while ridiculing the 'backward image' of 'Indians' in terms of fashion and style norms, also remark on the selective nature of the images: 'They follow up too late in India, they still wear flares, though I must admit they're not backward in everything, they're very advanced in technology but they don't show you those aspects of India'. One boy vehemently rejected the films, wishing to dissociate himself both from the films and from India, with the ironic comment: 'I didn't learn anything from the films apart from the fact that India is one of the most corrupt countries in the world', and later: 'That country has nothing to do with me any more'.

In discussions of this topic, representations of India in the British media were also often commented upon. These are seen as reinforcing an 'uncivilised', poverty-stricken image: 'documentaries shown in this country degrade India badly as well'. Strong resentment is felt at the circulation in the west of images of poverty, underdevelopment, death and disease, images which are seen to be linked to the 'degradation' of Indians in Britain where they 'get racist harassment'. Experiences of racism in Britain undoubtedly influence the range of meanings projected on to Hindi films, as they underpin responses to constructions of Indian society in all media. Boys especially show an understanding of how 'outsiders', for example their white peers, may rebuke Hindi films as 'backward' and 'ludicrous', but they also clearly feel estranged themselves from the sense of 'Indianness' and the 'India' represented in the films. There is an underlying awareness that the films, when viewed in the 'west', may function to confirm dominant, racist discourses on India and Indian/'Asian' people. Apparently, experiences of racism as well as such readings of the films are gender specific.

Western critics – academics and film enthusiasts alike – have either reviled or ignored Hindi films for nearly a century. This disdain and ignorance both springs from and feeds into racism. The fierce rejection of Hindi films as a 'genre', especially among boys, echoes western critical discourses. One 18-year-old boy's condemnation of Indian films was particularly eloquent:

> With the standards of media appreciation in the west it's hard to under-stand the sort of psyche that would appreciate these kinds of film again and again and again [. . .]. If you've been exposed to a film culture based on complex plots and detailed cinematography then you'd expect the same from the other culture and if it doesn't match up to that standard you don't want to see it any more [. . .] it's like driving a Morris Minor after you've driven a Porsche.

This coincidence of views does not confirm a 'truth' about the Hindi cinema. Rather it exposes a common frame of reference based on domi-nant western (Hollywood) film-making practices. Even where language presents no barrier, popular Hindi films subvert the generic conventions of western cinema and disorientate spectators whose expectations have been formed by western genres. For those who do enjoy Hindi movies, evidently the crucial source of pleasure lies in the skilful blending of certain generic ingredients: the screenplay, songs and music, the emotional appeal, the spectacle, production values and, of course, the stars. Deeper engagement with the films becomes apparent above all when narrative is discussed, revealing the pleasures involved in the viewing. At the same time, some further causes of resistance to the films become clear.

The popular Hindi cinema evolved from village traditions of epic narration and regularly and openly draws on the characters, dramas and structures of the mythological epics. Indeed many film-makers and theorists claim that there are only two 'metatexts', the *Mahabharata* and the *Ramayana*, and that every film can be traced back to these sources.

The 'ideal moral universe' which the films construct derives from the value system propounded by these epics (Thomas, 1985). Viewers' interpretations of the films and their affective engagement with them relies upon an understanding of this moral universe and its value system. Mishra (1985) sees Bombay films as transformations of the narrative structures inherent in these epics, the influence of which, he argues, goes beyond narrative form, for they must also be seen as ideological tools for the propagation of beliefs endorsed by the ruling classes. But it is the form and movement of the narrative that most distinguishes Hindi from western film – the balance between plot development, spectacle and emotion is very different. Spectacle alone risks losing an audience, so skilled narration involves swift transitions between various modes of spectacle, and the emotional involvement invited by the reassuring familiarity of narratives deeply rooted in Indian social, moral and psychic life (Thomas, 1985: 130).

One of the commonest assertions made by interviewees was that the films all have the same type of stories, and that they are therefore 'totally predictable' and not worth watching. Three basic narrative themes, popular in the late 1970s and 1980s, were repeatedly identified: (1) 'Dostana', where a bond of male friendship overcomes the desire for a woman; (2) 'lost and found', where parents and children are separated and reunited years later following a revelation of mistaken identities; and (3) 'revenge', where villains get their just desserts at the hands of wronged heroes (Thomas, 1985: 125). As interviewees observed, these themes are structured by the discourses of *izzat*. They convey a sense that ideal social and moral order involves living in harmony with fate and respecting the ties of family and friendship as well as wider social obligations. The narrative closure of contemporary films was often contrasted with the social-realist films made in the 1950s and 1960s, which are the object of renewed interest among young and old alike: in more recent films 'everything turns out all right and people have nothing to think about, nothing to cry about'. But interviewees who enjoy Hindi films reject the narrative structure typical of western films which are seen as 'continuous all the way [. . .] they just continue, no songs, no dances [. . .] that's why I find them boring'.

Pleasure is taken in the non-linear narratives, and the intricate and convoluted nature of storytelling in the Hindi cinema becomes apparent in attempts at narrative reconstructions. Hindi films are generally constructed around a number of climaxes counterposed with scenes of humour, spectacle and high melodrama. The narrative is driven less by a question of what will happen next but how it will happen. It is not so much that an enigma must be solved, but rather that a moral disordering must be resolved (Thomas, 1985: 130). Viewers expect to become emotionally involved with characters and this is a crucial part of the pleasure. Affective engagement is ensured not only by cinematic techniques which encourage identification but also through the songs which heighten the emotional impact of the film: 'The songs back everything up [. . .] they have real feeling in them and it's not just any old songs, they relate to the actual situations in the films, they get you emotionally involved and influence you'. As in melodrama, undischarged emotion is expressed through songs and music:

> Whenever that song comes on, I cry, I can't control myself [. . .] it's the father of a girl singing to her before she leaves her family to get married, he sings about how you are leaving us now and saying how when you were young I used to hold you in my arms, how I used to play with you [. . .] can't listen to that song without tears pouring out [. . .] and I think of my sister when she will be leaving us.

Fantasy, particularly romantic fantasy, is a chief source of pleasure for those who enjoy Hindi films. The songs and dances and their settings provide discrete 'dream-like' sequences and 'a moment of escape from reality'. This is especially the case among girls, although boys are probably reluctant to admit being charmed by romance:

> When I watch an Indian film, after that I'm in heaven but I don't relate to the real world like I did [. . .] they're in rose gardens and the music just springs up from nowhere [. . .] that's why people like watching them – to get away from the real world. What do drugs do? They take you to another world [. . .] so do Indian films but they're a safer way out of your problems [. . .] I wouldn't mind sitting in a rose garden like that.

Others take a more critical view of such fantastical scenes: 'they're fantasies for the poor, they show them what they cannot afford [. . .] they're satisfied with the songs [. . .] they [the film-makers] create the dream sequences for them'. They are also seen as exploitative and reactionary by more politically minded informants who compare recent films with the social-realist films of the 1950s:

> I think people could identify their immediate life with them [. . .] if they showed a farmer losing his crops after years of hard labour that was a reflection of life [. . .] there was nothing magical about it as it is now. After this period people didn't want tragedies they wanted fantasies, they wanted a means of escape, they wanted to break out of reality.

Many, however, even if they make such criticisms, recognise the cathartic and therapeutic aspects of these cinematic opiates. They are seen as enabling a temporary release from the tensions of everyday life and as helping viewers to discharge distressful emotions vicariously. One girl revealed:

> I'm scared of my parents finding out that I have a boyfriend but after I've watched a film, and listened to a few songs and calmed myself

down, I'm not scared of my parents any more – so they give you courage in a way.

Some girls find the films provide a source of support and encouragement, affirming their ideology of romantic love and legitimising their 'illicit' romantic liaisons through the power of feeling expressed by the lovers in the films. Some girls who are concerned about their own love and future marital relationships appear to seek confirmation in the movies that 'true love' can really be found: 'Sometimes we just sit there and wonder if there's a thing called love, you hear so many terrible stories of broken relationships and marriages [...] whereas in an Indian film you're so convinced that love is real [...] that it's true.'

Then again, western conventions of heightened realism are often contrasted with what are seen to be ludicrously unrealistic action and fight sequences in Hindi films. Anachronism is not easily tolerated: 'They'll show a man fighting for Independence – on a motorbike, with sunglassses and jeans – they should at least show him in the clothes of the period'. The implausibility of stunt sequences is rebuked where production values are low: 'It's stupid, motorbikes crossing lakes when you know it's a cartoon'. However, the criteria of verisimilitude proper to Hindi cinema appear to be based primarily on the skill exercised in manipulating the rules of the film's moral universe. Among regular viewers, accusations of implausibility are more likely to occur if the ideal codes of kinship duty are flouted than if the hero performs an outrageously unrealistic feat (cf. Thomas, 1985).

Despite the contradictory evaluations of Hindi films, most young people are encouraged to view and discuss the issues they raise with parents. For parents and grandparents certain films stimulate collective memories and nostalgia is a key part of the pleasure involved in watching them, especially the older, black and white movies which are available on cassette and also screened regularly on the local Indian cable or satellite channel. (The local cable channel Indra Dnush has now gone on satellite as Asia TV.) In a particularly moving account by a man in his seventies, tears welled in his eyes as he recounted:

> When we see black and white films it reminds us of our childhood, our schooldays and school mates, of what we were thinking, of what we did, of our heroes [...] and I tell you that gives us great pleasure.

Grandparents use the films to convey a sense of their past in India to their grandchildren, to tell stories of their youth and to describe what life was like for them. Elders regard most Hindi films as a powerful resource for educating their children in the values and beliefs that are seen to be deeply rooted in Indian culture and traditions: 'they teach not only the language but how "to be" in an Indian environment'. Young adults enjoy films which encourage discussion: 'films which bring out the contradictions in families, the arranged marriage system, the caste system and moral conflicts'. Thus the films serve both youth and their elders as tools for eliciting views on salient themes, especially the issues of kinship duty, courtship and marriage, the most intensely debated of all issues among children and parents. It would appear that Hindi films are used to legitimate a particular world-view but also to open up its contradictions. So, while young people use Indian films to deconstruct 'traditional culture', many parents use them to foster cultural and religious traditions. Some remain sceptical of parental attempts to 'artificially maintain a culture through film' but, successful or not, it is clear that the VCR is being used for the purposes of reformulating and 'translating' cultural traditions in the Indian diaspora.

DEVOTIONAL VIEWING: 'SACRED SOAPS'

As I indicated earlier, films serve the purpose of language learning, and elders also use them to impart religious knowledge. Parents encourage their children to learn their mother tongue at school but students, by and large, are not keen. Resources are scarce and few are eager to take up Hindi, Urdu or Punjabi as an examination subject. Literacy in these languages is not regarded as a useful skill. However, many young people are keen to develop oral/aural skills in order to communicate effectively with their elders and with relatives in Britain and in India, and films provide a way of doing so. Language is also a potent symbol of collective identity and often the site of fierce loyalties. In the context of a British society which constructs linguistic difference as a problem rather than as a resource, the desire to defend and maintain one's linguistic heritage becomes strong. Furthermore, in a community faced with religious diversity and at times division, it is not surprising that cultural identity is often construed as being based not only on linguistic, but also on religious, continuity. Religious or 'mythological' films are viewed for devotional purposes, particularly (but not only) in Hindu families, and their viewing is often integrated into daily acts of worship.

In recent years India's government monopoly TV channel, Doordarshan, has screened serial versions of sacred texts of Hinduism, the *Ramayana* and the *Mahabharata*. They have enjoyed unprecedented popularity not only in India, where some 650 million viewers regularly tune in, but also in the Indian diaspora where they are followed on cable TV, on video or, as with the *Mahabharata* in Britain, on broadcast TV. Some argue that these TV epics have exacerbated the trends toward Hindu fundamentalism and been exploited for political purposes: the BJP, the Hindu nationalist party, used several actors in these epics as candidates in various state elections (Chatterji, 1989; cf. *'We Have Ways of Making You Think'*, BBC2, 27 November 1992). However, in Southall, Hindu families have found them useful for helping their children deepen their religious knowledge and beliefs.

During my fieldwork in Southall, I was fortunate enough to be welcomed into the home of the Dhanis – à Hindu family – in order to watch the Channel 4 broadcast of Peter Brook's stage adaptation of the *Mahabharata*, which occupied six hours on a Saturday evening in November 1990. A few weeks later BBC2 began broadcasting Doordarshan's 91-part serialised version of the *Mahabharata*. So over a two-year period I visited them regularly on Saturday afternoons to watch it. The juxtaposition of the two versions, one Indian and the other 'western', led the Dhanis to perform a contrastive analysis. Our conversations and my observations during viewing formed the basis of detailed case-study of the reception of these two TV versions of the *Mahabharata* by the Dhani family (Gillespie, 1993b, 1994b). Here I shall highlight some of the key insights of this case-study and summarise its findings.

The *Mahabharata* and the *Ramayana* are the foundation myths of Indian society. They are said to permeate every aspect of Indian social life and to enshrine the philosophical basis of Hinduism and for centuries have served as an *ithisa* or a fundamental source of knowledge and inspiration for all the arts. In Sanskrit, *maha* means great; '*Bharat*' is the name of a legendary family, which in an extended sense means 'Hindu', or – extended further – 'mankind'. The *Mahabharata* is thus variously translated 'The Great History of India' or 'The Great History of Mankind'. It tells the story of a long and bitter quarrel between two groups of cousins: the Pandevas and the Kauravas. It recounts the history of their divine origins and the conflict over who will rule the kingdom. Towards the end of the epic Krishna, one of the most revered of Hindu deities, incites the Pandevas to go to battle against their cousins to restore order and achieve justice. The *Bhagavat Gita*, one of the most sacred Hindu texts which contains the essence of Hindu philosophy, records the advice which Krishna gives to Arjuna, a Pandevas, in a moment of self-doubt and weakness before going into the battle which is to decide the fate of the earth. Although few Hindus in Southall are familiar with the *Mahabharata* in its entirety, many know the *Bhagavat Gita* and, like the Dhanis, have acquired knowledge of its characters and story-line through its serialisation in popular cartoons and filmic versions.

The Dhani household consists of nine people: the mother and father in their late forties, five daughters aged 12 to 23, and two sons aged 11 and 18. They emigrated to Southall from Calcutta in 1978. The father and mother are employed in local catering firms. The family regularly views religious films and Mrs Dhani, in particular, will often stay up until the early hours of the morning to view them. She claims that religious films provide her with comfort and solace from life's everyday anxieties. There is a tone of playful guiltiness in her voice when, sometimes, she admits to having watched religious videos for some fifteen hours at the weekend.

The devotional viewing of religious films involves taboos, prohibitions and rituals, similar to those surrounding sacred places and objects. It is incorporated into the Dhanis' everyday lives as are their domestic acts of worship. For example, at the start of a religious film, incense is lit and when a favourite god such as Krishna appears, the mother will encourage her children to sit up straight and make a devout salutation. An extra *puja* (an act of worship which is generally performed three times a day; before dawn, at noon and in the evening) may be performed before or after viewing. Once a religious film has been switched on it must be viewed until the end out of respect. Food should not be eaten whilst viewing, except *prasad* or holy food that has been blessed. Viewing religious films is seen as a pleasurable act of devotion in itself and devotional viewing is arguably a mark of transformations in religious practices. However, these 'new' modes of TV consumption are nevertheless deeply rooted in Indian religious and cultural traditions, especially the iconographic conventions associated with the representation of deities (Guha-Thakurta, 1986), and devotional modes of looking, seeing and worshipping images deemed sacred (Appadurai and Breckenridge, 1992).

My first visit to the Dhanis to watch Peter Brook's production of the *Mahabharata* was marked by confusion and a crisis. I shall briefly describe the evening in order to set the scene. From the outset confusion reigned as the international casting and bleak, sackcloth costumes had the immediate effect of rendering their dearly loved gods unrecognisable:

RANJIT: That's Ganesha!
SEFALI: No it isn't, be quiet.
LIPI: That's Vishnu!
MALATI: Don't be silly, that's Vyasa.
RANJIT: But Vyasa is Vishnu.
SEFALI: No he's not, he's Krishna.

After twenty minutes or so Mr Dhani and his elder son went out proclaiming: 'It's no good it doesn't carry the meaning'. Mrs Dhani, her five daughters, youngest son and myself continued watching half-heartedly. A sullen and solemn atmosphere reigned and their lack of interest in the programme was evident. They began telling me of their love for the god Krishna and their delight in the TV serial the *Ramayana* which they had watched on video – which portrays the childhood of Krishna and tells the story of Krishna's incarnation, Lord Ram, and his wife Sita. After a couple of hours, part three of the production opened with preparations for the battle and with Krishna encouraging Arjuna to go to war. Silence fell and intense viewing began. The children appeared to become increasingly alarmed: 'Mum, why is Krishna telling Arjuna to kill his cousins? Why is he telling them to go to war?' asked Ranjit, the younger boy. 'You don't know who the goodies and the baddies are in this one,' said Malati. 'Why are we watching this anyway?'exclaimed Sefali. 'Tell me, who's enjoying it, shall we switch it off?' All eyes fell upon me: 'Yes, please do if you want to'.

It is difficult to convey the sense of relief and change of atmosphere that occurred the moment the set was switched off. I was troubled that they had been putting up with it because of my presence and, as I later discovered, indeed they had. Mrs Dhani and her two eldest daughters disappeared upstairs. I heard the sound of bells ringing and a horn blowing. Sefali explained: 'Oh, that's all right, they're just doing a *puja*'. Their displeasure and distaste for Brook's production was passed over quickly. 'Terrible rubbish!', Malati muttered. Soon Mrs Dhani and her daughters reappeared: 'Let's put *Sita's Wedding* on' (a film which tells of the wedding of Rama and Sita which occurs in the *Ramayana*). 'Yeah!' cried the children, 'Wait till you see it! it's fantastic!' By this time it was 10.30 p.m. so, fearful of overstaying my welcome, I replied that maybe I should come back: 'No! No! Mum says you must stay!' There was a joyful atmosphere as *Sita's Wedding* was put on. 'Why didn't we think of this before?' Munni cried. The mother sat on the floor with her two youngest children tucked under each of her arms as they all sang along to the opening song. When Ram appeared, they sat up and made a salutation: 'Thank God, I have my taste back again!' said the mother as we continued watching into the night.

The drama of this first evening at the Dhanis reached its crisis at the moment, highlighted by Ranjit, when Krishna's divinity and moral integrity seemed to be thrown into question. After performing the *puja* the Dhanis became receptive to viewing *Sita's Wedding*. This is perceived as a sacred text and was viewed accordingly in a devotional manner. However, the reasons why Brook's production was so distasteful to the Dhani family only became apparent to me in subsequent weeks, as we began watching Doordarshan's version and the Dhanis began doing a contrastive analysis of the two versions which was to last for several weeks. This contrastive analysis was quite spontaneous on their part but it was also, of course, encouraged by my presence – by their desire to understand the story themselves and to be able to explain it to me. I was an outsider being gently ushered inside their family, their home and their religion and this dynamic triggered an exchange between us of unparalleled depth and intensity in my fieldwork. We reviewed parts of Brook's production as they were curious to resolve the moral dilemma that confronted them as a result of Krishna's exhortation to the Pandevas to go to war against 'their own flesh and blood', as Ranjit put it. Malati got a copy of R. K. Narayan's shorter version of the *Mahabharata* and a text of the *Bhagavat Gita*, and so began our journey into resolving the enigmas and moral ambiguities it posed.

Brook's production was so distasteful to the Dhanis because, firstly, it flouted the iconographic conventions associated with the representation of Hindu deities. Certain visual codes, such as the use of colour to symbolise the personal and moral qualities of the gods, had not been respected in their eyes:

SEFALI: You can't even recognise Krishna, normally he's blue.

MALATI: Gunga and Bhisma normally wear white because it's a symbol of purity and truth.

RANJIT: Duryodhana should wear red shouldn't he because of his anger and the blood that gets shed.

Such systems of colour classification and symbolism are to be found in many ancient religions; according to Turner (1966) they provide a kind of primordial classification of reality. In fact the visual codes associated with the representation of Hindu deities have developed over centuries, but it was the introduction of popular, mass-produced prints which resulted in more fixed and stereotypical portrayals of the gods. Guha-Thakurta (1986) has traced the changing iconography of popular, religious picture production in India. He describes how the introduction of lithographic presses and colour printing led to the increased production of prints with 'gaudy and flamboyant colours, dazzling costumes and majestic backdrops'. The deities acquired a new solidity and roundedness. Theatrical postures and expressions also became part of the fixed stereotype of the gods. He argues that these developments contributed to the increasing humanisation and domestication of divinity.

However, for the Dhanis, more disturbing than the flouting of visual codes in Brook's production was the transgression of yet more deeply rooted cultural codes, such as the primary distinction between gods and humans. In their view the gods were not portrayed with due dignity or respect.

SEFALI: All gods are born into royal families. In the Indian one you can tell the gods from humans [. . .] and who is a king from the way he talks and behaves, you can tell by his strength [. . .] when like Krishna appears there's always joyful music. There are other things, like the king will always wear gold and the prince silver.

SEWANTI: Like in the Indian one you can tell a baddy because he will be wearing dark clothes and the music will have an evil feel to it [. . .] in the English one they've left it all to the language. In the Indian one everything contributes to the meaning – the way they speak and how they are spoken to, how they behave, what they wear, their clothes, their jewellery, everything.

MALATI: The respect is missing, like you would never hear Krishna being called by his name like that, it would always be Lord Krishna or Krishna ji. You would never hear someone call their elder by their name [. . .] people show Krishna respect in the Indian one by kneeling and kissing his feet [. . .].

SEWANTI: They've spoiled the picture of the culture [. . .].

MUNNI: There's no feeling in it.

MALATI: They borrowed the story but not the culture.

In contrast, in the Indian version, the representation of the Hindu deity conforms to traditional iconographic conventions and therefore can be worshipped on the screen, as are the gods in the popular prints which adorn every room in their home. Thus, for devotional viewing to occur, the image must be perceived as sacred, as entitled to and worthy of veneration. Brook's production violated the sacred aura of the gods as represented by conventional iconography.

The dramatic composition and weighting must also be correctly balanced in order to satisfy the requirements of devotional viewing. Clearly, the experience of viewing a 91-part serialised drama with many of the generic ingredients of the conventional melodrama or soap opera is quite different to that of viewing a six-hour televised theatrical production. Doordarshan's production is aimed at mass popular audiences whilst Brook's is targeted at middle-class theatre-going élites. Doordarshan's production allows for a close identification with the sacred characters which builds up over a lengthy time frame, and for a close involvement with the intricate inter-weaving of various narrative strands and subplots. The frequent moments of high melodrama and the often uninhibited expression of emotions allows for an intense affective engagement with the narrative enigmas and their resolutions. The Dhanis repeatedly drew parallels with their viewing of other soap operas: the cliff-hanger endings; the pleasurable anticipation of viewing; the mobilisation of knowledge of past events to interpret present dilemmas and to predict future outcomes; and the addictive nature of viewing. Yet more profoundly, the serial narrative form is able to represent the specific, epic and cyclical notions of time which constitute the philosophical core of the *Mahabharata* – which is seen to convey one cycle of birth, destruction and rebirth – the circle in which humans are caught until they reach spiritual union with the gods.

The role of the narrator also differs between the two versions in a culturally significant way. In Brook's production the story is narrated by Vyasa (an incarnation of Vishnu, one of the principal deities) who appears on screen. In the Indian version the narrator is Vishnu himself, but he is invisible and thus given a divine and mystical quality. He figures as a disembodied voice, seen only in the form of a shadow emanating from the heavens who, as Malati explains, represents Time itself: 'In the Indian one you see the shadow of the world going round – and that symbolises time and destiny – the shadow is telling the story and that shadow is Vishnu'. The Dhani children struggled to comprehend the deeper philo-sophical meanings of the text, particularly the Hindu concept of time, with the help of narrator who takes on an interventionist, explicitly didactic, role. The narrator provides the dominant discourse, guiding and leading the viewer to a 'proper' understanding of events and themes. Sometimes these passages of direct narratorial intervention were re-viewed repeatedly until a satisfactory understanding was achieved.

The Dhanis highlighted three moments in which the narrative weighting was markedly different in the two versions. The first was Bhisma's vow to remain celibate. Bhisma was the rightful heir to the throne but out of love for his father, renounced the throne and vowed never to have children who might contest the right to the throne of the sons by his second marriage. This crucial moment in the story transforms the fate of the world but, as Ranjit points out, Brook fails to understand its significance:

> In the English version they make it seem like it's just a little promise but in the Indian version, Bhisma's vow shakes the earth, thunder and lightning open up the skies. No human would be able to make a promise like that [. . .] I love that bit it's pure! If he does that for his father, imagine what he would do for his mother!

Similarly, the portrayal of Draupaudi's humiliation was considered to trivialise her suffering. Draupaudi, the wife of all five Pandevas brothers, becomes the stake in a game of dice between the enemy cousins, Yudhistira and Duryodhana. Yudhistira has a weakness for gambling and having lost everything else, stakes his wife and loses her too. She is then humiliated by the victor, who attempts to violate her honour; but Krishna intervenes and magically bestows her with a sari of infinite length, thus safeguarding her honour. This is another turning-point in the *Mahabharata* since her humiliation calls for revenge and intensifies the conflict between the cousins, later leading to the war. According to Sefali: 'In the Indian version the true strength of her character comes out. She questions all the men in court and gets her own revenge, in a small way, by shaming them'. Malati pointed out that the full extent of her humiliation is not even hinted at in the English version: 'For example, in the Indian one we know that she has a period because she's wearing yellow and that means she shouldn't even be seen in public'. Sewanti is equally disparaging: 'because they don't understand the respect she deserves they don't manage to put across just how badly she was insulted'.

It is interesting that the Dhanis' criticisms of Brook's production coincide with those of several Indian critics, such as Barucha (1991). Brook's production, according to both, lacks a clearly defined religious and moral frame of reference and is not contextualised within the social and ritual processes of Hindu culture and society; as a result, divine characters undergo a loss of sanctity. The Dhanis' criticisms became most intense at the moment when Krishna incites Arjuna to go to war – the moment which launched the crisis on our first evening together. The dilemma was later resolved through viewing the same scenes in the Indian version and the reading of supplementary texts. The Dhanis learned to rationalise the moral paradox that confronted them and to articulate some of the more profound philosophical themes. The didacticism of the Doordarshan *Mahabharata* enabled them to reconstruct the discursive register of the

Gita's teachings and to take pleasure in explaining its principles to one another and to me:

> MALATI: *Gita*, it's strange because it makes you see good in bad and bad in good.
>
> SEFALI: That's because everything depends on time. In the early stages of time human beings lived close to the gods and things were in harmony but then time moves on to a stage where humans move away from the gods and then chaos comes. Krishna was born into the Age of Destruction [. . .].

Whilst the actions of gods may seem immoral in the short term, in the long term they will be for the good. In Ranjit's words: 'Krishna's intentions are good. He knows that they had to go through a bloody war for the sake of justice, he does it to fulfil *dharma*.' Dharma, one of the most important principles to the Dhanis, refers to 'right action' or 'that which should be done'. It is the law upon which the universe rests; and it depends, as Sefali explains, on a cyclical conception of time: 'Humans are ruled by time and so is the world, not even the gods can prevent some things happening. The world has to fulfil its own destiny *in time*, like human beings – that is our fate, our *karma* – to be reincarnated until we are released, until we reach *nirvana*.'

Viewing the *Mahabharata* helped the Dhanis to articulate a cosmic view of the world which challenges and negates some of the certainties of their pragmatic everyday world. This latent conflict became especially evident when the complex ideas expressed about cosmic time, the ambiguity of good and evil, and the paradoxical actions of the gods were reduced again, later in the course of the discussion, to the simple, 'everyday' schema of a battle between 'goodies' and 'baddies', as when Malati explained that 'Krishna has taken sides with the Pandevas because [. . .] they are more holy than the Kauravas'. This simpler reading serves a consolatory function by giving a reason why Krishna protects the Pandevas (because they are 'good', unlike the Kauravas, and so are worthy of protection). Thus the more comfortable and reassuring everyday world-view is reinstated and the notions of good and bad reappear as unambiguous categories. Sefali: 'The *Mahabharata* makes you see life like it's a battle between good and evil, a battle for justice or *dharma* and when the equilibrium is lost you have chaos.' For the Dhanis, in their everyday lives, it is necessary to believe that human beings, at any stage in history, can escape chaos by moral action. Pragmatically, in the short term of personal lives, moral action is possible, through honesty, devotion and performing one's duty; but in cosmic terms, in the face of eternity, the distinction between good and evil disappears and what is more, moral actions themselves have unpredictable consequences. As Sefali explains:

Human beings have free will [. . .] destiny or fate don't control everything, neither do the gods [. . .] but you can't do something good with
the hope of getting a reward. You must first know what is right and then
do it but if you do something good you can't be sure the outcome will
be good.

In many aspects of their everyday lives the Dhanis apply religious ideas
and beliefs which were undoubtedly developed and refined by their viewing of the *Mahabharata*. Specific notions of time, fate and free will, destiny
and reincarnation frame their everyday perceptions but, in their contrastive analysis of the two versions of the *Mahabharata*, the Dhanis
explicitly articulated their understanding of the Hindu philosophical
and religious tradition in a way which illuminated, for them perhaps as
much as for me, key aspects of this tradition and so contributed to a further
shaping of their values and beliefs.

The highpoint of the entire epic came during the *Bhagavad Gita*
sequence when Krishna shows his universal form. The sheer awe with which
this sequence was viewed by the family was as remarkable as the images on
the screen. A low-angled tracking shot follows Krishna, surrounded by a
golden aura and, as he moves gracefully through the air, his figure expands
to dominate the screen and his multifarious incarnations successively
appear around him amidst flames and shafts of water. This represents for
the Dhanis a divine vision. It is as if Krishna makes an appearance in the
living-room. For the Dhanis, full of awe and wonderment, it is like *nirvana*
on TV: devotional viewing at its fullest intensity.

WATCHING 'WESTERN' SOAPS

If the viewing of 'sacred soaps' sustains and enhances a commitment
to religious and cultural traditions in some families, in others the viewing
of 'white', 'western' soaps such as the Australian *Neighbours*, the favourite
soap among young people in Southall, is another domestic ritual, one
involving both intimacy and censure. The distinction between the reception
of 'sacred soaps' and that of secular, 'western' soaps, between 'devotional
viewing' and what might be called 'devoted viewing', is indeed less sharp
than might be thought. As Chapter 5 explains in more detail, the reception
of 'western' soaps too is governed by a moral framework and implicated
in informal didactic practices which expose the cultural dynamics of family
life – though the issues involved concern the pragmatic ethics of everyday
life, lacking any cosmic dimension, and are more likely to provoke inter-
generational conflict. For young people in Southall, the regular viewing
of soaps encourages a sense of participating in a daily activity shared
simultaneously with youth audiences nationally and internationally.
In fact they feel themselves to belong to a wider youth culture shaped by,

among other things, watching *Neighbours*. At the same time their immediate, local concerns are projected on to such soaps and the cultural specificities of Punjabi family life inflect their readings, especially because of the ways in which their elders, in many cases, tend to censure *Neighbours* and their viewing of it.

Viewing soaps with siblings and, in many cases, with mother is by far the most common arrangement. It would appear that most mothers condone their children's regular viewing of *Neighbours* because it is a time, structured into the day, when they know their children will be settled down in front of the TV. Many young people recognise that mothers need a rest from domestic chores. 'Watching with mother' becomes a pretext for intimacy and conversation. But intimacy may be heightened by the act of sharing an experience regardless of what is shared. Given that some mothers understand and speak very little English, it may be the relaxed atmosphere of the viewing situation and the desire to be together, more than the soap itself, which is appreciated.

As with 'sacred soaps' and Hindi films, some mothers use the situation for didactic purposes; this is often interpreted as her way of showing her children that she cares and feels protective toward them. A sense of intimacy is heightened by passing moral judgements on the characters which often serves as a confirmation of shared values. Some young people do not feel that *Neighbours* relates to their lives, as Mandeep, a 16-year-old girl points out:

> *Neighbours* doesn't really relate to our lives cos it shows us things that we are not allowed to do, like all that teenage romance [. . .] it doesn't encourage us but it must do some boys and girls [. . .] you know it's like some of them think they must have a boyfriend and if you have one you're up in the air but if you're not into that, they think you're at the bottom of the sea.

But viewing with mother may just as easily lead to argument and censure as to intimacy. Translation is often necessary which some find tedious and difficult. Others claim that they find it very difficult to communicate with their mothers, as they simply do not understand young people's values. Amrit, a 16-year-old girl, claims that she prefers to watch *Neighbours* without her mother:

> I don't really like watching *Neighbours* with my mum cos you might start off OK but as soon as she sees something she doesn't like she's off [. . .] she'll start on you – don't do this and don't do that and I'll start arguing with her [. . .] and we might end up not speaking for three days over something which I think is quite trivial.

Moral issues feature prominently in family discussions about soaps. In some families the channel is switched over as soon as kissing or more explicitly sexual behaviour appears on screen. It is often younger members of the family, rather than parents, who quickly grasp the remote control in order to avoid embarassment or a row. Fathers are seen to be much more censorious than mothers. Mohinderpal, a 16-year-old boy claims that, while his father strongly encourages him to watch the news, 'He doesn't like us watching *Neighbours* [. . .] when I see kissing scenes with Scott and Charlene [. . .] I myself get the remote control and put it on the other side if my father is there [. . .] you have to'. To watch a 'kissing scene' in the presence of parents would prove to be too embarrassing:

> because what I've been learned is not to watch things like that but those things are more on TV so you can't help watching it. I don't mind if it's just my brothers and sisters and even my mum, she doesn't really mind, well she pretends not to notice, but never in front of my father [. . .] but I do get embarrassed if it gets carried away.

Evidently, some mothers are more tolerant in their attitudes because, having, in the words of Mohinderpal, 'grown up' alongside their children, they are closer to them and much more in tune with their interests and tastes. Some mothers have grown to like what their children watch or, at any rate, to like watching with their children. Such proximity and closeness to mothers stands in sharp contrast to the distance which often seems to characterise relationships with fathers. This pattern is reported by boys and girls alike.

Diljit, a 17-year-old boy, is expected to speak Punjabi at home, and when he and his siblings speak in English together, their father blames the television for influencing them to become 'more English'. He also believes that his children will eventually copy the behaviour they watch on screen and is outraged when young people are shown being disrespectful to their elders, kissing or arguing with siblings:

> He repeats himself over and over again [. . .] if someone's arguing on *Neighbours* he'll say, 'Do you have to watch people arguing?' and then he'll say, 'See! You're using the same words to argue with your family,' and then he thinks we're copying them.

Diljit disagrees with his father, dismissing as absurd his fears about the potential of soaps to inspire imitative behaviour; yet he does admire the way in which young people in *Neighbours* assert themselves to their elders:

> If there are arguments in *Neighbours* with parents and that, then I'll sit there and get even more involved [. . .] I'll sit there thinking, yeah I should have done that [. . .] I should learn to talk back to my dad, but, you know, it's very bad to show disrespect like that to your father [. . .] we're not allowed to backchat and argue with our dad but it's good to see how someone else can.

Many parents feel that their values are undermined by soaps like *Neighbours*; the only virtue of such programmes in their eyes is that they alert them to the temptations and traps that their children may fall into. Those commonly mentioned are squandering money in games arcades, smoking, drinking or taking drugs, dating and getting pregnant, and running away from home. Such potential threats make parents more vigilant and lead to censoriousness during soap viewing or, as in several cases I came across, to an absolute injunction against viewing *Neighbours*. In all these cases young people managed to subvert paternal strictures with impressive cunning. But neither parents nor their children wish to remain locked in battle, and mothers often act as mediators in such family disputes, alleviating tensions and pacifying the different parties. Thus 'watching with mother' frequently functions as a pretext for intimacy and communication, in which the reaffirmation of shared values negotiates with the articulation of aspirations towards cultural change.

Television as an object and a social experience is embedded in family life, and family relationships are expressed in and through the viewing situation. Soaps bring alternative sets of social behaviour and moral values into the heart of domestic life. In Southall, soap viewing has become a domestic, agonistic ritual which involves defining and redefining relationships with 'others' both absent and present: from the characters on the screen, who constitute a televisual presence, to the wider audience, an absent but implied cultural referent; from parents and the local 'community', to siblings and peers. But if soaps are a domestic ritual, mediating, shifting and (in some senses) dissolving the boundaries between the public and private, then viewing broadcast news implicates viewers in a further, national daily ritual, addressing them as citizens and members of the British nation.

LOCAL NEWS MEDIA

British national press and TV news coexists in Southall with a particular range of both local and international news media. The widespread availability and consumption of newspapers and current affairs magazines from or about the Indian subcontinent is a distinguishing feature of Southall's news culture. *Des Pardes* (Home and Abroad) – identified with the Khalistan movement – and the more conservative *Punjab Times*, for example, are among the prime Punjabi Sikh diaspora newspapers. Both are edited and produced in Southall, as are others. But whilst reading newspapers in Punjabi, Hindi or Urdu is rare among young people, listening to news and discussions about current affairs in a variety of South Asian languages, as well as in English, on the local radio station Sunrise is almost inescapable. Sunrise addresses its audience as British 'Asians' and aims, in the words of its chief executive, Avtar Lit, to 'preserve their unique cultural identity and keep them in touch with their mother country'. Sunrise is played continously in most cafés, restaurants and shops, as well as in most 'Asian' homes. Local folklore emphasises its ubiquitous quality: a common tale is that one can hear the same song or even a whole programme while walking the length of Southall Broadway. Sunrise has recently obtained a channel on the Astra satellite; it can now be received across Britain and throughout Europe and it is soon to go transatlantic. It provides an outstanding example of a local community station with international reach, serving the global Indian diaspora, thus reversing the more common pattern of the local consumption of transnational products.

Sunrise claims to be the eleventh largest commercial radio station in the UK and the most popular radio station in west London. It caters for a wide range of regional, linguistic and religious differences whilst attempting to maintain a broad-based appeal. News bulletins and current affairs programmes are transmitted in English, Punjabi, Hindi, Urdu and Gujarati. The primary emphasis is on news from the Indian subcontinent, local news stories and news concerning 'Asians' in Britain. It aims to appeal as much to a Glaswegian Sikh as to a Muslim from Bradford or a Gujarati in Wembley. It is often referred to by young people as a 'lifeline' or a 'voice' for the parents. Others, though, see Sunrise as a further index of their 'ghettoisation' in an 'Asian community' in London, in much the same way as the local Hindi video culture is held to cut the 'community' off from British society. By and large, young people prefer to listen to London's various independent radio stations, such as Kiss FM and Capital Radio, which target youth audiences. Even though most young people do not share their parent's enthusiasm for Sunrise radio, it is nevertheless their major source of news apart from national TV.

Music programmes comprise almost three-quarters of Sunrise's programming schedule. It caters for a variety of musical tastes: popular Hindi film songs; 'Asian golden oldies'; *ghazals*, popular renditions of Urdu love poetry; *qawwali*, an ancient form of Sufi devotional music; bhangra; and British pop. Samani (1993) highlights how 'preserving cultural traditions' and 'keeping young people in touch with their cultural heritage' through music is the aim of the presenters, who largely dictate the choice of music within the above pre-established categories. For most young people the choice of music is too narrow and too 'traditional'. Samani found that several presenters on Sunrise refuse to play ragga bhangra because, as one told him: 'we will forget our tradition [. . .] there will be no roots left [. . .] if we start spoiling our new generation, then who will put them right?' (Samani, 1993: 45). His research shows that Sunrise is not popular with most of the youth he interviewed, precisely because it chooses to ignore new forms of bhangra and other types of 'crossover' music currently popular among youth, such as fusions of *qawwali* with western pop rhythms. In young people's view, Sunrise caters for musical tastes in the parental culture and attempts to impose an identity upon them: as one of Samani's inform-ants protested: 'the very last thing we need is someone or something telling us who we should be' (ibid.: 56).

This is consistent with patterns in my own data which suggest that Sunrise is especially appreciated by mothers as an accompaniment to their domestic duties, and by grandparents who prefer to communicate in Punjabi and whose lives are based in the domestic sphere. However, one of Sunrise's programmes which is popular with all generations is a family phone-in called 'Social Introductions', broadcast on Sunday afternoons, where parents 'advertise' their 'eligible' sons and daughters on the marriage market. This practice is widely frowned upon because it implies that a family cannot find a suitable spouse for their son or daughter. Viewed as a sign of failure, it is said to spoil a family's reputation. Nevertheless, or precisely for that reason, it is widely listened to by youth and their parents alike.

Sunrise prides itself on the opportunities it provides for businesses wishing to sell to the 'Asian' community and no doubt it has contributed to a strengthening of commercial networks and local businesses. But young people's main interest in radio as a medium is in pop programmes and phone-ins, and it is only a matter of contingency that news stories are con-sumed. Patterns of radio consumption confirm the general tendency towards a preference for British and 'western', as opposed to Indian or Pakistani, media among Southall youth. However, it is also clear that, whilst few young people would tune into Sunrise voluntarily, many are in fact regular consumers due to their parents' interest, as with Hindi films.

If exposure to news stories through the local press and radio seems inescapable, the extent of broadcast TV news, equally, gives it an ineluctable quality. Survey figures, to my surprise at first, revealed that TV news is the genre most frequently watched and discussed in families in Southall (see Appendix 10). The four TV channels broadcast approxim-ately fifteen hours of news per day between them (at times when no exceptional circumstances, such as war, prevail). Nearly ten of these hours are broadcast on BBC1 and ITV, the channels most regularly viewed in Southall homes; and the shorter bulletins are often broadcast before favourite programmes like *Neighbours* and *Home and Away* (an Australian soap from the same stable). The sheer quantity of hours devoted to news and the strategic positioning of news bulletins in the schedules, as well as parental interest in the news, suggest that it would be difficult for most young people to avoid some news consumption, at least without making a wilful and conscious effort to do so. But these facts alone do not suffice to explain the survey results. Fieldwork research revealed that young people have compelling reasons of their own for watching news programmes with their families. As Chapter 4 explains in more detail, participation in the domestic ritual of news viewing is perceived to function as a kind of 'rite of passage' both to adult status and to effective British citizenship, particularly when young people are called upon by their parents to act as translators and interpreters of the national news agenda.

News viewing, like soap viewing, helps to structure daily routines and has become a domestic ritual in most homes. There are no notable gender differences in news viewing: only a slightly higher number of girls (77 per cent) than boys (73 per cent) report viewing news with their family on a regular basis. It could be argued that this is because girls spend more time at home, rather than because of their interest in news, but there is no evidence in the data to suggest that girls are any less interested in TV news or any less competent in talking about it. The only clear-cut gender difference to emerge is that girls and boys enjoy different types of news stories: girls like human interest stories while most boys state a preference for sports stories. News is generally seen as chief source of information about the world, a necessary link to the world outside the local community, and a prerequisite to functioning as a citizen in Britain. National news broadcasts address viewers as citizens, inform them of their rights and responsibilities, and foster a sense of national identity. So it is often in the sphere of news consumption and TV news talk that young people most clearly articulate the complexities and ambivalences of their relation to dominant, national modes of identification – complexities and ambivalences which are closely bound up with teenagers' ambiguous status, on the margin between childhood and adulthood. ll

'NOT THE TURKEY TYPE': CHRISTMAS AND TV

Many TV genres, particularly news and soaps, link families and media in daily rituals. Annual rituals, both national and religious, are also increasingly mediated through TV. Several researchers have highlighted the role of TV in shaping the experience of irregular civic rituals such as coronations and royal weddings: the simultaneous reception by disparate, scattered domestic audiences, engenders a sense of vicarious participation in national life (Chaney, 1986; Dayan and Katz, 1983). Annual 'British' rituals –notably Christmas, to a lesser extent Easter, and also key events in the sports calendar – may not always be 'performed events' in this sense, but they are key arenas for the construction of a sense of British national identity. The significance of this function of broadcasting for cultural minorities, who may otherwise have little access to mainstream British culture, is evident.

Belonging to the British nation and participating in national rituals, such as Christmas, are marked by a sense of ambivalence for most Southall families. The reader may assume that Christmas is not celebrated by non-Christian families in Southall, since it is of course a Christian feast and a western cultural tradition. It is true that in a religious and calendrical sense it has little relevance to Sikh and Hindu families who celebrate Diwali (the Festival of Lights marking the start of the new year), or to

Muslims for whom Ramadan followed by Eid marks the high point of the year. However, Christmas in modern Britain, that is, since Victorian times, has developed into a holiday celebration which embraces key cultural contradictions between the sacred and the secular, and between the public and the private.

Its historical raison d'être is that of a religious feast celebrating the birth of Christ, marked by religious rituals and symbolism (the crib, midnight mass, carol singing, etc.), and celebrating what are thought of as essentially 'Christian' values (love, charity, mercy, family unity). Thus in origin it is a sacred festival; but it is one which has acquired as much, if not more, a commercial and secular character. The blurring of the boundary between the sacred and secular opens Christmas up to being incorporated into Punjabi family life. Moreover, Christmas is both a public and a private feast. In the public sphere it is celebrated, in some form, ubiquitously and recognised as a national holiday. But Christmas Day itself is, for most, a highly private, domestic, family affair. Television brings together the public and private dimensions of Christmas in a spectacular way, enabling its public manifestations to be experienced in the privacy of one's home. For families in Southall, the rituals and symbols and the customs and traditions of Christmas are powerfully conveyed and represented by TV. Television, in giving access to the private and public, sacred and secular dimensions of Christmas implicates Southall families in its rituals.

TV viewing is also the principal activity at Christmas which brings most British families together for exceptionally extended periods of time. Christmas has become very much 'TeleXmas', as the various TV companies battle for viewers' attention with blockbuster movies, feature-length episodes of sitcoms, dramatic episodes of national soaps and the inevitable national ritual, the Queen's Speech. Families in Southall incorporate different aspects of its rituals and customs to varying degrees and in diverse ways. The following account was written by Kuljit, a 17-year-old Sikh girl, on her family's Christmas in 1989:

> Christmas is a Christian festival though my family does not follow the exact Christian way. We do have a party, not the turkey type, but one with food that we all like. We also give presents and cards and we invite family and friends over. We put a Christmas tree up and hang decorations on walls and ceiling. At Christmas we don't watch anything religious, us kids watch English films while our parents watch plenty of Indian movies which we hate because we find them so boring [. . .] we did watch some family films together like *Indiana Jones* and *Crocodile Dundee*. They also watched a programme called *Follow that Star* about an Indian actor named Amitabh Bachan who talked about his life, his family and his career.

Alibhai (1987) sees Christmas as posing particular problems for parents in Southall. She argues that the impetus to celebrate, to buy trees, lights and wrap and exchange presents comes primarily from children, who are the dupes of commercial interests, and she sees participation in Christmas by Southall youth and their families as a manifestation of oppressive, post-colonial, white power – a form of cultural racism:

There is a big difference between children sharing in the joys of different festivals of the world and being absorbed into the dominant religion of the country for six weeks of the year [. . .]. Behind the goodwill lies the central power relation where Christian social rituals dominate. (1987: 15)

She goes on to quote Arvind Sharma:

Everything about Christmas has to do with whiteness, the snow, the imagery [. . .] with messages of love in which you are not included because you are brown [. . .]. If I withhold this seductive festival from my son what can I offer to replace it? Most Asians feel the contradiction between longing and rejection. It's a party to which you have never been invited [. . .] so you either say I never wanted to go or you make your own parties which ape the real thing [. . .]. These imitation parties are [. . .] like wearing someone else's clothes.

Participation in Christmas can indeed be seen as yet another way in which the dominant culture exercises its power over the minority – a festival for the majority 'other' which simultaneously entices but excludes the minority. However, such views are not shared by many Sikh and Hindu families in Southall, many of whom now celebrate Christmas rituals in their own manner. For some, Christmas is an occasion for extended family gatherings and viewing popular American 'family' films, as Sanjeeb's diary illustrates:

Saturday December 24th: Today, me and my mum went to my cousins' houses to give their Christmas presents. Then we came home and done all the housework. Apart from that it was a quiet day. The only good film [on TV] was *Jagged Edge*.

Sunday December 25th: Christmas Day was great. All my relatives came round our house. We watched films on TV like *Back to the Future* and *The Empire Strikes Back*. I ate so many chocolates. We didn't cook a turkey because all my family are vegetarians and most of my relatives. Instead we ate food like pakora and samosas.

A more insightful analysis of the significance of Christmas for Punjabi families in Southall is offered by Baumann (1992). He argues, and my data would support his arguments, that Christmas is a domestic ritual which is centrally concerned with defining and redefining relationships with 'others'. To the children these 'others' are their peers and school friends, with whom they discuss and compare their own family's celebrations. To parents and elders the 'others' are fellow Punjabis, kin or neighbours, 'who assess the merits of going too far, or not far enough, in replicating an originally "alien ritual"'. There are further 'others': the 'English' or *gori* whom both adults and children know as the minority locally and the majority nationally. Thus, through Christmas rituals, not least patterns of watching TV, youth and their parents negotiate their subtly differing relationships to surrounding 'others'. The incorporation of a range of Christmas symbols and practices and differing perceptions of their significance are evident in the following statements, many of them excerpts from the Christmas diaries of several 16-year-olds, which were kept as part of a school project. Christmas rituals are not simply adopted but are often adapted and integrated into a family's own religious beliefs and practices.

Gita, a 16-year-old Hindu girl, looks forward to Christmas every year. Her parents incorporate their own religious worship into Christmas festivities, at the same time as feeling part of a wider 'community' of the nation:

> Well, in my household we do quite a lot of things for Christmas that's because we feel part of the community. I give out the traditional cards and presents while my parents do the same. This year in my house my parents put up the lights around a God they believe in to form the Christmas decoration.

This kind of adaptive celebration of Christmas is also common among Sikhs, as Paramjit, a 16-year-old Sikh girl describes. On Christmas Eve her family also celebrate the anniversary of one of their gurus:

> Christmas brings happiness and excitement. We all enjoy the day, just eating, watching TV and being lazy. One of the reasons that there is excitement is that on Christmas Eve it is Guru Gobind Singh's birthday and that makes Christmas a bit special. We go to the temple to pay respect and thank god for everything.

Jagdish, a 17-year-old Sikh boy, takes a broader view and expresses his hope for a greater religious tolerance among all religions. He clearly feels his own religion is little understood in Britain. In his view, TV can help to foster an understanding of 'other' religions at Christmas:

> TV is important at Christmas. Not only does it beat away stress or boredom but it teaches us to learn and understand and care about other cultures and beliefs as we would like other people to know about our culture too. But most of all it brings the family together, especially the soaps, we're a family of 'soapaholics'.

Although Muslims recognise Jesus as a prophet, most do not celebrate Christmas, as Nadia, a 16-year-old Muslim girl explains:

As we are Muslims we do take Christmas as a religious festival because
Jesus was one of our prophets but we do not celebrate it, we don't give
cards or presents. It does bring changes into our family because on that
day we are all at home together and we watch TV with cups of tea and
coffee in our hands.

Others appear to embrace the 'spirit of Christmas' and have a very
typically 'turkey type' of feast. Ranjit, a 16-year-old Sikh girl, describes
her family Christmas as follows:

I think Christmas is a time of giving and sharing and thinking of others
around you and putting all the bad things that happened over the past
year behind you [. . .] we have the traditional turkey, roast potatoes, wine
and Christmas pudding [. . .] we always listen to the Queen's Speech [. . .]
she speaks to you, sort of, personally, and you know she has her own
family problems, even though she's a queen but she makes you feel you
are really part of Christmas [. . .] then we all watched E.T., even my mum
[. . .] we were all crying by the end.

While probably few young people would agree with Ranjit's views on the
Queen, for many families she is an important symbol of the nation and her
family's ups and downs are followed by people in Southall as avidly as anywhere else in Britain. Most young people tend to joke about the royal family, referring to them as 'posh snobs' and imitating the upper-class accents
and behaviour. Only Princess Diana appears to be everyone's 'darling' and
is widely admired, by girls especially.

Family conflicts over what to watch on TV are as common among
Punjabi families as others and sometimes children's preferences take
precedence, as Ravinder, a 16-year-old Sikh girl, describes:

We watched E.T. My aunt and uncle had come. The adults found it
boring but we told them they should watch it as soon they'd be able
to understand the story-line. They discussed whether there really is life
on other planets. My mum thinks there is but nobody else did.

The chances of the family coming together over an American film are
more likely at Christmas, often with predictable consequences, as Daljit,
a 16-year-old Sikh girl, reports:

We watched a bit of Baby Boom but we switched it off when the
babysitter started bonking behind the sofa as the owner of the house
got home from work. My dad put on an Indian film, Beta Beta, the
same old moralistic values came up again but this time the issues
included respect for elders and love between brothers and sisters
and how they should treat each other and not argue all the time like me
and my brother. My dad gave us a little lecture and we didn't talk
much after that.

The religious and national rituals of Christmas, through the mediation of TV, both incorporate and are incorporated into Punjabi family life in London. Youth and their parents selectively adopt and adapt a range of customs and practices associated with Christmas, redefining their relations to a range of significant 'others', both present and absent. Such cultural interactions and transformations are typical in plural societies. However, not only the religious and national festivals of the dominant culture are selectively appropriated and transformed. I shall end this chapter with an example of the more subversive and liberating appropriations of the media in Southall youth culture, one which defiantly challenged the locally dominant use of the annual religious ritual of Diwali as an occasion for the affirmation of Indian cultural heritage.

DIRTY DANCING AT DIWALI

Diwali, the Festival of Lights, is celebrated with great rejoicing in October each year in honour of Lakshmi, the goddess of wealth. It marks the beginning of the new year for Hindus and Sikhs alike. In most families, a ritual purification by water is followed by much dancing and music. In Southall, on the night of Diwali every house in every terraced street places candles along the low outside wall which separates the front garden from the pavement, and the skies are lit with magnificent firework displays. These firework displays are themselves an innovation in customary practices at Diwali, facilitated by the close proximity of Guy Fawkes Night, celebrated on 5 November throughout England: this is the only time in the year when fireworks are widely available in shops. Local schools usually close to enable families to celebrate, but most schools organise Diwali concerts, not unlike Christmas concerts in form, where performances of 'traditional' Indian dancing, singing and music are conventional. Typically, groups of girls learn the dances from a popular Hindi film and mime to songs, while boys play a range of Indian musical instruments.

At the high school where I worked, the deputy head, regarded by his students as a very 'strict' Sikh, had made himself unpopular because of his attempts at 'preserving religious and cultural traditions'. According to many students, he was 'going too far', chastising students for cutting their hair, condemning girls who wore skirts or the slightest touch of make-up and generally imposing a very strict regime. He also placed great emphasis on Indian performing arts, especially at Diwali. One year (1990) a group of 14- to 16-year-olds surreptitiously decided to change the Diwali concert repertoire and to perform a dance routine from the film *Dirty Dancing* – a 'rite of passage' film which had maintained an unparalleled degree of popularity since it hit the box offices in 1987.

Dirty Dancing is set in an American holiday camp for teenagers in 1963. It traces a girl's passage from innocence to sexual maturity, and from ugly duckling to beautiful dancing princess, through a romantic encounter with the dancing instructor. Freed from parental constraints, dancing, especially sexually suggestive 'dirty dancing', is enjoyed each night by the kids at the camp. The essential values of the film concern loyalty and friendship, and its major crisis occurs when the girl faces a conflict between loyalty to a friend and to the values of her parents – a theme to which most young people in Southall can easily relate. Patrick Swayze, an extremely popular film star among local girls, is the star dancer. His dancing partner gets pregnant several weeks before the final concert which marks the end of the summer camp and in which they are due to perform their star turn. Jennifer Grey, the female star of the film, obtains the money for an abortion from her father, refusing to tell him what the money is for out of loyalty to the girl. She simply asks her father to trust her.

Much of the film is about the preparations for the concert. Without his partner Swayze is at a loss, but Grey, of course, steps in. Initially they are simply dancing partners but soon they become intimate. They devote every waking hour to practising the dance for the final night. Further problems arise when Grey's father, a doctor, is called to the scene of the girl's botched abortion. Thinking Swayze is the father and that his daughter used the money to protect him, he forbids his daughter to have anything to do with him. Swayze is then sacked after being accused of theft by a jealous admirer. Grey stands by him and pleads his innocence to her father and the manager. When they refuse to believe her, she reveals that he could not have been responsible for the theft since she slept with him on that night. Her father is appalled.

All is very gloomy when the final night comes and the concert proceeds in a very dull manner. But Swayze returns, making a dramatic entrance. With all eyes upon him, he spots Grey sitting in a corner with her parents, declares that 'No one puts my baby in a corner,' takes her hand and leads her up onto the stage. He stops the proceedings, grabs the mike and tells everyone that they will do the last dance together. He publicly declares his love for her, saying that their love is not based on instant attraction but grew from their mutual respect and loyalty – values very close to the hearts of Southall youth. The dramatic climax arrives as they perform their duet to 'I've Had the Time of my Life' – a lively flamenco/rumba mix involving intricate steps and an intense erotic charge. The high point of the dance is the 'lift': he jumps off the stage, she runs down the aisle and makes a dramatic leap to fly up into his arms. The party takes off and everyone starts dancing – including two apparently staid old ladies in fur coats. All misunderstandings are cleared up as the father admits to them both that he was wrong, thereby declaring his approval of the romance.

Just as in the film, Amit and Jaspreet, who were chosen to do the dance routine, rehearsed every night after school for six weeks. They learned the steps from the video by repeatedly watching it. The whole process of rehearsing began to emulate the film itself – especially the problem of getting the steps right and doing the 'lift'. They could not practise the lift standing waist-deep in a lake, as in the film, but went to Southall Park, and practised it using park benches. Their performance was an outstanding success. The school audience went wild; students whistled, shouted, hooted, clapped. They had never seen such a skilled and daringly erotic performance by a boy and girl together. Boys do not usually dance at concerts and so Amit was considered brave and was praised for this, especially as he performed so well. The lift was met with cries of delight, and as Jaspreet twirled around in the air, the deputy head (rather than throw off his turban and dance, like the old ladies in furs, as someone jokingly suggested later) stalked out in disgust and rage – a triumphant victory for all youth present.

This appropriation of a western popular film was both unusually planned and unusually confrontational, setting out to challenge the culture of authoritative elders through a public performance and celebration of allegiance to the values of an idealised version of 'western youth'. As I have indicated, the choice of *Dirty Dancing* for this purpose was far from accidental, since the film itself is centrally concerned with conflicting loyalties to peer group and parental values. The jokingly suggested alternative response by the deputy headteacher might indeed be taken to imply a wish for this conflict to be resolved as it is in the film: a desire for the bearer of paternal authority in the school to emulate the filmic father's final acknowledgement of the legitimacy of the young stars' behaviour. In many respects the differences between peer and parental cultures, and various kinds of attempt to negotiate between 'Indian' or 'Asian' and 'British' or 'western' systems of representation, values and beliefs, structure the viewing patterns reported by young people in Southall. Certainly this process can be conflictual. But as the aspects of the local media culture which I have outlined in this chapter indicate, outright confrontation is much rarer – certainly in domestic settings – than processes of debate, accommodation and adaptation, in which young people, mothers, fathers and grandparents take up contextually variable positions in response to their viewing. What can be discerned overall is a complex process of many-sided negotiation between the cultures actually and televisually present in Southall, a negotiation which is reflected in patterns of TV talk in youth culture. The following chapters explore in more detail the negotiations which take place around some of the most significant TV genres, starting with the case of TV news.

Chapter 4

Coming of age in Southall:
TV news talk

One of the most surprising findings of the Southall Youth Survey was that TV news is reported to be the genre most frequently watched and discussed by young people and their parents (see Appendix 10). Yet interview and observational data consistently show that the majority of young people do not enjoy watching news and find much of it uninteresting and difficult to understand. This paradoxical feature of their TV consumption can be explained partly by the fact that news viewing is a domestic ritual in most homes and therefore some news viewing is inescapable. There are, however, more compelling reasons. Competence in understanding and talking about TV news is perceived as a marker of becoming adult and as a way of gaining access to the world beyond their own immediate or local experiences. No matter how boring they find particular bulletins, great significance is attached to TV news as a genre, because it is seen as an invitation to the world of adult affairs. Most young people are motivated to watch news because they wish to graduate to adult competence in the genre. This suggests that, contrary to the findings of media research carried out among adults (Morley, 1986: 162), consumption of TV news is an age-specific rather than, or at least as much as, a class or gender-specific activity.

As indicated earlier, the consumption of news in Southall is characterised by competing and culturally diverse sources of news and types of news stories. In Southall, adult competence requires an ability to understand and discuss news from the Indian subcontinent in Punjabi, Hindi or Urdu. Yet young people are often more competent in understanding British news broadcasts than their parents. Translation of British news broadcasts by young people for their parents and grandparents is thus a characteristic feature of news viewing in many families. Translation activities confer status and a degree of responsibility upon those who are able to act as an interpreter, especially when it involves explaining legal and civic rights and responsibilities, and who can move with ease across cultural and linguistic barriers. Such competence facilitates the transition from child to adult status in London Punjabi families. Knowledge of the world is normally passed from elders to children. In migrant cultures, the power relations involved in this process may be partially reversed when young people's linguistic competence enables them to acquire fuller knowledge of the surrounding culture and society.

In this context, becoming adult is not only linked with competence in the reception and translation of news stories but also involves the ability to locate oneself within various social categories (gender, generation, 'race', ethnicity, etc.) and across multiple frames of reference: national and international, local and global. This favours the development of the 'cosmopolitan' consciousness discussed by Hannerz (1990). National news tends to address its viewers as citizens, especially (but not only) at times of national crisis or war. However, London Punjabi families find that their status as national citizens is often undermined or challenged by racist and discriminatory practices and attitudes: their sense of 'belonging' to Britain is frequently problematised, and their political and cultural affinities are inextricably bound up with their colonial past and post-colonial present. Young people display deeply ambivalent attitudes to the idea of national identity whether framed as 'being' 'British' or 'Indian' or 'Pakistani'. As I shall demonstrate in this chapter, self-conscious ambivalence towards received notions of national, ethnic and religious identity is linked with increasing awareness of the interconnectedness of local and global affairs, and with the development of a pluralist ethos; and these in turn are perceived by many as a sign of becoming adult.

My arguments about the role of TV news in the transition to adult status in Punjabi families are elaborated here with reference to young people's talk about specific news events which were intensely debated during my fieldwork. The chapter details why becoming adult is associated with competence in the genre of news, explaining how adult status is achieved in the family context. It goes on to describe the interplay of local and Indian subcontinental politics, analysing how young people negotiate religious and 'racial' tensions in the context of Southall's own particular 'news history' and political culture. This section focuses on young people's reactions to the news coverage of an alleged racist murder in 1989–1990. Young people's sense of class and political identity is then explored through a focus on British national politics, highlighting responses to the poll tax and Margaret Thatcher's resignation. Finally, the inter-relationship between global and local news events, and the ambivalent positions of identification that young people experiment with, are analysed through an examination of the reception of news of the Gulf War (1991).

Young people's 'news talk' shifts fluidly from discussion of a news story, to representations of that story, to the realities of their own lives. It plays a significant role in processes of collective identity formation, providing a context and a resource for young people's experimentation with self and group definitions. Collective identities, as I have already pointed out, are neither fixed, impermeable expressions of origins nor entirely self-appointed as some postmodernist commentators have recently suggested. Rather, collective identities are constructed processually in ways that are both highly structured and context-bound, in terms of class, 'race', ethnicity, gender, religion, age, locality and other factors. Through collective processes of TV news reception, political and cultural values are discussed, collective identities are negotiated and aspirations towards cultural change expressed.

Even at age 16 or 17, young people's comprehension of the main, extended evening news bulletins is limited. They perceive TV news as an adult genre based on adult discourse and, more particularly, as a middle-class genre. The vocabulary, accent and speech patterns, the authoritative mode of address, the middle-class language register, the assumption of knowledge, the length and detail of the bulletins are cited as factors which impede comprehension. Few 16-year-olds possess the linguistic or cultural competence necessary to understand political and economic news in particular. This can be explained by the limited nature of political and economic education in secondary schools. Very regrettably, English schools generally fail to provide an adequate framework in which political and economic information can be processed. As a result a high degree of selectivity is evidenced in the attention paid to different news stories and in the type of news bulletins watched.

Breakfast news, the shorter five-minute bulletins, regional news, and the simplified, entertaining children's news programme *Newsround* are the initiation ground from which a subsequent interest in news develops. Human interest and crime stories attract most attention, although some boys watch sports news daily. Many teenagers rather shamefully admit that they still watch *Newsround*, hastening to add that this is because their younger siblings do so. However, it is clear that they also watch it because, while aspiring to adult status, they still like to retreat into the more cosy, reassuring world constructed by children's programmes. (The following quotations are taken from a taped discussion among a group of 16-year-old girls.)

AMRIT: I still watch *Newsround* and other children's programmes cos it gives me a break from the hectic life you lead and it makes you feel like a kid again and you can have a laugh instead of having to face the responsibilities of hard work and being a 16-year-old adult.

Amrit highlights the disjuncture between emotional, intellectual and physical maturity. For although many 16-year-olds want to be treated like adults and indeed, like Amrit, refer to themselves as adults, they find sustaining adult-like attitudes and behaviour difficult. Amrit is the eldest daughter in the family; like many eldest daughters in Southall, she has assumed considerable responsibilities in her family since both of her parents work. She looks after her siblings, cooks and helps take care of paying bills and other household administrative duties. Her self-perception as a young adult is related to culturally distinctive concepts of childhood, youth and adulthood. Many parents from the rural villages of the Punjab do not operate upon a concept of adolescence, which is a typically western notion. By the age of sixteen one is potentially marriageable, and this is the chief marker of distinction between childhood and adulthood. Thus, while youth is recognised as a category of experience, the lengthy period of transition, of experimentation and rebelliousness that characterises adolescence in modern western culture is not regarded as normal by most Indian parents.

TV news offers to young people the promise of becoming adult, of gaining access to, and an understanding of, the world of adult affairs. Asked to explain the importance of news, young people offer a number of answers. News is valued as serving a relativising function: without news about the wider world, people would remain locked into their own small communities and stay ignorant. It is seen as a prerequisite to functioning as a citizen in British society: news informs one about changes in laws and one's duties and responsibilities as a citizen. Furthermore, it is said to heighten awareness of notions of political freedom, democracy and equal rights. It should be noted that the fieldwork was conducted during 1988–1991, a period of international political turbulence which enhanced consciousness of global change, uncertainty and risk. News events such as the fatwa pronounced against Salman Rushdie, the Tiananmen Square massacre, the collapse of the Soviet Union, the fall of the Berlin Wall and the Romanian revolutions, the release of Nelson Mandela and the Gulf War (identified as the most important world events of the period by informants) raised far-reaching questions about freedom, democracy and human rights, which young people in Southall discussed and reflected upon.

From a young person's point of view, limited experience of the world and increasing curiosity about it finds expression in the desire to become competent in the news genre: to increase one's awareness of, and ability to talk about, the world in which one lives, in spite of the difficulties and boredom often associated with the task:

> SANGITA: You feel kind of grown up when you talk about the news, you know, it's serious, and you have to take some things seriously, but a lot of the time we just muck about, laugh and joke so talking about news is a way of growing up.

TV news serves as a kind of linguistic role model and an initiation into public and political discourse for young people, who like to imitate, ridicule and learn from public speakers. Picking up vocabulary, idioms and ways of expressing ideas, they claim, helps their language development:

HERJINDER: [. . .] like often, you know, we might have a good idea but we've got a childish and babyish language, whereas if we decorated our ideas with more fancy words we'd make more of an impression [. . .] when you watch the news you get amazed at all the big words they use but you get a sense of how they are supposed to be used and that gives you another approach it sort of helps you to express yourself.

However, there is some ambiguity attached to the desire to become competent in the genre. This is because the world, as constructed by TV news, is not a safe or secure place but one full of threats, misfortunes and disasters. TV news plays upon fundamental anxieties about one's security in the world and thus frequently provokes fear (Smith, 1985), as well as evoking more complex notions of trust and dependency (Giddens, 1991). Such feelings of anxiety are often countered at the end of each bulletin by formal conventions, notably the requisite light-hearted closing sequence ('And finally . . .'), which returns viewers to the relative safety of their own homes and encourages a sense of relief that at least no disasters have, as yet, befallen us:

GITA: To each and every one of us TV news is an important part of growing up, without it [. . .] we wouldn't be aware of our surroundings [. . .] we wouldn't know about the terrible things that happen to people in poor countries [. . .] we should be grateful for our lives [. . .] it's a link up to the world.

Knowing about 'terrible things' is part of growing up, part of an adult world which parents usually want to protect their children from. According to informants, parents want their children to retain 'childlike purity and innocence' until they are of an age when worldly, adult matters can be understood. In many parents' eyes, TV already gives young people too much insight into the world of adults. Yet most consider it important for their children to watch the news in order to extend their general knowledge and reap educational benefits. Parents also use the news viewing situation to warn their children of the dangers and threats that may confront them, exploiting it – as they do others – for didactic purposes.

BEING *CHUST* AND *SIANI*

Many parents expect their children to have reached maturity by the age of sixteen and to be able to demonstrate this in their speech and conduct. From the age at which they become potentially marriageable there are pressures upon young people to gain recognition and acquire adult status in the parental culture. However, this is not simply a question of marriageability, it is also very much dependent upon one's ability to assume an adult role in the family and this is associated with interpersonal communication skills. The ability to discuss news events and issues competently and confidently is one signal to parents of becoming adult.

Initiation into adult circles of communication is facilitated by acquiring *chust* status. According to my informants, this word has a number of connotations. It means being able to gain respect in adult company by being 'quick, showing wit and getting your point of view across'; 'being able to talk well and fit in with everybody'; 'being able to talk well in Punjabi and in English'; 'knowing when to be serious and when to joke'; 'knowing how to talk to elders'; 'being informed and able to express what you know in an adult way'; and 'being able to answer adult questions safely without causing an argument'. In other words the term encapsulates a set of skills, personal qualities and values associated with becoming adult: intelligence and sociability, tact and discretion, respect and deference. Thus to be *chust* is to acquire status through an internalisation of culturally specific codes of communication with elders – although in the Southall context, the competences involved also become those associated with 'cosmopolitanism' in Hannerz's sense, since they include skills in translation, in the literal sense as well as in the extended sense defined earlier (see Introduction, pp. 18–22). Bilingualism is important since it enables young people to act as interpreters, mediators and even arbiters in family disputes and decisionmaking. By watching the news with parents and being able to discuss it with them, young people show initiative and demonstrate to their parents that they want to be treated more like adults:

> PERVINDER: By watching the news, your parents know that you've gone through a stage, that you can talk in an adult way, you watch them talking about the news in an adult way and then you begin to fit in you don't seem like a child any more [. . .] they treat you as a *chust* kid, you know, grown up.

The counterpart of *chust* is *siani* which, according to informants, means 'wise and sensible', 'quiet and reserved', 'modest'. If one is *siani* one gains acceptance in adult circles. Some claim that *chust* and *siani* are gendered concepts. For example, a boy who is *chust* will know that with female elders his verbal interaction should consist of jovial, witty and humorous banter. However, this would be deemed inappropriate in the presence of male elders where talk should be more serious and worldly. Girls claim they are encouraged to be *siani*, in the sense of 'restrained', in verbal interaction. However, one's position in the family hierarchy may also affect one's *chust* or *siani* status. Eldest sons and daughters tend to be more likely to be perceived as grown up, but if one does not develop the necessary communication skills then that status is denied. Also, girls often speak better Punjabi than boys because they use it more at home with their mothers and female relatives. Thus the desire to graduate to adult competence in news is not gender specific. Rather, it is dependent upon one's intellectual and communicative competence. But it also requires an interest and competence in news about the Indian subcontinent.

'HERE' AND 'THERE'

The priority and sense of urgency given to news about India in the parental culture is reiterated by many informants. It is seen to be a link to their 'country's roots'; feelings of attachment to India and nostalgia remain strong despite settlement in Britain. Political turmoil in the Punjab in the last decade has been an added incentive. Many families have relatives there and fears about their safety are often intense:

AMRIT: Like, recently, the main disaster area is in New Delhi and I've got my mum's sister who lives there and a few months ago we heard that my uncle and my cousin didn't come home and my aunt was really scared [. . .] but they were safe [. . .] when she wrote and told us we were really scared for them [. . .] so when things like that happen you want to know what's going on there.

The anxiety among Sikhs in Southall about obtaining reliable news from the Punjab in the 1980s was partly due to perceived distortions, inaccuracies and omissions in the coverage by Doordarshan and AIR, the main Indian news channels, which in many people's eyes exacerbated Hindu communalism and portrayed Sikhs generally as 'terrorists' (Singh, 1985). The Punjabi diaspora press widely reported such distortions, encouraging close scrutiny in Southall of different accounts in various Hindi, Punjabi and English-language media. The BBC was often seen as uncritically accepting the line of the ruling Indian Congress Party; but at other times, especially when reporting restrictions were imposed, it was seen as offering the only source of impartial accounts of events.

A young person's interest in news from the Indian subcontinent is shaped by several key factors. Interest is likely to be higher where there is: direct experience of the country; competence in Punjabi; a degree of religious and cultural knowledge; parental encouragement; and close affective links with kin locally and in the Punjab. The idea that India is the family homeland and the fear that some day one may be deported were also given as reasons for maintaining links with India via news. The type of news story, its topicality and currency in local communication networks may be just as important in generating an interest:

PARAMJIT: Yeah, I'm interested in news from India because India is also my home [. . .]

SURINDER: [. . .] even though we're British we still care about what happens in India.

FARZANA: I think it's important for people to know what is happening in countries that their parents came from because you never know, one day you might have to go back there.

Many parents try to foster an interest in news from India in their children, as they do in the values and traditions of their 'culture'. Especially among those 'twice-migrant' parents who experienced expulsion from East Africa, the fear of being repatriated one day remains intense. The following exchange highlights the contradictory and ambiguous attitudes to Indian news, and indeed to showing any interest or becoming involved in it, among this group of 16-year-olds. Both Tejinder's and Dalvinder's parents are East African Sikhs, and their comments are quite typical of children from 'twice-migrant' families.

TEJINDER: My parents get annoyed if I don't take an interest in Indian news, they say, 'What will happen if you get chucked out of this country and you have to go there?', they go, 'It's interesting watch it!' but I can't really be bothered.

INDERJEET: My parents don't really say that to me.

AMRIT: Mine do too, but I don't have an interest in news from India, my parents do [. . .] I do have some concerns cos I've got relatives living there [. . .] you want them to be safe but other than that I don't really care.

DALVINDER: I don't know anyone who lives there, I've never had any contact with them so I don't care what happens there [. . .] I don't feel that India is a part of me.

ONRAY: Yes, actually it's pointless knowing about something there when you're here.

Chorus: Yeah.

ONRAY: But in a way it's OK knowing about political issues down there, and the state the country is in but what's really important to you is what happens here, it's here that counts.

AMRIT: But what happens there can affect what happens here.

INDERJEET: [. . .] the only reason I'd watch news about India is if I were going on holiday there, just to see if it was safe enough.

TEJINDER: I don't have any interest in news from India, it doesn't affect me but if something important was happening I'd want to know about it [. . .] I was born in Britain and I've lived here all my life so what happens here in Britain does concern me.

The group consensus is that *here* counts and *there* does not. Group dynamics play a role in consolidating this consensus of uninterestedness: it is just not 'cool' to be interested in the Indian subcontinent, and some young people summarily dismiss its inhabitants as *pendus* (a pejorative term for 'peasants'). The prevalence of negative attitudes towards India among some young people is considered by child migrants, such as Navdeep (17), to be based on a lack of experience and knowledge about the country. He explains:

you see a lot of people don't want anything to do with India, they think Indians are all *pendus*, they don't really understand that India is a big country and you do get the poor but there's a lot more to it [. . .] I really learned a lot there [. . .] I really picked up the whole image of the language, religion and culture and if you don't know the place you don't see how brilliant life can be there [. . .] I wouldn't mind living there one day.

Yet Tejinder's comments, in particular, reveal not only the importance attached to subcontinental news by her parents, but also her own, only half-admitted, dissent from the consensus. 'Twice-migrants' are doubly removed from India and so more likely, as in Dalvinder's case, to have no close kin there – but they are also more sensitive to the insecurity of their status in Britain.

News issues which are important to parents are thus often much less significant to their children, or only unwillingly recognised as such, because many feel that events in India have little relevance to their lives here. They frequently express a desire to move away from such parental pre-occupations and to live more fully in British society. Many young people feel themselves to be 'doubly sheltered', not only through living in a Punjabi 'community' where exposure to the wider 'white' society is extremely limited, but also in the fact that elders endeavour to curtail the influence of 'white' society and culture. Therefore, among certain young people, the greater the pressure from the parental culture to maintain an interest in Indian news and culture, the greater the tendency toward 'westernisation'. The juxtaposition of 'here' and 'there' as both unrelated and as interrelated is a source of tension for young people. For whilst some may not see India as a part of themselves or their lives, events in India, as we shall see, can and do have direct effects and repercussions on local life. This growing awareness of the interplay of Indian subcontinental and local politics through the media of the Indian diaspora is an integral part of the diasporic experience, which young people respond to in very different ways.

Interest in Indian news is not the only factor involved in graduating to adult competence: an ability to talk about it in Punjabi confers additional status in families. But many young people do not possess the necessary linguistic skills for this, and find it difficult to understand Punjabi news broadcasts on Sunrise radio. Often they are not literate in Punjabi and so cannot read the Punjabi press, which forms a central part of their parents' news consumption. The situation is commonly reversed when it comes to British TV news because young people are, very often, more competent than their parents in understanding and discussing news in English. Thus young people often already possess a degree of 'adult' competence in British news, which exceeds that of many parents. As a consequence of this, translation of British TV news for parents and grandparents by young people, is a characteristic feature of news viewing in many families. This allows them to demonstrate varying degrees of competence in adult news and assists them in acquiring adult or *chust* status. Grandparents and mothers are most often mentioned in this connection. However, translating the news for one's father is by no means rare:

> HARJINDER: [. . .] my dad, he's fifty, and he makes a lot of valid points but he doesn't know how to put them across in English so then he starts going on in Punjabi [. . .] but, like my brother, he doesn't have adult language in Punjabi so he'll call me down and I'll try to put across in the simplest and clearest way what my brother is trying to say [. . .] you see, to have language in an adult way matters a lot for whether they see you as a *chust* kid [. . .] a *chust* kid will know the language [. . .] if they ask you something then you'll be able to answer and then go on and tell them more [. . .].

Translation can be a difficult and annoying aspect of news viewing for young people:

> DILJIT (17):   The moment he [Dad] sees Asians on the TV, not on *EastEnders*, he wants us to watch, he calls us down and we've GOT TO watch it and even if you're in the bath or something he'll start shouting 'There's something on about India and I don't understand it, come down!' – there are a lot of Indians in this country who don't understand the news, even though they've been here quite a long time.

But being able to summarise or translate the key points of a news story, engage in dialogue with adults, form opinions, take a stand on issues, and even challenge and attempt to change elders' views makes a young person feel 'grown up' and encourages others to perceive them as such.

Learning these skills also involves learning about, and indeed redefining Southall's local 'news history', especially as this history implicates national and international politics in a number of ways. The following sections focus on young people's responses to issues in the spheres of local, national and international news, though in each the interpenetration of all three spheres will be apparent.

'RACIAL' AND RELIGIOUS CONFLICT: LOCAL NEWS

Southall has its own particular news history and political culture in which debates about the representation and interpretation of local events are conducted. Young people construct their own version of that news history according to their own experiences, a version which, in certain ways, challenges the accounts of their elders, particularly when issues of 'racial' and religious conflict are discussed.

Parents who emigrated to Southall in the 1950s and 1960s faced major problems of racial discrimination and racist violence. In 1976 Gurdip Singh Chaggar, a Sikh schoolboy, died as the victim of what came to be seen as the first racial murder to take place in Southall. His killing led to the setting up of Southall Youth Movement (SYM), whose members broke with what they saw as their parents' pacifism and reluctance to cause trouble. They were prepared to defend their right to live peacefully in Southall at all costs. In 1979 the National Front, who were active in the vicinity, organised a public meeting on St George's Day. Violent confrontations ensued between National Front members, the Special Patrol Group (SPG or riot police) and local youths. In addition to more than 1,000 arrests and countless serious injuries, a teacher, Blair Peach, was killed by a truncheon blow from an unidentified SPG officer. Then in 1981 a skinhead rock band appeared in the Hamborough Tavern on the borders of Southall, bringing with them hundreds of National Front supporters from all over London. The perceived collusion between the police and the National Front had not been expected and, after a skinhead youth assaulted a Punjabi woman, SYM and local youths stormed the pub and burned it down. This was a symbolic act which marked a turning-point in Southall's history. Further opposition to the presence of 'Asians' in Southall became untenable. It had become an 'Asian' town that could defend itself (Bains, 1988).

Since 1957 the Indian Workers Association had been active in responding to the problems experienced by local people in the spheres of housing, employment and immigration. During the 1980s a plethora of state-funded community groups emerged, which aimed to combat racism and racist violence. The most prominent were Southall Monitoring Group (SMG) and Southall Black Sisters (SBS). These and other groups were run by committed activists who in many cases had been politicised by involvement in the street fighting of 1979 and 1981. The groups were of various left-wing persuasions, competed for scarce resources, mainly in the form of local authority funding, championed different causes in the struggle against racism and often came into conflict with one other. Bains refers to them as 'professional ethnics' and 'career militants', describing them as a new intermediary force between local people and the state, whose vociferous claims to 'represent' the militant demands of their 'community' secured them state funds and 'fat salaries' (1988: 240). However one chooses to perceive them, they kept alive the memory of the murders of Gurdip Singh Chaggar and Blair Peach and continued the struggle against racism.

At the same time vigorous antiracist (and antisexist) policies were thrust upon public institutions by local politicians, especially the Greater London Council (GLC). In Southall schools, positive discrimination in employment and promotion, and the requirement to implement such policies, provoked much resentment among many of the (mostly white) teachers. But many pupils also felt that the heavy emphasis on the issue of racism was counter-productive: it did not, as far they were concerned, relate to their everyday experiences. The official discourse of 'antiracism' promoted by the GLC and others, with its one-dimensional view of racial antagonism, its tokenism and the questions it begged about legitimate political representation, has been much criticised. By and large it simply served to reinforce existing relations between the state and its 'minorities', failed to win popular support and became a favourite target of ridicule in the popular press (Mercer, 1990). Certainly by the late 1980s the policy had alienated many young people in Southall.

By the later 1980s, few 16-year-olds had any knowledge of the dramatic events and tragic murders which took place during the 1970s. Nor, they claim, do they have very much direct experience of racism except when venturing outside Southall. Whilst 'race' thinking is commonplace, racism is not an everyday reality for people in Southall, as it is for, say, Bengalis in Tower Hamlets in the East End of London. Indeed, Southall developed its distinctive character partly as a response to the racism of British society (Gundara, 1986). Awareness of racism in the wider society exists, but to widely varying degrees; and the political activism of the various antiracist groups found few supporters among the youth of the Thatcher years. Surprisingly perhaps, most young people claim that religious sectarianism, rather than racism, is the most disturbing aspect of local life and the key source of conflict.

My 16-year-old informants' first experiences of Southall appearing on national TV news date back to the storming of the Golden Temple in Amritsar in 1984. In response to increasing political unrest in the Punjab, Indira Gandhi sent in troops to root out Sikh 'terrorists', arresting Bhindranwale and other 'extremist' Sikh leaders whose ambition was to establish an independent Sikh state – Khalistan. These tactics proved counter-productive, and led to Hindu–Sikh communal clashes on an unprecedented scale. Indira Gandhi's centralisation policies, the intervention by the national centre in federal state politics and intolerance towards aggressive minority demands continued to fuel the Punjab crisis (Brass, 1991). In 1986 Indira Gandhi was assassinated by her Sikh bodyguards. These events were extensively televised and had marked repercussions for young people, as they became aware of how political and religious conflict in the Punjab and India could affect their lives. This group of girls express a typical response:

SEEMA: We started watching the news at the time of the storming of the Golden Temple and the assassination of Indira Gandhi.

MONICA: Everybody watched the news at that time, I remember it so clearly, everyone was glued to their sets, we were only about seven or eight years old at the time.

INDERJEET: It was horrible, it was, like all our parents' lot, like they forgot they were all Indians and that they spoke the same language and [. . .]

MONICA: [. . .]that they had things in common and that.

INDERJEET: They started causing trouble with each other [. . .]

SEEMA: [. . .] and then it got into the schools, the Khalistan thing, like you've got Sikhs and Hindus at school and it was like people going overboard.

MONICA: People started making their own gangs, little kids, you know it was unbelievable, shouting Khalistani slogans.

SEEMA: It went on for quite a long time, in fact, it's still here.

INDERJEET: It made you sort of realise that religion can be a bad thing sometimes.

SEEMA: People should keep it in their homes and in the gurdwaras, not bring it to school.

In a town where Hindus and Sikhs had coexisted peacefully under the umbrella of an 'Asian' identity, these events threatened to create a rift between them. This sense of a common 'Asian' identity, created in the British context as a pragmatic solution to earlier collective problems of discrimination, under the maxim 'strength in unity', emphasised similarities rather than differences and was now under threat. This was particularly disturbing for young people for whom religious differences, though clearly recognised and considered significant, were not usually a source of conflict and, indeed, were underplayed in the school context. However, religious differences began to manifest themselves in new ways. One of the local gangs, the 'Holy Smokes', exploited their Jat Sikh identity, and their strength in numbers locally, to parade a fierce warrior image – playing upon an ancient heritage which equates Sikhs with warriors. They paraded themselves as supporters of the more fundamentalist sections of the separatist Khalistan movement, and some even sported orange turbans to symbolise their allegiance to the cause. They conducted local 'warfare' with their rival gang, the '*Tuti Nangs*' (a more heterogeneous group comprising male youths from various other castes of Sikhism, Hindus, Muslims, London Caribbeans and whites). During the height of these clashes (1984–1988), the often violent or criminal activities of these gangs were constantly in the local, and occasionally the national, news.

Although the 'Holies' were admired and feared by many local youngsters, they were also frowned upon by those Sikh youths who argued that, in fact, most of the 'Holies' who called themselves 'Khalistanis' knew little or nothing about their religion or about the political issues involved in the

Khalistan movement, unlike some of their more respected Sikh peers. In their view, a 'pure Sikh' understands and adheres to the basic tenets of Sikhism and adopts the 'the five Ks' – the distinguishing features of Sikh identity and symbols of Sikh brotherhood. Although originally they may have had practical significance, they are now endowed with exclusively symbolic meaning: *kes* – long, uncut hair, a mark of spirituality; *kanga* – a comb, a sign of disciplined spirituality; *kirpan* – a sword, a mark of dignity, self-respect and power, and a means of protection; *kach* – short trousers, a mark of self-restraint and abstinence; and *kara* – a bracelet, signifying the *chakra*, a circle, symbol of eternity. As Jagjit, a 16-year-old Sikh boy explains:

> Narinderjit, now he's a pure Singh and he's a Jat and he's done the five Ks and that's what I mean by pure and because he's been brought up that way, he knows about religion and politics and he can talk about it and when he talks you just wanna listen cos you know, he don't bullshit like Sati and that lot who even though they're Jat and shoot their mouth about being Khalistanis and Holies and all that, know nothing.

Many young people witnessed with dismay how religious politics in the parental culture could interfere with their peer relations and many, as in the following exchange between two 16-year-old Sikh boys, expressed their outrage at the storming of the Golden Temple and their embarrassment at local celebrations upon the assassination of Indira Gandhi. Mohinderpal expresses a commonly held view: that TV news reports of these events were responsible for exacerbating religious conflict in Southall:

MOHINDERPAL: I think Asians have done worse to us than white people have, like Hindus, they destroyed our temple, that was our holy place for centuries, that's more than a white person can do in 100 years and now Hindus and Muslims are begining to fight over a temple in Kashmir [. . .]. When they were covering the Golden Temple on TV, they should have shown something from the Hindu point of view as well, they focused too much on Sikhs hating Hindus and that. TV brought the war over here – look at that guy from the Maharajah restaurant [on Southall Broadway], they say he got shot by Sikh extremists.

DILJIT: Everyone was arguing at my gurdwara, I was so embarrassed, arguing in the gurdwara! It was sad man, they were giving out sweets and opening champagne in the streets when Indira Gandhi got murdered, they were giving out boxes of *ladhu* [sweetmeats] free man!

MOHINDERPAL: And what is even worse, it was a holy man that shot her and that's embarrassing to our religion.

DILJIT: How can people be so sick as to celebrate someone's death? [...] and when Bhindra Wallah [a Sikh holy man and leader of the Khalistan movement] died they had all these processions.

MOHINDERPAL: Young people, they were even worse, there were a lot that were happy that she died and they lit fireworks and they showed all that on the news it was so embarrassing man!

An especially deep ambivalence and conflict was experienced by some young Sikhs of the castes considered 'low', such as Chures and Chamars. Not having found a place of respect within the Sikh hierarchy, over the years many members of these castes have gravitated towards Hinduism and worship in Hindu mandirs. Without a clearly distinct Sikh or Hindu identity, such young people found this religious–political conflict a source of deep distress. This was intensified further by the fact that their ambiguous status was deemed an affront by those who reacted to events by asserting an even stronger religious identity.

So, for young people in Southall in the 1980s, their formative involvement in local politics and news centred on the problem of religious sectarianism 'imported' from the subcontinent. From an early age many young people developed a sensitivity to news portrayals of political turmoil in India and of the local repercussions of such news, marked by a keen awareness of how 'others' (implicitly British people outside Southall) might come to perceive their 'community', its political and religious conflicts and themselves. It is in the context of this very brief outline of Southall's news history and political culture that their responses to news of the chilling murder of Kuldip Singh Sekhon must be seen.

A worker at Heathrow Airport and a part-time local cab driver, Kuldip Sekhon was stabbed fifty-four times by a young white man, Stephen Croker, in the late hours of the night of 10 November 1989. He had picked up Croker from the Golf Links housing estate, on the borders of Southall, to take him to a nearby estate in Cranford. Two days later Croker was picked up by the police and admitted to drinking and drug-taking on the the night of the killing. At first, there seemed to be no obvious motive for the murder. The victim had not been robbed: £75 and a gold watch were found on his body. But the kitchen knife which Stephen Croker had used upon Kuldip Sekhon had been brought from his home. Had he planned to use it? Several weeks after the murder the rumour that Southall had seen another racist murder began to spread. Southall Monitoring Group (SMG) posed this central question: would Kuldip Sekhon have been killed if he had been white?

SMG organised a fundraising support campaign for the family. They networked with other antiracist groups locally and nationally and sought to bring this murder to the public's attention. It was, they claimed, a symbol of all the other (they cited fifty) racist murders which had occurred in Britain during Margaret Thatcher's premiership. Due to protracted autopsies, the funeral did not take place until January 1990, while SMG's multimedia campaign kept the murder and the question of its racist motives in the forefront of people's minds. The murder became the focus of many grievances about racial harassment and violence, both locally and nationally. This reawakened many fears among adults which were not shared by young people – fears of a revival of racist attacks.

Feelings came to a head when, nearly three months after the murder, Kuldip Sekhon's funeral was arranged for 31 January 1990. SMG wanted to make this a public and media event that would pierce the conscience of the nation and demonstrate local outrage at what was undeniably, for them, a racist murder. The body was brought to the local community centre where it lay in state, as had the body of Gurdip Singh Chaggar. Some 500 people were present to pay their last respects. The full horror of the murder was revealed as a procession of local people glanced at the decomposing corpse, scarred with knife wounds, amidst camera crews jostling for the 'best shot'. Much as the showing of Indira Gandhi's body lying in state for three consecutive days on Indian TV inflamed passions in India (Singh, 1985: 168), the public display of Kuldip Singh Sekhon's body inflamed passions in Southall. The subsequent funeral procession and protest march brought an estimated 3,000 people onto the streets of Southall. Local shops closed their doors and pulled down their metal security grilles. The procession was broadcast on BBC1 South East and ITV Thames regional news on the evening of the funeral. Given the time-lag between the murder and funeral, most young people had already formulated opinions and responses to the murder. Media coverage, local knowledge of actors, rumour, folklore and fantasy all contributed to produce various accounts of the murder. However, direct experience of the funeral-cum-protest march and the media coverage of it that evening generated considerable debate on the following day at school.

The immediate response was related to the family tragedy. Here was a respectable Sikh father who drove a cab to bring in extra money for his family. He was a good family man with five daughters. The fact that he had five daughters was considered to augment the tragedy. Young people asked how his widow would cope with bringing them up. How could she marry five daughters with respect and therefore with dowry? The family tragedy, rather than the allegedly racist motivation of the murder, preoccupied most young people.

Comparisons were made between the BBC and ITV coverage on the morning after the funeral procession, which led to discussions of representations of Southall on TV news more generally. This is an extract from a discussion between two girls and a boy in the sixth-form common room:

DALJIT: The BBC news, sort of, put across that it was a racist murder and that everyone in Southall is up in arms about all the racist murders that happen here but that's a bit misleading isn't it, cos it's the first one that's happened here for years, I mean murders happen everywhere but they really blow it up when it's an Asian community.

AVTAR: But it's always the same whenever Southall comes on the news it's always about racism, it's as if anyone in Southall could be murdered, like Southall's a really dangerous place to live.

DINESH: I hate the way they always show crowds of people marching on the street with banners and protesting and [. . .]

AVTAR: [. . .] yeah, did you see all the people pushing and shoving to get into the Dominion Centre? They sort of portray people like *pendus* and they go hundreds of people 'flooding' the streets, and 'angry crowds' it's like they have no respect for the man or his family, it's like Asian people are always causing trouble.

DALJIT: But the ITV they presented it like it was cos he was a cab driver and that, you know, it's cab drivers who are at risk cos they drive around alone at night with money.

AVTAR: But they still showed all the people protesting and marching [. . .]

DINESH: [. . .] and all the bloody police, that's another thing, whenever Southall is in the news there's always vanloads of police around as if any moment there's going to be war, I mean, it was the man's funeral [. . .]

AVTAR: [. . .] he should have been shown more respect.

DALJIT: But it's like the Southall Monitoring Group were speaking on behalf of all people in Southall and really that's biased.

DINESH: Well, they've done a lot of the campaigning and it was them that got the BBC to come along in the first place.

DALJIT: How do you know?

DINESH: Amrit told me cos she was involved in the campaign.

DALJIT: I feel really sorry for the man and his family but I think they've blown it up out of all proportion.

DINESH: It's just like reawakening old wounds.

AVTAR: There'll be a white backlash I bet you.

DINESH: Not round here but in places like Greenford maybe.

Regional TV coverage is seen to confirm dominant representations of the 'Asian community' as an 'alien' presence, a 'problem' and locus of 'trouble' in need of policing, and also as a 'community' of 'victims'; the representative status claimed by the SMG is questioned; and the centrality accorded to race, racism and race violence in local politics, and particularly in national representations of Southall, is regarded with scepticism and sometimes dismay. Reacting with disenchantment after years of antiracist campaigns, young people frequently express criticism of the tendency to 'reduce everything to racism'. In this case, many preferred, for a number of reasons, to think of the killer as a 'madman'.

Most young people were ambivalent about the alleged racist motives behind the murder, unlike some of their elders. While some agreed that racism may have been an element to the murder, they were extremely wary of what they saw as the 'media hype' surrounding the funeral and were concerned about Southall's 'image'. Not that they remained unmoved by the murder, but many argued that Mr Sekhon should be given due respect and that his murder should not exploited by SMG and others for political purposes. They saw the campaign as a deliberate attempt to open old wounds, which would serve little purpose, but possibly unleash a 'white backlash', targeted at 'Asians' living in white areas. Whilst this was the dominant view, there was a group of sixth-formers who became actively involved in the campaign and who expressed their alarm at the lack of support they had received from the school and local authority, which refused to close the school on the day of the funeral, although students were allowed to attend it if they wished. They were angered that there had been no public inquiry into this and other racial attacks and murders, and saw this as part of a more general attitude on the part of the British government and media to turn a blind eye to the problem of racist violence.

More generally, racist murders are seen to be a relatively rare phenomenon and difficult to prove. For most young people the central tragedy was murder. Many pointed to the other local murders; that of Pushpa Bhatti, a woman who was murdered in Southall Park; and that of Surinder Gill, a wealthy businessman. They asked why their more politically active peers and elders did not respond in the same way to these murders. The answer they received was that these were not racist murders. And so many young people concluded that among political activists, murder is only worth protesting about if it has racist motivations; whereas for many young people with little experience of racism, a murder is a murder. Most young people remained sceptical or ambivalent about the racist motivation behind the murder, as this exchange between two 16-year-old Sikh boys demonstrates:

NAVDEEP: They think it was a racist murder but no one knows for sure, OK, the guy has a record of involvement with the National front [. . .]

AMANDEEP: He was supposed to have told his girlfriend the day of the murder that he was going to 'kill a paki'.

NAVDEEP: He was also out of his mind on drugs [. . .].

AMANDEEP: No one really knows for sure and that's why they've made such a big thing of it.

NAVDEEP: I think it's the same thing that happened ten years ago, you know, those two murders, Chaggar and what's-his-name Blair Peach [. . .] it brings it all back and everyone remembers, it all happens again and it's always the same issue, racism, that's what gets people up in arms, they've made it into a huge media event but I think religious conflict in Southall is a more serious issue but Southall only ever gets on the news when it's to do with racism, crime or the gangs.

The murder of Kuldip Sekhon was, for many young people, their first encounter with the possibility of a racially motivated murder on their doorsteps and as such was a very disturbing experience. Once again Southall was in the news. Whilst some used the situation to vent their feelings about racism, most recoiled from the vociferousness of adult campaigners who, unlike 16-year-olds today, had spent their youth fighting racism on the streets of Southall. The following exchange between two 16-year-old Sikh boys highlights a common pattern of response:

KULDIP: Because they can't prove everyday racism, people cover it up, so if something major like this happens, they try to cover the rest of the issues around it, they bring the media into it, and in doing that they tend to blow it right out of proportion.

TALVINDER: Really I suppose they've made a martyr of Kuldip Sekhon [. . .] he now symbolises all racist murders.

Obviously, this was a very traumatic event and it is impossible, here, to do justice to the depth of feeling involved, nor to the integrity of most adults and young people alike in their collective attempts to make sense of this tragedy. I have tried to present a pattern of response among many young people locally and to highlight how this murder forced young people to confront the problem of racism from the point of view of their elders and local activists. In doing so, they articulated their own positions in relation to Southall's news history at that particular conjuncture. No doubt their reaction may also be explained by the very real fear of confronting not only the idea but the possible reality of a racist murder.

To this day the central question, posed by the youth and elders of Southall as by the national press, remains unanswered ('Was Kuldip Sekhon Killed Because of the Colour of His Skin?', *Independent*, Magazine, 13 October 1990). In July 1990 Croker was sentenced to life imprisonment for murder at the Old Bailey. Neither the police, the judge nor the jury claim to have found any evidence to suggest it was a racially motivated murder. In contrast, SMG claim to have discovered two separate complaints against Croker for the racial harassment of Asian families on their files. Ealing Racial Equality Council also knew of Croker as a member of a skinhead gang, with a background in drugs and solvent abuse, frequently in trouble for smashing Asian shopkeepers' windows as well as for fighting in pubs. He also had a conviction for assaulting an Asian youth. Croker himself, it appears, gave nothing away throughout the investigations and trial. He claims that he does not know why he did it; and neither do the youth of Southall, but they would mostly prefer to believe that it was the act of deeply disturbed character rather than the cruelest manifestation of racist violence. But perhaps there is also an element of hope in taking such a position, for they, undoubtedly, want to look, not back but forward, to an adult life in Britain unmarred by racism.

NATIONAL AND CLASS POLITICS: THATCHER AND THE POLL TAX

More than any other issue at the time of fieldwork, the poll tax (officially known as the community charge) and Margaret Thatcher's resignation – the two being very closely linked in most minds – provoked young people to articulate a sense of their family's class or socio-economic position in British society and, by association, their party-political allegiances. The importance attached locally to Margaret Thatcher's resignation will come as no surprise to anybody familar with the serious hardship that the tax brought to many Punjabi families. 'Asians' throughout Britain were affected by it with particular severity because of the prevalence of relatively large households. To clarify the picture, in one informant's household five adults became eligible to pay the local poll tax, increasing their liability from £265 (under the previous council tax regime) to £1,820 – an increase of £1,555 or some 600 per cent. It is not hard to see why the news of Mrs Thatcher's resignation was welcomed. For most, it meant not simply an end to her 'reign' as prime minister but above all the possibility of the abolition of the poll tax. The resentment among young and old alike is highlighted by this exchange between three 16-year-old girls:

AMRITA: Everyone's really pissed off with the poll tax, five people in my family have to pay it, it's crazy, where do they think we get the money from?

PERMINDER: Everyone's complaining about it, it's not just people in Southall who are complaining though, look at all those people who smashed the place up in London.

AMRITA: Yeah, but Asians are more badly affected because we've got larger families.

BALJIT: Even little kids know about it, like my little brother he wants a new pair of trainers but my parents can't afford them and he keeps saying, 'Come on Mum?' and she says, 'Look at the poll tax we have to pay, that's why we can't afford it'.

Many young people claim that their parents relied on them to translate the news about the poll tax, to explain the situation to them and to deal with the community charge forms. Certainly, many young people have such 'adult' concerns thrust upon them at an early age.

Southall is traditionally a Labour-voting area where a certain amount of antipathy to any Conservative government, and to Margaret Thatcher in particular, might be expected. Many parents remember her comments about Britain being swamped by 'alien' cultures, her tightening of immigration control and her general antipathy to the presence of 'immigrants' in Britain. There is a widespread view among young people that the Conservative government is racist and a conviction that a Labour government would provide better public services and support the poorer sections of society better than the Conservatives; also that Labour would be more sympathetic to the concerns of 'Asians' in Britain on such issues as immigration control and racism.

Financial reasons alone are insufficient to explain the widespread jubilation about Mrs Thatcher's resignation. The 'Leadership Battle' itself was a compelling story, and most informants' accounts and reconstructions focus on the 'showdown' or the 'shaming up' of a woman with power. There was a certain amount of gloating over her fall from exalted heights, intrigue at the conspiratorial conduct of her Cabinet colleagues and amusement at what was perceived as her public shaming. But this was matched by an equally firm admiration for the 'dignity' of her departure, particularly among girls with strong personal aspirations, such as 'high achievers' in school. Indeed, many girls, despite loathing and resenting her policies, stated that they saw in Mrs Thatcher a powerful symbol of a woman who had succeeded in a 'man's world', and expressed great respect for her strength of character and leadership.

As we have seen, articulating a political viewpoint and being able to take a stand on issues of public importance are associated with being 'grown up'. In matters of British national politics, young people's views are however strongly influenced by those of their parents as well as by the socio-economic circumstances in which they find themselves, as is indicated by these girls' discussion of Mrs Thatcher:

GITA: She's ruled our country ever since I can remember and I'm so glad that I won't hear her nasty voice and see her ugly mug on TV any more, that's the best news of all.

SAIRA: But she was such a strong leader, she had the power to shatter people, look how she behaved in parliament, she could cuss people down badly, I suppose that's why she was called the Iron Lady.

GITA: That's true but she took her power too far.

SURINDER: My family hate her.

SAIRA: Since the poll tax everyone has had problems with money.

GITA   We've all been affected in one way by her cruelness and greediness.

SAIRA: She was a strong woman but she was uncontrollable.

SURINDER: If she didn't resign, she would have taken shame [. . .].

GITA: I think she was badly shamed up anyway, she came out on the steps and said she was gonna stay put and the next day bang she's gone. [All laugh.]

Young people are well aware that, in the not-too-distant future, they will have the right to vote and this acts as a further incentive to involve oneself in matters of national politics. There is also evidence of an increasing interest in ecological issues – some claim they would rather vote for the Green Party:

RANJIT: Most of us just about manage to pay the mortgage [. . .] her policies have affected me, like in school, there's not enough books to go round, they've affected my family cos now four people have to pay the poll tax and we're skint, they have affected my dad cos he has had to wait so long for his operation.

FARZANA: That's right! I mean, it's all right for the well-off innit but it's difficult for working people.

PARAMJIT: Yeah, but anyone would think she was the bloody Queen of England the way she behaves, like when she starts mouthing off, you'd think she could never do anything wrong.

RANJIt: I tell you one thing, I'm not voting for any bloody Conservative when I'm eighteen, I'd rather vote for the Raving Monster Loony Party.

The majority of my informants consider their families and themselves to be working class and supporters of the Labour Party. But it is really only in the context of national politics that the word 'class', with its typically British connotations, has any meaning to people in Southall, where as we have seen, religious and caste distinctions predominate. By 'working class' young people usually mean several things: that their parents are employed in low-paid, manual or semi-skilled jobs, or unemployed, or 'poor'; they vote Labour; they do not 'talk posh'; and they have not benefited from further education.

But a sense of being working class is modulated by other factors. First, for Hindus and Sikhs, the social hierarchy is founded upon the principle of caste, which links notions of spiritual 'purity' with one's designated occupation and status in life. Thus a person may be seen to be of 'low' social class but of high caste status. There is, however, some contention as to whether those of Jat caste, traditionally landowners and farmers and top of the hierarchy in the Punjab, have been displaced by the Ramgharia caste in Southall. Traditionally these are 'low-caste' craftsmen who, after migration to East Africa and then to Britain, are more urbanised, educated and generally speaking, better able to adapt to life in Britain. Thus 'low' caste is not necessarily linked to 'low' social status as it is in the Punjab: traditional notions of caste are being challenged in Britain and several, often contradictory, criteria of status may operate at any one time. Second, the opportunities opened up to many youngsters by their families' thriving and successful businesses may bring economic wealth but not a consequent rise in status, according to caste principles. Third, the strong tendency towards upward social mobility among 'Asians' generally, together with the high level of aspiration among young 'Asians', means that generational differences in perceived social class are prevalent within many families, especially where higher education has lead on to professional careers.

Therefore class identity is not a straightforward matter for Punjabis in London. Nevertheless, articulated in relation to national politics, it remains a very significant facet of social identity, and in this respect there is no evidence that cultural, religious or ethnic identifications, 'old' or 'new', are erasing class identity. The issue of the community charge and Mrs Thatcher's resignation, more than any other news events, encouraged young people to articulate their position with regard to the Conservative government of the day and, in the great majority of cases, to confirm the locally traditional allegiance to Labour party politics and sense of being working class. But young people in Southall take up such positions provisionally, in relation to particular issues, in particular contexts and ambivalently: for a range of other forms of identification are open to them (or thrust upon them), each of which is subject to dislocation by others, and only some of which can comfortably coexist or be combined in stable hybrid forms. It was in talk about the Gulf War that the complexities involved in processes of identification surfaced most clearly.

AMBIVALENT POSITIONINGS: THE GULF WAR

For Southall youth and their families, TV coverage of the Gulf War highlighted the contradiction of being addressed by the news media as part of the British nation, while at the same time the national status and loyalty to Britain of 'Asian immigrants' was being more insistently questioned than is usually the case in public discourse (for a fuller discussion than is possible here, see Gillespie, 1994a). The outbreak of war precipitated an intensification of debate among young people in Southall about national, political, religious and ethnic allegiances. One of the most persistently surprising aspects of the discussions held by young people in the first weeks of the Gulf War was the constant shifting of categories used to describe the adversaries. The opponents on either side of the equation vary, as at various moments the war is seen to be a confrontation between the Middle East and America; Christians and Muslims; east and west; Arabs and Allies; blacks and whites. In their discussions young people experimented with a variety of positions, moving across and between these categories. Initially, however, attention focussed on the dramatic coverage of the 'precision bombing' and ambivalences were played down in favour of a more generally humanist approach. I shall begin by describing some of the more general responses to the war, and those which are age and gender related, before proceeding to an analysis of young people's experimentation with identities.

One of the most immediate and obvious effects of the outbreak of the Gulf War was the sudden change in personal and domestic routines. Many young people in Southall claimed that their families, like those elsewhere, were glued to their TV set during the first week of the war. Those who had cable TV (20 per cent of the survey sample) felt themselves to be especially privileged, since CNN's coverage of the war was considered far superior to that of the national news networks. But the sense of exhilaration that some derived from CNN's dramatic, live footage was countered by a pervasive feeling of nervousness. War provokes fear, especially fear of death. The initial Allied attacks led to anxieties that the war might spread to Britain, even to Southall. Some, usually younger teenagers such as this 15-year-old Muslim boy, seemed confused as to whether it was a nuclear war:

> ADNAM: They're not only destroying a country but also the world, all of them, all these nuclear war planes that they're hitting is, in the end, going to destroy the world. It's frightening, I don't want to die young! In the end they're probably going to destroy everyone [. . .] sometimes I have a feeling that I'm going to die cos it's just possible that they shoot something over here or in the middle of the core of the earth and they might just destroy us all.

Adnam's apocalyptic vision rather dramatically expresses the more general sense of fear and uncertainty about the possible consequences of the war that were prevalent among many of the younger teenagers in its first week. Anxieties about growing up in a world already 'spoilt' by adults were frequently expressed: 'We're young and we have open minds, older people tend to have tunnel vision and have fixed ideas and this leads to conflict [. . .]' (Kirit). Empathy was most clearly aroused when the victims of war were perceived as family members. Indeed, it is as if the poignancy of the human casualties of war is only fully appreciated with reference to family tragedies. The irreparable and enduring consequences of the war, especially in breeding hatred in the world, were often discussed in an emotionally charged atmosphere during school breaks, especially by girls. Sameera, a 16-year-old Muslim, said:

> Those people out there who are dying, they are ordinary people, like us, they are mothers and fathers, sons and daughters, you feel for them whether they're Muslims or Christians, black or white, I mean, they're all human beings.

However, several weeks later, a widespread shift in attitude was apparent. The war had become 'boring'. Some complained that some of their favourite programmes, like *Home and Away* and *'Allo 'Allo*, had been cut in favour of war coverage. Others felt that the TV coverage was excessive and that the war was dominating their lives at home and at school. However, the language of war remained as a new set of military terms and idioms was acquired, undoubtedly encouraged by the tabloid press, and put to use in everyday talk. For example, one girl, suffering from an outbreak of acne, was approached by a boy who jibed, 'That's a pretty bad Scud attack on your face'. She slapped his. Young people also became familiar with a new cast of political, military and journalistic characters who they could exploit for the purposes of insult. Gulf jokes, from the sick to the silly, began to circulate and humour became a common way of dealing with war, especially among boys. Some enjoyed pointing out ironies in the situation, in this case incidentally implying a disidentification with the British nation: 'Britain built all these bunkers for Iraq and now [laughs] the silly bastards can't even blow up their own bunkers'. Such casual and lighthearted talk was typical of the very competitive style of interaction among some boys for whom scoring a point or 'having a laugh' in an all-male peer context takes precedence or who would be seriously challenged by any deeper or more serious discussion of the issues.

Clear gender differences emerged in perceptions of news coverage and in patterns of identification with the military and journalists. The parallels which have been pointed out by many cultural critics, between the TV representation of the Gulf War (and other recent wars) and the imagery of video games appear to have played a role in these gendered responses. TV viewers consume close-up images of distant wars in the security of their homes. Responses to the outbreak of the war and its imagery reveal a shifting sense of involvement and detachment, proximity and distance, threat and security. In an essay on the Falklands War, Williams (1989) refers to the 'culture of distance' which TV has helped to create. He argues that very precise images of 'wars of distance' are already built into contemporary audio-visual culture and that these serve to blunt our perceptions and sensibilities:

In every games arcade we can press buttons and see conventionally destructive flashes on targets [. . .] What difference is represented when the flash of a hit can be remembered to contain and to be destroying a man? [The pervasiveness of such imagery] may already, in many minds, have blurred the difference between the exercise and the actuality, between the rehearsal and the act [. . .] for it is one of the corroding indulgences of the culture of distance that to the spectator the effect, at least, offers to be the same. (1989: 16)

That the media contribute to a desensitising of our responses to human tragedy, or compassion fatigue, has long been argued by media effects researchers. Such arguments need to be treated with some caution, as does any implication that viewers somehow confuse or cannot distinguish between a real, televised war and a video-game war. However, it seems that at times a blurring of the difference certainly occurred, especially among boys, for whom playing video games is a daily activity. Thus Williams's argument needs gendering. The seductiveness of the imagery of this technowar was clearly apparent among boys, many of whom expressed a fascination with war technology – a fascination which boys' comics and action-packed war videos, as well as games, have partly created and heavily exploit.

During the first week of the war, it was quite common to hear some boys engaged in an enthusiastic debate about the relative merits of Scuds and Patriots and the thrilling nature of 'precision' bombing. In reply to a comment that the war was getting boring one boy retorted: 'No way man, the war's all right, all right as long as the blowing up and killing goes on!' This kind of 'gung-ho' remark was more common among the disaffected 'dossers', or 'low achievers' of the school who would not, or could not, debate the war at a more sophisticated level. It was also an attempt to shock and attract attention in the presence of peers and of myself – perhaps more a product of rivalry among boys wishing to present a 'hard' image than genuine insensitivity to the casualties of war. Yet many boys did become intrigued by the images of 'spectacular destruction'. For example, Perminder complained that she had not seen her boyfriend since the outbreak of the war:

He doesn't come to school any more, he just stays at home, glued to the set, and his mates go round and they sit there all day waiting for another Scud missile attack. I think there's something gross about that myself [. . .] and now all he talks about when he phones is Scud missiles, interceptors and all that. I don't know what he's going on about half the time.

Certainly teenage boys in Southall, socialised into a video culture of macho heroics (Sylvester Stallone, Arnold Schwarzenegger and Co.) consume many more war-based videos and video games than girls. Boys display their fascination with images of war, violence and aggression and appear to find warfare far more compelling and fascinating than girls. Several girls criticised boys for treating the war like a video game: 'It's just like a film but we know this is real. In films war is glorified but here it's not [. . .] some of the boys treat it as if it's just a video game, they don't seem to care'. As many young people pointed out, it was easy in the early days of the war to ignore its human casualties since the visual emphasis in news reports was on the military technology. Gita exclaimed:

All you see are Scud missiles flying around in the sky and interceptors colliding in space – it's like *Star Wars*. You never see anyone being killed, just buildings being destroyed, it's as if this was a war without human beings.

Further gender differences emerged in the patterns of identification. Nobody identified with 'war leaders'. Boys tended to identify most with the pilots who acquired heroic status, expressing sympathy with them because of the dangers they faced. The most compelling TV interviews were considered to be those with pilots returning from sorties, still flushed with excitement and fear, who talked openly about the air attacks. Their accounts of the war were seen to be more authentic than any others. For girls, the point of identification was the TV journalist Kate Adie. She was admired as a heroine, a 'woman at war', willing to brave danger so that the viewers 'back home' could be informed.

GURINDER: I think Kate Adie's great, she's stuck there in that army hut. It must be rough for her but I think she's a really good reporter [. . .] she seems to get to the bottom of what's going on [. . .] I bet a lot of the soldiers fancy her in her camouflage uniform [giggles].

The nurses were a further point of identification for many girls:

KERENPAUL: Humara keeps saying that she wants to go there as a nurse and we tease her that she only wants to go for all the dishy soldiers [. . .] I would go, not for the soldiers [laughs] but to help people. I would, I really would like to go [. . .] if anything watching the Gulf War has shown me that being a soldier is not glamorous or fun, it's a job in which people get paid to kill others.

These gendered points of identification with protagonists in the war as televisual spectacle, linking to other points of identification in audiovisual culture (video war games and war videos for boys, women TV reporters and hospital dramas for girls), suggest efforts to deal with the disruptive and anxiety-provoking nature of the war or its coverage, by resorting to already familiar genres. But, at least for more reflective individuals, these strategies could only momentarily suppress awareness of the political complexities of the war, and of the ways in which they were personally implicated in these complexities, as citizens of Britain whose 'Britishness' is only one facet of their cultural identity. It is time to turn to young people's criticisms of the war coverage, their concerns about the local effects of the war, and the contradictory and ambivalent positions which they experimented with in relation to national and cultural identity, in the course of discussions about the war.

Clearly, to follow the war news in any detail required a degree of competence and motivation, which some young people simply did not possess. It was noticeable that in the sixth-form common room, where much of this data was gathered, the most serious and extended discussions of the war and its coverage took place among A-level students who very consciously brought their subject knowledge, notably of history, economics and English literature, to bear on discussions. Far from taking an uncritical view of TV's coverage of the war, most young people seem to adhere to a conspiracy theory of the media. The most common refrain was that the news is biased: 'It only shows you one side of the story, it makes out that everything that the Allies do is right!' The news coverage of the Gulf was seen as little more than propaganda:

PRITPAL: A lot of my friends they just believe what they see in the news but if you didn't question the news it could brainwash you, I mean how do we really know what's going on? How do we know that the government isn't misleading us? [. . .] They said that the Allied attacks had 80 per cent 'success rate', now they're saying that 80 per cent 'found their target' but didn't necessarily bomb them, so that's the news misleading people innit?

Others commented upon the prevalence of images of bloodsoaked Israeli casualties and the absence of images of Iraqi casualties; the abundance of images of 'successful' Allied attacks and absence of 'successful' Iraqi attacks; the time and space given to justifying the Allied intervention as legitimate and lack of attention given to Saddam Hussein's point of view; the portrayal of American war leaders as heroes and of Saddam Hussein as a villain, 'a Hitler', 'The Butcher of Baghdad' – labels circulated by the tabloid press.

HERSH: I limit myself to news about the war because I know there's a lot of propaganda and that it's not really truthful [. . .] for example, I heard that the Ministry of Defence has issued a 32-point plan for censoring news.

Most young people realised that the war was censored on both sides and that TV's coverage of the war was selective, biased and partial. But this was necessary, they variously argued, for the sake of national security; to keep up public morale; to sell newspapers and fill air time; to avoid a public backlash by those who have relatives risking their lives and fighting out there; and to reinforce public opinion that the Allies are right. The old cliché – truth is the first casualty of war – was reiterated by many. Most realised that truth is filtered and as Kashif stated: 'News, like a poem, has to be interpreted'.

Critical distance is also apparent in comments about the portrayal of the Iraqi people:

JAGDEEP: It's as if the ordinary Iraqi people have no dignity, they are not given the dignity of human beings and that's not right, that makes me feel sad because it's as if their lives are worth nothing but the life of one British soldier is precious.

Those – a minority – who gave their full support to the Allies were seen to have derived all their views, exclusively, from the media. Having no alternative source of information, they were regarded as victims of propaganda:

ABJINDER: [Among my friends] the ones who think America are right are the ones who've been watching the news and taken it for granted, they've taken all their views from there and been influenced by it quite a lot so they're not really thinking for themselves and they haven't got any other news or views to compare it with, they just soak up the propaganda.

The economic as well as the human consequences of war were discussed, not simply in terms of the rise in the price of petrol, but also in terms of local employment. As Heathrow Airport is one of the main local employers, within a month of the outbreak of war, hundreds of parents were made redundant or had their hours reduced due to restrictions on air travel. Security at the airport tightened dramatically and parents brought home news about armed police on patrol; fears of terrorist attacks at the airport, and elsewhere, were rife, and many young people expressed fears about their parents' safety. Clearly, the local repercussions of such a devasting global event also serve to mediate responses to the war and its representations, bringing it closer to home and reminding young people of the interdependence of the local and global spheres.

The war provoked a heightened sense of vulnerability to racist attack and awareness of the threats posed to young people's religious identity, as well as their ambivalent nationality and citizenship status. Many young Muslims were deeply worried about the effects of the war on their religion and its possible consequences for themselves. News of the summary deportation of a number of Muslims from Britain led to fears that they, too, might be deported. The imminence of Ramadan, a forty-day period of fasting from sunrise to sunset, was another focus of concern:

ADIL: This war is going to badly affect my religion, soon it will be Ramadan and there should be peace – Muslims are taught that we shouldn't fight one another – it says so in the Koran – they shouldn't be fighting.

Some were distressed that the war would violate the sanctity of Mecca, the most sacred place of worship for Muslims worldwide. It would, some argued, prevent Muslims from performing the *haj*, the pilgrimage to Mecca which all Muslims are expected to make in the course of their lifetime. Others worried about the presence of 'Christian' soldiers in Mecca and the likelihood of their eating pork and drinking alcohol, which are strictly forbidden by the Koran.

Differences between parental and peer viewpoints were also most intense for young Muslims, who often expressed the need to find a delicate balance between the two, though rarely so poignantly as did Kashif:

> For me the war is a conflicting factor. I come to school and the Gulf War is somewhere and then I go home and its different. My mother she sees the war on TV and she tells me I should even go and fight if need be [. . .]. She is on Saddam Hussein's side, like she preaches that Islam is behind Saddam Hussein and she is behind Islam. It's like here [school] I almost live in both worlds, here, it's like 'our side' and then I go home and and it's like 'Saddam Hussein is Nawab' [prince] and stuff. At home I have to keep the family order so I can't exactly have opposing views to my parents, like showing them opposing views and when I go to a highly English area, I have to keep social order, you know, whatever the public view is, you might have your own views but you can't express them as well. I might say I'm for Saddam Hussein and then 4,000 English people will come down on me [. . .].

Kashif is clear on the nature of the contradictions experienced by many of his Muslim peers:

> The news talks about the anger of British Muslims and their loyalty to Islam but what is a British Muslim? Is he more British or more Muslim? You can't exactly have an equal choice of both, it's difficult to say but I think I'm more westernised, I wouldn't say I'm British because we're in two societies at the same time, one is Islamic society, but not to the true extent, and the other is westernised society, but bearing away from it. If you look at the small things in these societies they are totally different, like your behaviour, your duties and your role in the family.

Kashif is both 'westernised' and Muslim in varying degrees in different situations. He shifts his position according to context in order, as he says, to keep both the family order, based upon Islam, and the social order, based upon western views. Trying to cope with the variety of roles he has to play and the expectations demanded of him is assisted by the distinction he makes between his public and private selves. In front of his father he will confirm his role as a 'pure Muslim' in order to avoid conflict and resentment. Similarly, at school he finds that he takes the Allies' side: 'Like here when I say "we" I mean the Allies but at home I say "them" '.This shifting of positions according to different contexts is commonplace; indeed, the ability to deal with contradiction, ambivalence and ambiguity pragmatically, while as far as possible remaining true to oneself inwardly, is seen to be a sign of maturity. In Southall, this type of skill is another facet of the adulthood associated with understanding news. Kashif accepted that his strategy was necessary to 'keep the peace' and 'social order'.

Many young Muslims questioned the legitimacy of the war and the justifications for the Allied interventions given in the British news media:

'Kuwait stole Iraqi oil during the Iran/Iraq war and so they owed Saddam Hussein money which he was entitled to'. Similarly, although few young Muslims actively support Saddam Hussein, they try to understand his point of view. Some held him in some esteem for standing up to the powerful forces of the west which are seen to dominate the world. Farida: 'In a way Saddam Hussein has already won the war – he has done the impossible, he has stood up to the west and in most Arabs' eyes that means he has won!'

A further set of opposed standpoints is derived from parents' views of the war, which are premised on sharp distinctions drawn between the East and the West, and often reflect their allegiances within Indian sub-continental politics. Navdeep, a 17-year-old Sikh boy:

> I get quite a lot from my parents [...] they have lived through past experiences and they know for a fact that there is a divide between East and West, so when we listen to them we get their image as well, so we think within that frame as well and I believe that they've gone there just to show western superiority [...].

It is partly through news viewing in the family that young people gain insight into their parents' political views, since this is a context in which political opinions are often expressed. Nirmal, an 18-year-old Hindu boy:

> My dad overreacts to everything on the news, especially Indian politics [...] he keeps going on that the British are making all this propaganda about Russia cos, you know, India is an ally of Russia.

Indian subcontinental politics is relevant to many parents', and therefore also young people's, views. During the Cold War India was seen to be an ally of Russia, in contrast to Pakistan which received American support. Thus young Hindus and Sikhs claimed that parents of Indian background tended to have an anti-American stance already, which made it easy for them to be critical of the Allies. Anti-American views of course do not coincide at all with the dominant accounts of the conflict circulated by the British media which supported and justified the Allied attacks. As Shelley, an 18-year-old Hindu boy, explained:

> Our dads are anti-American because of the way they dominate the world and think they own the world. They think they are the world's policeman [...] they have their own theories about why America is involved in the Middle East and like in the Pakistan–Indian border dispute, America is supplying Pakistan with weapons, they seem to have a lot of proof so they believe it [...] they say the Americans are evil [...] watching the news with my dad, it's a one-way slag off of America.

It is not surprising, then, that many young people in Southall take a critical approach to the western media's portrayal of the war. Their parents' past experiences of colonialism and the struggle for independence, followed by migration and settlement in Britain, have sensitised them politically in ways which differ markedly from the average member of the British public. The argument, prevalent in the media at the time of the Gulf War, that the American presence in the Middle East is justified as an act of retaliation against Iraq's violation of the UN agreement and in order to protect the human rights of Kuwaitis, was given short shrift by many, such as this 16-year-old Hindu boy:

HERSH: They [the Americans] don't really care about the people or the human rights, there were no human rights in Kuwait or Saudi Arabia, Saudi Arabia has been condemned by Amnesty International for torture and in Kuwait only 7 per cent of the population have been allowed to vote [. . .] I think they should have human rights and that those people should not be killed because they happen to live in a certain country.

The notion of human rights returns repeatedly in discussions: this is doubtless connected with the fact that at age fifteen all these students study the topic of human rights in their Humanities lessons. Thus a conception of human rights combined with a widespread condemnation of war, *per se*, was the basic stance adopted by most young people. This also fed into their views on the 'racial' and racist dimensions of the conflict.

Many young people in Southall felt threatened by the rise in racist attacks in Britain and in America which accompanied the war. As Anopama, a 16-year-old Sikh girl exclaimed:

It's not just Muslims that are being attacked! Did you hear that Sikhs were attacked in Chicago, Sikhs were attacked! Sikhs were threatened because people thought they were Iraqis, we're all Pakis as far as some people are concerned.

It was felt that the war itself could be seen as a 'race war', and the consequent sense of vulnerability – though more pronounced among parents than young people – emerges clearly in the following exchange among a group of Sikh and Hindu girls:

ANOPAMA: Doesn't this Iraqi war seem like a 'race' war? [chorus of 'Yeah!'] It's like two different races fighting against each other but America just doesn't want to admit it, they cover it up.
REENA: What if there's a huge backlash here?
ANOPAMA: If the war started here where would we fit in? We call ourselves British [. . .]
REENA: No one cares if we're British or about where we come from, we're just all coloured.
HERJINDER: We're not British and we're not Indian, if you went to live in India you wouldn't fit in there.

ANOPAMA: We can't fit in, we can't, if I'm here I'm a Paki and there I'm a *gora* [white person] in my jeans, innit?

HERJINDER: We can't think their way, there are a lot of differences between east and west.

ANOPAMA: We can take the best of both worlds but if there was a rift between India and England where would we fit in?

REENA: We think west laws here in school and we go home and they inflict east laws on us there.

ANOPAMA: When Saddam Hussein calls for a holy war where does that leave us Sikhs and Hindus?

The heightened sense of vulnerability and insecurity that the Gulf War provoked is revealing of deeper ambiguities concerning definitions of self in relation to significant 'others'. The fact of being addressed by the news media as a member of the British public was severely undermined by the rise in racist attacks around Britain and the widespread questioning of Muslims' loyalty to Britain and to the Allies during the war. The war coverage heightened young people's awareness of how they are perceived by 'others', members of the British public in particular; and this in turn generated debate about the vulnerability of their position in Britain, and about the difficulties of 'fitting in' both 'here' and 'there' – in India and in Britain, at school and at home.

The Gulf War and other international, national and local news events, mediated by multiple, culturally diverse information channels, impinge in various ways on life in Southall. The debates precipitated by such news events – or rather, by such plural news coverages and the diverse interpretations of them – prompt teenagers to become acutely conscious of the diversity of positions they are obliged, invited or able to choose to take up, in varying contexts, as members of internally diverse diaspora 'communities' and as British citizens. They find themselves constantly needing to ask 'Who am I?', 'Where do I speak from?' and 'Who is speaking on my behalf?' as well as 'Who is speaking to me?', and they answer these questions differently, and often ambivalently, in different circumstances. The skills involved in negotiating these questions of identity from context to context are learned in the process of graduation from child to adult status in the eyes of families and peers; and this process is accelerated when, in response to dramatic public events, young people are (or feel) called upon to take up explicit positions as if to resolve ambiguities and ambivalences, which, however, remain. Of all events, war most powerfully insists on a thinking in terms of stark binary oppositions – us and them, friend and foe. Such terms reveal themselves as woefully inadequate to the complexities of these young people's sense of hybrid national and cultural identity.

Chapter 5

Neighbours and gossip: Kinship, courtship and community

The conventional western soap opera constructs a 'symbolic community', weaving together the everyday lives of its inhabitants in a fine web of intricate relationships between kin and neighbours, friends and enemies. The proximity of people's lives, their closeness in time and place and in their relationships, generates narrative conflict and movement. In key respects, the soap opera embodies many of the characteristics of local life in Southall: the central importance of the family; a density of kin in a small, geographically bounded area; a high degree of face to face contact (a 'knowable community'), and a distinctive sense of local identity. Similarly, the proximity and contiguity of kin and neighbours generates much of the distinctiveness of social life in Southall.

The arguments presented in this chapter centre on the homology, which is perceived by many of my informants, between life in Southall and life in the Australian soap opera *Neighbours*. They frequently commented, in particular, on the multiple relationships between local gossip and soap gossip: the term 'gossip', in young people's talk, serves to structure the symbolic community of the televised fiction as well as that of real Southall, and it also provides the metaphorical linkage between the two.

Soap operas are seen by Southall viewers to be intrinsically based on gossip. Much information is passed between characters, and of course to the viewer, in the form of gossip. A stereotypical gossip character figures prominently in most soap casts: she (invariably it *is* a woman) both drives forward onscreen narratives by spreading information within the fictive community, and in the process relays information to the viewer. In *Neighbours*, at the time of fieldwork, this function was performed by Mrs Mangel (later by Hilary). Mrs Mangel, the elderly woman who observes, reports and censures young people's behaviour, incarnates for Southall youth the network of relatives and neighbours, particularly aunts and other female elders, who act as the moral guardians of their neighbourhood and whose 'gossip' is feared as a force of constraint of young people's freedom. Her character, indeed her very name, became the symbolic linchpin of the connectedness of Southall and Ramsay Street (the fictional setting of *Neighbours*).

The reception of soaps is also characterised by the speech forms of gossip. Viewing generates gossip among young people about the characters and their actions. And this soap talk is also fuelled by soap gossip published by the tabloid press, which adds further dimensions by playing with the double existence of the characters within the soap text and the actors outside it. In the case of *Neighbours*, several stars of the show – Jason Donovan, Kylie Minogue and Craig McLachlan – are also pop stars, whose images and star personalities are circulated in diverse media texts. Thus gossip within the soap, gossip circulated by a variety of other media texts, and gossip generated locally by both the soap and other texts, are all integrated into young people's everyday and TV talk. And finally this talk itself is, in general, conducted in forms which they themselves refer to as gossip.

Young people's everyday interpersonal communication is informed in significant ways by their soap viewing, not simply in its content but also, more significantly, in its form. As I shall demonstrate, the very structure of the soap and the cognitive processes of reception it entails are closely akin to the processes whereby gossip is transformed into rumour in local communication networks. This offers an explanation for something that puzzled me for a long time during fieldwork, namely, the way that young people move so fluidly and seemingly unselfcon-sciously between 'soap talk' and 'real talk'. The two are inextricably linked and, to an outsider, often indistinguishable. The parallels which young people themselves draw also help to explain why the reception of *Neighbours* is so easy and pleasurable.

Some readers, no doubt, will find it surprising that young 'British Asians' should engage so avidly with an Australian soap featuring an all-white cast. The popularity in Britain of *Neighbours*, and its stable-mate *Home and Away*, has even been ascribed to the latent racism of British society by media commentators. Bruce Gyngell, an Australian TV producer, was quoted in the *Guardian* (2 November 1993) as claiming that the appeal of these shows lay in British audiences' nostalgic pining for an all-white society (which he located in the 'pre-immigration' era of the 1960s!). But Southall's *Neighbours* fans evidently have compelling reasons for identifying with the soap's young protagonists, which override 'racial' differences. They draw on the soap as a cultural resource in their everyday interactions both in the peer culture and with parents and other adults, as they endeavour to con-struct new modes of identity for themselves. In order to understand why and how they do so, it is necessary to look more closely at the main features of 'soap talk' and gossip in general; at gossip and rumour in Southall in particular, as young people living there perceive it; and at the homology between the form of soap narration and gossip as a social speech form.

SOAP TALK

TV genres bring a range of discourses into play and employ particular ways of speaking: popular entertainment programmes work with colloquial and vernacular speech while news, current affairs and documentary programmes employ more formal modes of address. These differences play a major role in cementing affinities between particular audiences and genres, such as that noted by numerous researchers between soaps and women (Hobson, 1989; Geraghty, 1991; Morley, 1986). Most of this research has focussed on adult women, showing, for example, that one of the key pleasures that women find in soaps is the validation of their own kind of talk (Brown, 1987: 22). This validation works in two ways: the programmes use the same forms of talk that the women use among themselves; and they provide additional material for the 'small talk' and 'gossip' that bond female friendships. Both these forms of validation are involved in soap viewing and soap talk among Southall youth, and we shall return to them shortly.

A large part of the enjoyment which is derived from watching soap operas lies in talking about them with other people, a talk which predominantly takes narrative form (Hobson, 1989). While TV may be viewed in the home, talk about TV outside the home with friends at work or in leisure completes the process of communication. Pleasure is derived from exchanging views and opinions about programmes with friends and colleagues:

> Talking about soap operas forms part of the everyday work culture of both men and women. It is fitted around their working time or in their lunch breaks. The process takes the form of storytelling, commenting on the stories, relating the incidents and assessing them for realism, and moving from drama to discussing the incidents which are happening in the 'real' world. (Hobson, 1989: 150)

Retelling soap opera stories gives viewers the opportunity to be storytellers, enabling them to extend their repertoires as storytellers and at the same time to inflect stories gleaned from TV in ways relevant to their own lives. Hobson also highlights the ways in which women's talk among friends and colleagues brings the interests and concerns of the private sphere into the public domain: the fusion between the two domains characterises such talk. And indeed, it is often the talk about a soap which determines whether someone will begin watching it in the first place. Thus viewing in the private context and patterns of sociability in the public context mutually shape one another: 'When a storyline is so strong that it is a main topic of conversation it is reason enough to get someone watching so as not to be left out of the conversation' (Hobson, 1989: 161).

Such views are reiterated by my informants who claim that, for example, peer pleasure and pressure led them to start watching *Neighbours* in order to participate in everyday conversations. Thus *Neighbours* is part of young people's shared culture and acts as a collective resource through which they compare and contrast, judge and evaluate the events and characters in the soap and those in 'real' life. They make assessments about the validity of what happens in the soap and compare it with what a character should have done or what they or others might have done in the same situation. As Hobson argues, because the subject-matter of the soap operas is so familiar to the viewers, there can be a free flow of information in talk as people work on 'collaborative readings' of the TV text which are informed by, and inform, their own social experiences. It is the interweaving of fiction and real experiences that perhaps most of all characterises the nature of soap talk:

> It is the talk about TV programmes and the relating of those programmes to the everyday life of viewers that moves TV into a further dimension from that which ends at the viewing moment. Indeed, talking about TV programmes and what has happened in them is essential in making a programme popular and part of the cultural capital of general discourse. (Hobson, 1989: 167)

The collective nature of reception as evidenced in soap talk is also commented upon by Seiter *et al.*:

> What we found in our interviews over and over again was that soap opera texts are the products not of individual and isolated readings but of collective constructions – collaborative readings, as it were, of small social groups such as families and friends [. . .]. It seems then that the soap opera, not least because of the strong need it creates for collaborative readings, has considerable potential for reaching out into the real world of viewers. It enables them to evaluate their own experiences as well as the norms and values they live by in terms of the relationship patterns and social blueprints the show presents. (Seiter *et al.*, 1989: 233)

Soap talk in Southall is largely enjoyed as a peer group activity. Though many young people discuss *Neighbours* and other soaps in the family, as was explained in Chapter 2, 'watching with mother' evokes a pleasurable sense of intimacy, but there is often the risk of parental censure. In talk among the peer group, especially among intimate friends, young people can be less guarded about their opinions: 'You're just more relaxed, you can say what you want, you can swear and use your own language, you can be more yourself and say what you really feel'. In this context, soap talk – the construction of collaborative readings plays important functions in cementing friendships. And here, as we shall see shortly, it also serves as a means of discussing personal and family issues indirectly.

Existing audience research strongly supports the notion that soap talk is a gender-specific activity, more or less exclusively confined to women and girls. The characteristics of soap talk are sometimes described in ways which suggest that it exemplifies 'female' social virtues. Thus Thorne *et al.* (1983), for example, identify:

> recurring patterns which distinguish talk among women from mixed-sex and all-male groups: mutuality of interaction work (active listening, building on the utterances of others), collaboration rather than competition, flexible leadership rather than the strong dominance patterns found in all-male groups [. . .]. (1983: 18)

My data problematises this established notion somewhat, indicating that both girls and boys engage in soap talk, though different results emerge from different research methods – a significant finding in itself in terms of the debate on methodology.

In interviews, boys generally denied any interest in soaps, dismissing them as 'sissy' programmes and professing not to discuss them with peers. Interviews with girls confirm that, while many boys are in fact keen viewers of *Neighbours*, they tend not to discuss the programme, at least not with girls:

> SAIRA: You don't really know what boys are really like, they don't discuss *Neighbours*, they think it's a sissy drama, they discuss computers, the latest films, video piracy, sport and boring stuff like that, they don't like discussing relationships.

So interview data suggests that soap talk is much more a feature of female than male communication. Boys claim that, if at all, they tend to talk more about the amusing incidents, the gags and repeat funny lines. But fieldwork observation provided much evidence that no such gender distinction exists, or that it is at least increasingly permeable. Soaps like *Neighbours* appeal successfully to teenagers as a whole, with characters of both sexes providing strong points of identification for male and female viewers. The characters and their dilemmas were discussed with pleasure and animation both in all-female groups and in mixed-sex groups, where issues of gender relations were extensively thematised. I also found some evidence that boys indulge in soap talk both with close female friends and in all-male groups, though more secretively. Thus while gender distinctions still affect the perceived acceptability of soap talk, the exact equations set up by some researchers between female viewers, female patterns of social interaction and interest in relationships, emotions and problem-solving, and soap as a 'female genre', do not appear to obtain in Southall.

We saw earlier how, in the domestic context, viewing soaps such as *Neighbours* may lead to intimate as well as censorious talk. In the peer group, soap talk frequently involves the veiled discussion of personal and, in particular, family problems, as these are displaced on to soap narratives. Young people themselves see talking about soaps as important because it allows them to talk about their own problems, indirectly, through a particular character or situation. A sense of family loyalty would inhibit most young people from talking directly about their own family problems, except perhaps with the closest and most intimate of friends, and even this is very rare. The culturally central concept of *izzat* (outlined above, p. 38) prohibits public discussion of private family issues, and so soap talk often allows tensions to be ventilated, serving a therapeutic function, as informants see it. The key emphasis of such talk seems to be on how problems get solved:

> GITA: In school or at home we often have teenage problems which relate to our soap [. . .] but you don't talk about your own family except to really close friends maybe [. . .]. By talking to friends you come to an understanding [. . .] you can think back to what a character did and see if they did things the right way [. . .] we discuss the problems and how they get solved.

This is a highly culturally specific function of soap talk in Southall, the importance of which can hardly be overestimated.

Soap talk is also seen as a way of bonding friendships, since, in discussing the problems that characters face and how effectively they deal with them, one is giving expression to norms and values in terms of the concrete experiences of others, where more direct or abstract expression of norms would be difficult:

> GURVINDER: It's important to talk about soaps and share those experiences with friends because your friends get to know you better, they can understand what your views are, how you think, what you believe, what you're having difficulties in and what your weaknesses are, you get closer.

Soap talk facilitates discussion of a range of topics, such as the attractiveness of certain male characters, which would be taboo in parental company:

> PARAMJIT: After watching *Neighbours* we always talk about it the next day at school, we talk about the sexy male characters like Henry and his muscles, and other things like how stupid Bronwyn is for not speaking properly to Henry [. . .] most of the things we talk about we wouldn't discuss with our parents for obvious reasons.

Young people identify with the situations in which particular characters find themselves:

> REENA: Discussing *Neighbours* with friends can be important at times because sometimes you feel as if you are in the same position

as a certain character and have to stick up for yourself and say what you think.

Especially for girls who have little direct access to people outside their kinship and peer networks, soaps are seen to provide an extension to their immediate social experience:

> MEENA: Some girls, especially those who lead sheltered lives, are always talking about soaps and they're always talking in that kind of soap style, you know, 'Oh dear what's the matter? Do you want to talk about it? Can I help you?' [. . .] they want to talk problems [. . .] for those girls, who don't do much else, soaps are really important.

But, one should add, soaps are also 'really important' to many young people in Southall who do not lead particularly sheltered lives by local standards.

The local importance of *Neighbours*, then, lies in the various functions served by talking about it. Essential to all these functions are processes referred to by researchers in terms of 'identification'. The relationship between viewers and texts is often conceived of as one whereby the text offers certain 'positions' for the viewer to identify with, primarily in relation to characters in the soap:

> Viewers may identify with certain characters, seeing themselves as in that character's shoes; they may regard them as a role model, imitating that character's behaviour in order to gain some of the rewards which that character is shown to enjoy; or they may recognise aspects of a character as similar to a significant person in their own lives, engaging in [. . .] 'parasocial interaction', watching the action as if playing the opposite character, as if the character were interacting with them directly. (Livingstone, 1990: 22)

Thus identification is seen as a psychological process whereby the viewers either project themselves on to characters and their situations or dilemmas; or else, in the reverse case, the characters and situations are appropriated and used in mimetic or imitative fashion. My data on soap talk and 'real' talk suggests that these two processes are related to each other in a much more reciprocal and socially complex way, and furthermore that the psychological dimension is not primary.

The word which informants most commonly use to describe their relationship to the text is not 'identification' but 'association'. They claim that they 'associate' themselves and or their friends with characters, situations, feelings and problems. They link and connect aspects of the social world of *Neighbours* with their own and attempt to accommodate and integrate their perceptions of the soap world into their own and vice versa. In this process, it is not in fact characters *per se* that provide the essential point of identification, but, on the one hand, a perceived social world seen as a generational entity – the social world of teenagers – and on the other hand, the very processes of narration involved in 'reading' the soap, in talking about it, and in talking about their own social experiences and aspirations.

The creation of meaning through the interaction of texts and readers is best conceived as a process of negotiation and struggle (Livingstone, 1990: 23). The processes of negotiation which are manifest in young people's soap talk are of central concern here. Talk about their viewing allows for the negotiation of what is and what ought to be both in their own social lives and in the soap world. It involves both realism and fantasy and is centrally focussed on questions of morality. These negotiations are partly facilitated by the continuous soap text which refuses closure and allows viewers to adopt a 'wandering' point of view. As Allen suggests:

> The perspectival openness of the contemporary soap opera diegesis enables it to accommodate a far greater range of 'negotiated' readings than other, more normatively determinant forms of fictive narratives. Furthermore, this openness helps account for the broadening of the soap audience in recent years to include more men, adolescents and college students [. . .]. Becoming a competent reader [. . .] requires a unique investment of the reader's time and psychic energy [. . .]. Watching soap operas is a social act as well as an engagement with narrative text. (1985: 147–148)

It is precisely because viewing and discussing *Neighbours* is a socially shared act and experience that young people can draw upon it collectively to make sense of their own lives. Yet the talk arising from their viewing, whilst recognising certain similarities, more often tends to emphasise differences between the soap world and their own experience. The parallels which do exist between the soap world and the social world of Southall are less a matter of substantial similarity, than of formal characteristics of narration and narrative structure.

So as far as substance or content is concerned, three thematic areas dominate in young people's talk about their viewing: family and kinship relations; romance and courtship rituals; and neighbourly relations in the 'community'. In exploring these relationships in *Neighbours* and contrasting the forms they take with their own experience, young people are actively and creatively negotiating the most important sources of social tensions in their lives. Within and across these domains, they are exploring generational, gender and cultural differences. I shall examine each of these thematic areas in turn, although it is the overlap and competition between them which drive the narratives both of these young people's lives and of the soap. But first, it is necessary to examine more closely the role of gossip in these real and fictive narratives.

SOUTHALL GOSSIP AND RUMOUR

Gossip and rumour are seen as one of the greatest threats both to a young person's freedom and to family honour, or *izzat*, in Southall. Gossip among adults is seen to be more pernicious, malicious and harmful than among young people since it usually has more far-reaching and dangerous consequences. It is very rare that peer gossip will be revealed to parents because complicity among youth is high. One of their most consistent condemnations of Southall concerns the pervasiveness of gossip among adults and the instrumental role it plays in social control, especially in the surveillance of gender relations.

In most of the relevant literature, gossip and rumour are conflated. Though there is a degree of semantic overlap, there are important distinctions to be made which are significant for my argument, distinctions which are not just 'academic', but belong to the culture of Southall. According to informants, gossip consists of fragments of information about the private lives of people known to those who share it. It is exchanged among a group of intimates, in a small social network, and usually concerns violations of social or moral norms. Gossip becomes rumour when such fragments accumulate and are pieced together to form a narrative which then circulates in a much wider social network. Thus a rumour is public knowledge which comes into being as a result of a process of collective interpretation performed upon gossip. As public knowledge, it may concern individuals not known to its recipients and transmitters, who accept it as a socially sanctioned – if not necessarily accurate or true – account of an event.

Academic work on gossip and rumour has tended to arise in local studies, particularly ethnographies. Lest the reader be tempted to suppose they are peculiar to the Punjabi community in Southall, it is worth briefly highlighting a few earlier studies. Blumenthal (1932, 1937) recognises gossip as a characteristic feature of small-town life (in this case in Chicago) and draws up a typology of different types of gossip. Bott (1957) highlights the importance of gossip among women in London working-class families with close-knit social networks and segregated conjugal roles. She describes the pressures upon women to conform to local standards and to participate in gossip networks if they wish to reap the rewards of companionship. She concludes that gossip is one of the chief means whereby norms are stated, tested and affirmed. Paine, in general reviews of the anthropological literature (1967, 1968), argues that gossip is an informal and indirect sanction which is employed where the risks of open or formal attack are too high. Evans-Pritchard, in his ethnography of the Azande (1937), describes how situations of ignorance or uncertainty produce tensions or suspense which may result in gossip. He shows how the very belief in witchcraft creates anxieties which are periodically discharged as gossip and accusations. Cohen (1980, 1982) links carnival with gossip among Afro-Caribbeans in London's Notting Hill and argues that it is a means by which individuals and groups may 'contest territory' in physical and social space.

Festinger *et al.* (1948) suggest that rumours, on the other hand, are propagated when individuals pass on stories which enable them to express anxieties that might otherwise remain unacknowledged. Leinhardt (1975) proposes that 'fantastic' rumours are necessary to resolve complexities in public feeling that cannot be readily articulated at a more thoughtful level. Firth's (1956) research among the Tikopea led him to suggest that certain types of rumour serve as social instruments by which individuals or groups attempt to improve their status, while Smith (1985) sees rumour as a process of negotiating shared meanings, rather than a product of social organisation. Shibutani (1966) is one of the few academics to distinguish between gossip and rumour, alluding to their different temporal and spatial patterns and to the larger number of people involved in rumour. His concern is primarily with the latter, which he regards as 'a recurrent form of communication through which men [*sic*] caught together in an ambiguous situation attempt to construct a meaningful interpretation of it by pooling their intellectual resources' (1966: 17).

Let us now turn to the specificities of gossip in Southall. Young people often complain bitterly about the close surveillance they feel themselves to be subjected to in public life in Southall. Some young people see gossip as resulting from the close-knit kinship and social networks. One of the survey questions asked respondents to agree or disagree with a list of statements about Southall, culled from comments we had often heard people make (see Appendix 4). Seventy-four per cent agreed that 'nothing in Southall can be kept secret'; 69 per cent agreed that 'everybody watches what everybody is doing'; and 45 per cent agreed that 'Southall is too isolated, it's like an island'. These results are particularly telling, since none of the other statements was confirmed by more than one third of respondents. The figures support much of the qualitative data.

Many young people see gossip as a means by which parents compete for public recognition of their family honour or *izzat*. The following exchange between two 16-year-old boys in an informal school context makes this clear. They are discussing their families and Southall:

DEVINDER: Indian culture . . .

MALKIT: Yeah . . .

DEVINDER: Indian culture, I'll tell you what Indian culture is, it's respect, respect and more respect.

MALKIT: [laughing] That's true and it's even worse in Southall because you're surrounded with different, er, not different religions, mostly Sikhs [. . .] but Sikh families [. . .] it's kinda like there's more tension between them to keep respect.

DEVINDER: I think Southall is just one big gossip, I mean you can't even [...] I mean you might not even know the woman but it could be your mum's, friend's, sister's, daughter's, friend's friend and by the time you've got back home, you don't know how it's got back home but you walk in the door and your mum says 'Where have you been? Someone told your auntie that you've been flirting with girls on your own!' and I just wanna laugh but it makes you really angry to why they're saying it and it's even worse for girls [...]

MALKIT: [...] and it's always the same woman, not a man [...]

DEVINDER: [...] and when you watch a soap you think of that woman and when you think of a soap you think of that woman and that's why you begin to hate that person in the soap, like when they show Mrs Mangel and Madge is having a go at her and then I think of this aunt on my road that I really hate cos she's an old gossip and it makes you feel good and you wish you could have a go at her yourself.

The connection between soap gossip and Southall gossip is most force-fully demonstrated by the local appropriation of Mrs Mangel, the key gossip character in *Neighbours* at the time of fieldwork. She is seen to embody everything that one would despise in a neighbour. She gossips. She has no sense of loyalty. She talks behind people's backs with malicious intent. She is an interfering busybody who twists and distorts events in order to put people down. While purporting to uphold the moral values of the community, she shows a prurient interest in any aberration of social or moral codes of behaviour. Among young people the term 'Mangel' has entered everyday usage as a term of abuse for anyone who gossips: 'Oh! she's a right Mangel!' can be heard commonly, even long after she had actually disappeared from the soap (to be replaced by Hilary as the gossip character). The term still has wide currency and her character has taken on almost mythic proportions: she is the 'evil eye' and the 'maligning mouth'. The appropriation of the Mangel metaphor is revealing of a specif-ically local response to *Neighbours*, as the anxieties of young people in Southall are projected onto the Mangel character as the embodiment of the significant threat that gossip poses to their lives.

The threat of having a gossip interfere in one's life is most acutely felt by girls, since family honour or *izzat* ultimately depends on the chastity of daughters. Gossip in the parental culture is typically exchanged by women about girls. As Diljit, a Jat Sikh boy put it: 'Girls are the heart of a family's *izzat*.' *Izzat*, with its contraries *beijjit* (disgrace; adjective *beizzat*) and *sharm* (shame), denotes a key value which underlies norms in Punjabi culture, representing a cluster of religious, social and moral meanings which link kinship duty and the sanctity of family life, a family's internal moral integrity and its social standing in the community. It is a focus of status competition between families in Southall. I referred earlier (in Chapter 3) to the widespread perception among Southall youth that women are the 'carriers of tradition', a role expressed in the cultural power they exercise in the home. Women are deemed primarily responsible for maintaining religious and moral traditions, and this role allows them considerable leverage in challenging their formal subordination to patriarchal power through informal means. Much depends on personal skills in asserting oneself in various ways, not least through posing a threat to *izzat*. For in one sense, *izzat* is a matter of male pride, enjoining men of honour to behave with fearless independence and to control and protect their female kin. A woman who challenges male authority threatens his honour, and male *izzat* depends on women behaving with modesty and segregating themselves from the male world. But *izzat* is also attributed to families, not just to individuals. As Ballard puts it: 'The advancement of their corporate *izzat* is one of the most important goals which South Asian families set themselves' (1982: 186). This is best achieved by arranging prestigious marriages for daughters with men of the same (or a higher) caste. And so, at first sight paradoxically, women play key roles in marriage negotiations, for:

> In the rigorous pursuit of an ideal which intrinsically subordinates them, women gain influence not just over other women, but over men. But all would be lost if any public acknowledgement were to be made that this is the case. (Ballard, 1982: 186)

Thus in the field of marital arrangements, women – both mothers and daughters – traditionally have considerable power at their disposal.

However, as the young bride is 'given' to her husband's family and she has rights to dowry wealth, which she must share with her in-laws and which must be acceptable to them, very heavy financial pressures face the bride's family – especially in the case of low-income families. This system places power in the hands of the boy's family rather than the girl's. And in Southall, the high density of Sikhs living locally, and specific challenges to traditional norms and values that have arisen through migration and settlement in Britain, mean that competition between families for respect and respectability is very intense. This is also reflected in rival families 'out-bidding' one another in the lavishness and stylishness of coming-of-age and marriage rituals.

The traditional system has meant that, for centuries in the Punjab, unmarried girls have been prohibited from freely associating in public with boys who are not kin by blood or marriage, i.e. potential marriage partners. A girl's reputation has to be impeccable if she is to be married honourably, and it can be seriously damaged if she is known to have a boyfriend or, in some cases, if she is merely seen 'hanging around' or 'chatting', let alone 'flirting' with boys on the high street or elsewhere in public. A girl's reputation may be speedily sullied by a casual aside, such as the phrase (accompanied by a 'tut-tut') *kuriānbar phirdian* (literally, 'about outside') or *awara gardi* ('roaming', 'wandering'), referring to girls seen unchaperoned in public. Settlement in Southall and exposure to British and American norms associated with courtship and marriage has meant that such prohibitions are not easily maintained.

The perceived permissiveness and moral laxness of 'western' values with regard to gender relations and sexual relationships are felt by many parents to be extremely threatening. In representing modes of behaviour deemed permissive, television and soaps like *Neighbours* are seen as particularly threatening: as potential enticements, to be avoided at all costs. But 'transgressions' increasingly occur, placing great strains on family life. In some cases they are countered by a tightening of restrictions on young people's, especially girls', behaviour. Such stress and strain is further heightened by the difficulties of controlling information about private family matters or about one's children's misdemeanours. Gossip about transgressions of norms poses a major threat to families.

From the parental perspective, gossip is a powerful means of social control because its focus on violations of moral codes, norms and values serves to reinforce them. Furthermore, gossip helps define status relations, establishes various degrees of closeness and distance among people and draws boundaries between insiders and outsiders: in short, it is a key arena of the mediation of culture and society.

In the peer culture, highly differentiated views of gossip and rumour are current. There are ambiguous attitudes and feelings toward gossip depending on whether it is harmless, idle chatter or sheer malice. Gossip is perceived as a gender-specific way of talking: whilst boys may gossip, girls are seen to be better at it and to take it much further than boys. It then often turns into 'bitching', a kind of malicious talk, on its way to rumour, which spreads much more. According to both boys and girls, male talk is only intimate among very close friends and its substance does not spread beyond an immediate, close-knit circle. As one 16-year-old girl comments:

> AMERJIT: Girls tend to take gossip much further than boys, we really bitch behind each other's backs, but then when we see each other we go, 'Oh! Hi! how are you' [. . .] the boys tell us off and say we take it too far, you know, we'll keep going on about it, repeating it, exaggerating it or adding to it.

Boys claim they do not gossip:

> AMANDEEP: We only talk about boys who get on our nerves otherwise we ignore them [. . .] when there's friction, you know, like someone bad mouthing someone behind their back, we are more likely to confront the person, girls wouldn't, they'd just gossip or bitch.

In one peer network, comprising approximately fifty 16-year-olds, which I studied closely, six main friendship groupings were apparent, typically segregated according to gender, year group and course of study (these were all A-level students), except for one mixed group containing three dating couples. Each group exhibited a similar structure: a core intimate group, usually consisting of the highest status members, comprising anything from two to four people, and peripheral groupings of two or three members around this core. Attached to several of the groups was an outsider of low status, invariably a girl. These girls, feeling at times outcast and seeking attachment, moved more freely than others between groups and between its core and periphery subgroups. They were generally disliked and seen as 'stirrers' and 'spies', since they were in a position to overhear, eavesdrop and abuse private information about others. This person, referred to as the *chugli* (a spiteful gossip), transgressed the boundaries of loyalty in relaying information across groups. In doing so she hoped to acquire (momentary) status by being privy to knowledge that no-one else in a particular group had. So whilst she was a useful source of gossip, she was much maligned. Gossip causes trouble between the different groups as they vie for status, recognition, admiration and popularity; but gossip is also the vehicle of that struggle.

Several female informants talked of their compulsive urge to make revelations through gossip: to enjoy the momentary prestige and excitement that the revelation of 'juicy gossip' brings. The thrill brings little enduring satisfaction:

AMRIT: Sometimes you just wanna let it out, you have to tell somone, you just can't keep it to yourself [. . .] like if something happens I've just got to tell Dally [her best friend] and I'll say don't tell anyone [. . .] but then I won't be able to keep it to myself so I'll tell Sanjeeb and within no time I've told ten people and to each one I've said 'don't tell anyone else but . . .' [. . .]. I don't know it's just the excitement that you know something that the others don't [. . .]. I suppose it puts you in a position of power because you've got to be the first to tell.

DALLY: But you lose that power once you've told them.

AMRIT: Yeah that's true, the power and the excitement only lasts for a few short seconds.

DALLY: You not only lose your power but that other person loses their trust.

In the peer culture both boys and girls are the subject of gossip. The key subject is romance and 'dating':

RUPINDER: It's mainly about who fancies who, who's going out with who, the problems that they have, how far they go, you know what

> I mean, who's about to break up, who's just broken up, what people are wearing, how they do their hair, who's getting drunk, bunking, rucking, who's a slag and who's a sap, who's got shamed up [. . .] you know, that sort of thing.

Many young people distinguish between gossip and rumour mainly by virtue of the fact that gossip is seen as private talk and rumour as a story for public consumption. In the language of social science, rumour is gossip transformed into a narrative by storytelling processes which involve the social construction and dissemination of a narrative in a specific communication network through a variety of 'verification procedures'. These procedures filter the narrative, subjecting it to a levelling of detail by omission and, conversely, a sharpening of detail by selective retention (Firth, 1956). Thus, through a social and cultural process of collective interpretation and refinement, an incident is converted into narrative material for more general transmission.

So rumour, in my informants' terms, is gossip made public. Gossip never gives the whole story, only fragments. Thus – like narration in soap operas – it creates information gaps which recipients are more or less desirous to fill in. Recipients of gossip hear fragments of information from a limited or one-sided perspective and are usually little concerned about the accuracy or veracity of what they hear; and in the absence of additional information, verification is difficult. Rumour is less easily confined and controlled since verification procedures have already attributed the story with some legitimacy and authority, though not with an author. Whilst the author of gossip is known, being identical with the speaker, rumour is characterised by authorial anonymity since it is a social construction. Thus there is a dissociation between the speaker and the message such that the speaker cannot be held responsible for the story. A rumour is therefore openly and freely discussed without reservation and without the kind of intensity of confidentiality that accompanies gossip. No trust or loyalty is required on the part of the recipient who is therefore free to spread it:

> RUPINDER: A rumour is common knowledge, it's, how would you say, it's an unproven story but you don't care because everyone wants to believe it, in any case it's hard to prove or deny [. . .]. Take the rumour about Ruby and William, I mean the whole school, the whole of Southall knew about that. It all started when she bunked school for a week, people started saying she'd left home and run away with William and when she didn't come to school for two months it seemed true cos no one saw him either, then some said that she was living at his house and some said that she's got sent down India [. . .] you know, her parents are really religious and strict and that's happened quite a few girls round here [. . .] then the rumour went round that she was pregnant, but no one really knew and then there

was talk of an abortion, even her best friends were discussing her pregnancy, which I thought was really bad, anyway, the rumour ended when shc came back to school a few months later, but no one really ever knew if it was true or not, although everyone suspected that she had an abortion, she's living back at home now.

As this example shows, initial gossip leaves information gaps which are later progressively filled through the acquisition of new information; incoming clues spark off new hypotheses which are later confirmed, rejected or held in suspense. Red herrings may be introduced and divert attention. Time-gaps in the acquisition of new information cause delay and during this period the basic elements of the story may be embellished, exaggerated or distorted, depending on the moral or affective investment of those participating in the construction of the rumour. There is a tendency to speculate and elaborate a rumour (especially when faced with scepticism) until it acquires some narrative coherence and plausibility, and to assimilate fragments according to an established narrative theme. Young people often use either previous rumours or soap narratives as models. In Southall these are mainly rumours of girls running away from home, rumours about girls dating or marrying a boy of different religion, caste or colour, and rumours about pregnancy and abortion.

Several versions of the Ruby–William rumour prevailed for a while until one version gained widespread credence. Even though it was perceived that the rumour ended upon their return to school, talking about the rumour did not end, because despite the ascendance of a 'received' version, a margin of doubt remained that allowed for continued speculation. Such rumours become part of peer folklore and are resurrected whenever gossip starts about someone else's misdemeanours. Thus past rumours and soap storylines provide narrative frameworks through which new rumours may be interpreted. Insiders, people with privileged knowledge (e.g. the girl's sister and her friends), play major roles in the construction of rumours. They talk confidentially to others, who may then be pressurised to tell other intimate friends or may voluntarily proffer such secrets, and so gossip shared by insiders becomes a rumour which returns periodically to them for verification and assimilation. In this case, harmless gossip about truanting was transformed into a rumour which later became one of the biggest scandals of the year in the peer culture. This particular rumour also formed the narrative of one group's own soap production on video in my Media Studies course. Ruby's sister, Bally, was a member of the group that produced a soap closing sequence entitled 'Freedom At Last'. Ruby played herself, and although the rumour was never openly referred to either at the planning stage or during the production, all involved, including myself, shared a public secret. The perfect irony of their own 'real-life' fiction was that it transformed a scandalous rumour into a triumph of freedom: the courting couple triumphantly escaped the strictures of gossip and parental control by running away.

Gossip and rumour about transgressions of norms poses a major threat to families and this explains why the issue of gossip is so prominent in the lives of young people locally and why it is so central, especially for girls, to their engagement with the soap genre. But if gossip is a threat it is also an activity, a way of communicating which is indulged in and enjoyed by many and which varies from harmless chatter about people to the spreading of scandal and slander. Turning now from gossip and rumour in real life in Southall, to soap narratives, we will see that specific textual features of the soap genre encourage the interpenetration of 'soap talk' and 'real talk' as varieties of gossip.

SOAP NARRATION AND GOSSIP

Narration is the process whereby story material is selected, arranged and represented in order to achieve specific effects. A *narrative* or story is the product of such processes, present in the mind of the recipient. The distinction between the story that is represented and its representation goes back to Aristotle's *Poetics*, but it was most fully theorised by the Russian Formalists, using the terms *fabula* and *syuzhet*. In Formalist theory, the *fabula* (sometimes translated as 'story') is the imaginary construct which we create progressively and retroactively as we perceive the *syuzhet* ('plot'), which consists of representations of actions and events arranged in a dramaturgical process. A *syuzhet*, then, consists not of the narrative text itself but of those organised elements, clues and prompts which recipients perceive in the text and put together, framing them within temporal, spatial and causal relations, to construct a *fabula*. In Bordwell's words, the latter:

> is a pattern which perceivers of narratives create through assumptions and inferences [. . .], the developing result of picking up narrative clues, applying schemata, framing and testing hypotheses. The viewer builds the *fabula* on the basis of prototype schemata (identifiable types of persons, actions and locations), template schemata (principally the canonic story format which briefly involves: setting plus characters – goals – attempts – outcome – resolution) and procedural schemata (a search for appropriate motivations and relations of causality, time and space). To the extent that these processes are intersubjective, so is the *fabula* that is created. In principle viewers will agree either about what the story is or upon what factors render it ambiguous. (1985: 49)

The *fabula/syuzhet* distinction is relevant to this discussion of soaps and gossip in a number of ways. It usefully focusses attention on the processes of narration, unlike many other theories of narrative: for here we are concerned with the cognitive and intersubjective activities of the viewers not just during, but also after viewing. The cognitive processes described by Bordwell, when applied to the continuous narration of the soap genre, express their results in talk which young people perceive as a form of story-telling, and which they refer to by the term 'gossip'. Also, the processes involved in converting gossip into rumour, described a moment ago, are very closely akin to the processes of *fabula* creation. Both involve a range of activities directed at the construction of a coherent story out of available fragments of information. This offers a way to explaining why the teenage viewers' identification with the soap *Neighbours* is more an identification with the processes of narration and with gossip than with particular characters *per se*, as is conventionally perceived.

The experience of viewing *Neighbours* is seen by young people as similar to hearing gossip. *Neighbours*, like most other soaps, privileges verbal over visual discourse. The low production values, cheap sets and naturalistic camera techniques do not make it visually exciting in the way that certain American soaps such as *Dallas* are. Low-budget soaps like *Neighbours* bear the traces of their generic origins in radio, where the emphasis on dialogue was seen to be compatible with the housewife pursuing her domestic chores whilst listening. Thus, apart from a few attractive characters in whom teenagers find some visual pleasure, the key engagement with *Neighbours* is with the dialogue.

Given the proximity, intimacy and intensity of family and neighbourly relations in *Neighbours*, much of the dialogue involves private, intimate talk between family, friends and neighbours, very often about other people behind their backs. The complex interweaving of different story-lines in the continuous narrative depends on a constant succession of revelations about the secrets and past and present lives of characters, and speculation about their futures. For young people in Southall, this way of talking is equated with gossip. In the following spontaneous exchange about soaps, in a classroom setting, four girls and one boy (Onray), all aged sixteen, discuss gossip in soaps and in their own communication:

INDERJEET: All soaps are really bitchy, it's just like talking behind someone's back.

ONRAY: Yeah there's a lot of spite in soaps.

DALVINDER: But isn't that what we do in real life?

ONRAY: What?

DALVINDER: Talk about people behind their back.

INDERJEET: Not as much as they do in soaps.

DALVINDER: Come off it! We do!

INDERJEET: But they base their story-lines on it.

DALVINDER: We might not do it straight but you can't say we don't do it.

TALVINDER: We all do, everyone does.

AMRIT: I gossip.

DALVINDER: I spend my time gossiping, you can't say that you don't talk about somebody, even if someone is there in the room, you still talk about them behind their back, even if you're not saying anything bad about them, just general conversation, you're still talking about someone else, it's just a way of socialising.

AMRIT: Like when you get together with your mates and you say, 'Wanna hear the latest?'

TALVINDER: AND gain attention for a while.

INDERJEET: You can even make it up and gain attention.

DALVINDER: Valid point!

The definitions of gossip presented here confirm those quoted and discussed earlier. The transition from talking about soap gossip to real gossip is made with relative ease, while the distinction is upheld between gossip which is malign and that which is harmless. This exchange demonstrates the formal parallel which these young people draw between soap gossip and real gossip. For them, it is not simply that soap characters gossip, as they do, but that soap storylines are based on it, as are many of the stories that they construct in course of their everyday lives.

Soaps are characterised by oral forms of storytelling, defined by specific time-structures, which fragment narration across a longer time frame than is the case in any other genre, and thus extend suspense and heighten curiosity over days and weeks rather than hours. This bears similarities to the stories which are constructed by young people through fragments of gossip which accumulate on a daily basis and may go on to acquire the currency of rumour. This relates to one of the most important features of soap narration: the way in which knowledge and information is distributed between the characters in the diagesis and between characters and viewers.

What Barthes (1975) refers to as the 'hermeneutic code' involves the establishment and resolution of questions and enigmas, and the delicate balance between denying readers (or viewers) information, and revealing it. Soap viewers are placed in a privileged position of knowledge through the shifting narrative point of view and the seeming omnipresence of the camera. But at any moment viewers also lack significant information as a result of narrational strategies which generate information gaps, as well as the conventional cliff-hanger endings. Viewers, like the recipients of gossip, are in possession of secret knowledge that is shared; and this in turn catalyses speculation about how a character will react when this knowledge is revealed to them. As is often the case in melodrama (Neale, 1986), the question of the distribution of knowledge between characters and audience is crucial. In conjunction with the timing of revelations which determine the future or fate of a character, powerful affective reactions can be produced by the viewers' privileged position – notably, in melodrama, by what Neale calls the 'too late' syndrome, where tears are generated when a character finally discovers what the viewers have long known, but is helpless to intervene to alter their own or others' fates.

As Buckingham points out, in an argument which dovetails with mine: 'the pleasure of gossip about soap opera is the pleasure of sharing secrets to which only a select few are privy' (1987: 64). In his view too, the essential identification is with the processes of narration; *what* is revealed may be a source of great fascination in itself, but it is the *process of revelation*, both within the narrative and in its subsequent reconstruction in discussion, which constitutes the most important source of pleasure. In soaps, multiple enigmas are initiated, developed and resolved at different rates, and so the viewer's curiosity is in a constant state of arousal. Curiosity is partially appeased by the information to which the viewer has privileged access. As with gossip, we know intimate secrets of characters' lives, we know which other characters share this information, but we also know that those wishing to conceal their secrets are unaware that we are privy to this knowledge. This places viewers in a position of power in that they know something others do not know – but also in a position of powerlessness in that they are unable to use this knowedge, unlike with real-life gossip, to intervene in the course of events.

Soap viewers' activities involve the processing and manipulation of information in a way that differs markedly from those required by other texts. The continuous narrative means that regular viewers are in possession of a great deal more knowledge about characters and past events than in any other genre. In the case of *Coronation Street*, it may stretch back over 30 years. The broadcast life of *Neighbours* in Britain was five or six years at the time of fieldwork; thus, many 16-year-old viewers would have been watching *Neighbours* on a daily basis (on weekdays) for nearly one third of their lives. It is not surprising therefore that young people learn to live with television families, like the Robinsons, the Bishops and the Mangels, almost as extensions of their own lives. The range and depth of background information which viewers accrue over the years facilitates the cognitive and verbal activities during and after viewing. Buckingham (1987) summarises these succinctly: recollecting past events that we have seen; imagining past events that we have not seen; formulating hypotheses about future events; testing these hypotheses in the light of new information; making inferences in order to explain actions and events; processing new information; developing or consolidating our knowledge of characters and judging these characters and their relationships. All these cognitive activities which take place while viewing form the basis of the verbal discourse in which young people engage in both the domestic and peer contexts. These are very similar to the processes, referred to earlier, that gossip undergoes in becoming rumour: briefly, the levelling of detail by selection and the sharpening of detail by omission. Moreover, the characters of the soaps are themselves involved in these processes of story construction and evaluation. The cross-cutting connections between the large number of characters populating the dense social networks of soaps offer multiple perspectives to viewers, which they take into consideration when making their judgements about any particular scenario. The cliff-hanger endings and the suspense that is generally created through the processes of narration further encourage speculative talk about characters and their relationships. Hence young people's marked tendency to perceive soaps in terms of gossip and to identify with the processes of narration rather than with any individual character.

However, this is not to say that the pleasure of *Neighbours*, for Southall youth, lies in the formal qualities of its narration alone. As I have already suggested, its viewers are also keenly interested in certain aspects of the thematic substance of its narratives. The following sections address the ways in which my informants, in their talk about 'community' relations, kinship, courtship and marriage, draw on the soap as a resource for the comparative evaluation of their social and cultural experiences, and for the articulation of aspirations for change.

'COMMUNITY'

Young people compare and contrast neighbourly relations in Southall with those in *Neighbours*. They do so by juxtaposing notions of 'how things are' and 'how they ought to be'. The theme song suggests an idealised mode of conduct, and when young people sing it, they do so with ironic inflexions:

Neighbours, everybody needs good neighbours
With a little understanding you can make a perfect plan
Neighbours are there for one another
That's why good neighbours become good friends

Neighbours everybody needs good neighbours
Just a friendly word each morning makes a better day
Neighbours should be there for one another
That's why good neighbours become good friends.

In fact this ideal is constantly threatened by feuds between neighbours in the soap narrative which, merely in order to continue, actually depends on an interminable succession of misunderstandings and conflicts between neighbours. Rajesh and Kulbir are 16-year-old boys. They both watch *Neighbours* regularly. They compare what they see as a rosy state of affairs on Ramsay Street with their own experiences of neighbours. The following extract is taken from a taped conversation they had about soaps:

RAJESH: It's like living in a dream, innit? Because everyone gets on so well together.

KULBIR: Everything happens in Ramsay Street.

RAJESH: It's an ideal way of living innit? Cos all the neighbours get on and that, they get on really well and they're always there when you need them – take my neighbours for a start, I don't know when man, we ain't spoken to them since I don't know when man, them on the right-hand side, we spoke to them when we moved in but we ain't spoken to them since, they're stuck up and that innit?

KULBIR: It's like where I live innit?

RAJESH: In Ramsay Street that's how you wanna be innit?

KULBIR: Yeah but look at it, it's a closed street, it's a dead-end street innit?

RAJESH: Yeah.

KULBIR: Well I got cousins living in a dead end street and they don't get on with their neighbours the way they show it.

RAJESH: Yeah but it's just fiction innit? Who gets on with their neighbours that way, tell me?

KULBIR: Nobody.

RAJESH: Exactly!

They make a straight comparison between neighbourly relations in the soap and in their own lives and the ideal nature of neighbourly relations in the soap is dismissed as 'fiction'. They do not mention the conflict and mis-understandings which propel the narrative forward, although they must be aware of them. This might be due to the high incidence of short-term conflicts which get (more or less) speedily resolved compared to the rela-tively few long-term conflicts which remain unresolved for months or years. By contrast, in real life and in Southall, neighbours are not seen to get on well. They may be 'stuck up' or just as likely, they may be deliberately excluded from domestic and family intimacies. (This is certainly not unique to Southall with its concerns regarding *izzat*. According to *Social Trends 1990*, 82 per cent of the British population claim they would not have moved into their home if they had known who their neighbours were.)

The contrast between how things are and how one would like them to be is evident when Rajesh comments that 'Ramsay Street is how you want to be'. But neighbourly intimacy and support in times of trouble could militate against the primary value of family honour. This is also apparent in an exchange between Camila and Sukhi, both 16-year-old girls. However here there is a reversal of the previous situation. In this case it is not the neighbours who are 'stuck up' but the speaker's family who need to protect themselves from gossip and interference. The exchange took place in an informal group discussion in a Media Studies lesson, while watching the title sequence of neighbours. Camila's dislike of her own neighbours becomes apparent, though, like many exchanges, this begins in earnest only to end in farce. As the title sequence, showing all the neighbours gathered around the Ramsay's swimming pool, appears on screen, the girls are singing along to the theme song: 'Neighbours should be there for one another ... ':

> CAMILA: But oh my god! [laughing] Neighbours gossip! My neigh-
> bours are horrible, they're always looking out the window watching
> what we're doing, they're Mangels.
> SUKHI: Yeah, real neighbours don't always get on so well, I mean
> what do neighbours share?
> CAMILA: Swimming pools! ... even their knickers! [raucous laughter]

Whilst this last comment is an obvious send-up, a way of gaining attention and esteem among friends whose main preoccupation is 'having a laugh', the point is clear: real neighbours are more likely to gossip about you than share things, and thus hardly behave in the ideal way portrayed in the title sequence. This raises questions about 'neighbourliness' in a town which is often constructed by outsiders as a 'community', and within which the term 'community' is also frequently invoked in a variety of senses.

Neighbours offers models of, and opportunities for talking about, the tensions which exist between families and their neighbours. The delicate balance between privacy and sociability is a tension that requires working through by neighbours and friends in any local area, but this tension takes on culturally distinctive hues in Southall, where there is a very high premium on privacy and where gossip poses a particular threat. These factors are somewhat at odds with the notions typically implied by invocations of 'community'. In Southall, this term is often used to express a range of meanings: from a sense of 'belonging' and loyalty to a place, to the sharing of similar backgrounds and values; from the sense of a shared social and geographic boundary, to a distinctiveness from other local areas. However, notions of 'community' are highly ambiguous and largely mythical, for internal cleavages of status, gender, generation and, most crucially in Southall, religion, are more significant markers in daily life than is any supposedly unified 'community'. Indeed, the term is typically invoked when inhabitants feel some threat from the outside, or when a spokesperson elects him or herself to speak on behalf of the 'community'. In such cases the sense of 'community' is strengthened and for a short while differences are forgotten.

Whilst individuals may consider themselves to be part of a 'community', and many young people in Southall do, in the sense that they have a strong sense of shared local identity, they also consider themselves members, respectively, of several different 'communities' which coexist within Southall, 'communities' of religion and cultural heritage. And it is the networks of actual social relations, maintained both within and outside the local area, which count when it comes to questions of the control of information about family life, questions of *izzat*. The high density of kin living locally and the closely knit nature of the associated social networks form the basis of the communications networks that exist.

Social ties may be strong, as well as highly competitive, between families whose members attend the same place of worship or the same place of work; families of school friends; and families formerly from the same village in India, who are treated 'like kin', ostensibly, although relations are not subject to the same binding obligations of unrestricted reciprocity which apply to 'true kin':

> GURINDER: We stay close to families who have come from the same village in India, if you can imagine these families lived together for hundreds and hundreds of years and often have the same ancestors going way back, they used to do the same jobs, they were the same caste, they shared their experiences over time and that makes you very close and that closeness usually continues in England, they are more like real neighbours but they don't live next door.

In the parental culture the ideals of community and neighbourly relations are crystallised in the word *baradari* (or 'brotherhood') and founded upon village life in India, where historical, regional, religious and caste similarities forge a very deep sense of solidarity and belonging. These relations have become idealised in 'exile', partly through the influence of the nostalgia propagated by Hindi films in which, as we saw in Chapter 2, traditional village life is represented as 'morally pure' in contrast to the corruption of modern city life. Such ideals are hardly to be realised in the urban context of Southall. Ballard, discussing second-generation South Asian-British youth, argues that:

> Although everyone accepts that family loyalties should be sustained, the value of participation in more far-flung social networks of extra-familial kinship is looked upon with increasing scepticism, especially since they tend to generate a suffocating traffic of gossip and scandal. (1982: 196)

There is nevertheless an attempt to maintain village ties where they exist, and close friends are certainly treated in many contexts as if they were kin.

In some ways the social networks of certain families in Southall bear some residual features of those in Punjab villages, where component families within the local group are so closely connected and related that they are clearly marked off from external relations. In such networks, privacy is at a premium: it is not something that has been valued or even experienced traditionally, but it has become an imperative as a result of the dislocations of migration and settlement. If one adds to this the general lack of individual privacy which is a feature of extended families, one can begin to appreciate how families encapsulated within activities known to so many cannot escape the informal sanctions of gossip and public opinion. In this sense, the 'community' of Ramsay Street appears, to Southall youth, to represent an alternative ideal, even though this perception might not seem to do justice to the less than idyllic neighbourly relations which actually obtain in the narrative.

KINSHIP

Whilst young people's own families and those in their social networks provide their primary frame of reference about family life, soap families extend this frame of reference and offer alternative sets of families which young people use to compare and contrast, judge and evaluate and, in some cases, attempt to critique and transform aspects of their own family life. As we have seen, migration and settlement in Britain has meant that Punjabi families are undergoing significant changes in their economic, social and moral environments. Punjabi family life is recognised by young people to be based upon sets of norms and values, duties and responsibilities, roles and expectations, rules and regulations which differ in certain fundamental respects from those which apply in 'white' families. In some families these are being revised, whilst in others there is an attempt to maintain more or less strict adherence to traditional family norms and values. Thus parents differ markedly in the degree of conformity to traditional values they expect of, and attempt to impose upon, their children; young people too vary considerably in the degree and nature of the rebelliousness or conformity they express verbally and or in their behaviour.

Despite this variety, and change and adaptation, certain fundamental features of kinship organisation prevail, albeit in modified form, in conjunction with certain sets of norms and values. The very high density of kin living in Southall is a distinctive feature of local life. In the youth survey (see Appendix 2), 34 per cent of respondents reported more than ten cousins living in or near Southall; 36 per cent of Sikh respondents reported grandparents living in or near Southall (Appendix 2a); over one third of households have between six and eight people eating together. These figures point to a prevalence of larger households and suggest that one in three is a three-generational household. The very high density of kin ensures that the principles of binding reciprocity, respect and co-operation (rather than self-interest) prevail, even though many families are now breaking into smaller household units.

The relative complexity of kinship ties (compared with white families) is evident in the extensive kinship terminology which young people have at their disposal and which they use to delineate, with precision, an individual's position in the family. Thus four kinds of uncle and five kinds of aunt are distinguished by terms which express, for example, the distinction between the father's elder and younger brothers. This has consequences

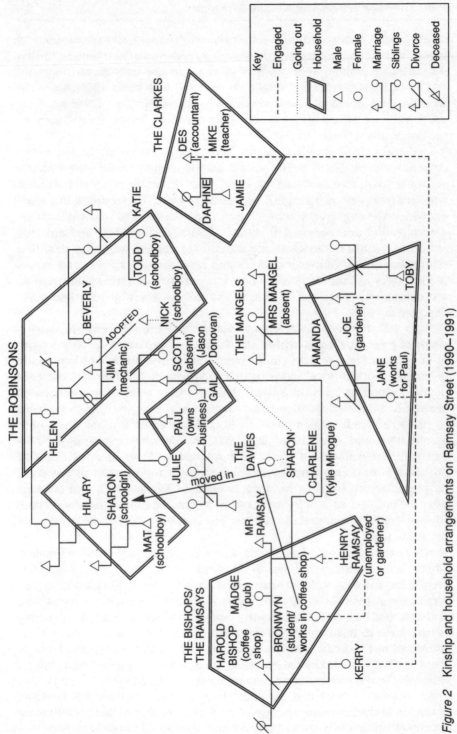

Figure 2 Kinship and household arrangements on Ramsay Street (1990–1991)

for their perceptions of kinship relations in *Neighbours*, as competence and speed in defining kinship relations with precision assists them in understanding soap families. One group of 16-year-old girls constructed a kinship and household diagram for *Neighbours* (p. 167) with great ease, displaying an impressive depth of knowledge about the kinship ties. Their informal talk while they were working on this diagram is one of the main sources of the comments reported below.

In Punjabi families individual needs or desires are subordinated to the demands of *izzat*. Many young people find themselves in a position where, at home, parents claim the superiority of Punjabi cultural traditions and family values over English or 'western' ways. Experiences at school or when viewing *Neighbours*, they claim, encourage individual self-determination and personal freedom. Whilst most parents and children alike are sceptical of the wholesale adoption of western ways, it is clear that established norms and values, duties and responsibilities, roles and expectations, rules and regulations are up for negotiation as far as young people are concerned. 'Soap talk' is one of the means whereby such issues are negotiated.

Soap talk further allows young people and their parents to discuss changes in gender roles within the family. Approximately 70 per cent of mothers are now in paid employment outside the home, predominantly in manual work in local industries (see Appendix 1c). Only 28 per cent define themselves as 'housewives'. In theory, at least, this has allowed greater financial independence for women and in some families served to challenge traditional domestic roles. However, it is clear from both quantitative and qualitative data that conventional expectations prevail and that women and girls are burdened with an unequal share of domestic duties. Furthermore, women are over-represented in low-paid, part-time labour, often without the benefits of a contract. Those mothers who are in full-time employment often do gruelling amounts of overtime to supplement the household income and are, in some families, the main breadwinners.

All these factors, moral, economic and social, exert pressures on families. There are marked variations in the ways in which different families respond to and deal with challenges to traditional family norms and values. Yet at age sixteen the family and wider kin are the primary source of love and affection, as well as of control and constraint in one's life. Young people have to develop verbal bargaining skills if they are to assert their individual needs on the family stage and if they are to ensure some involvement in decision-making about their lives with regard to their future, especially in the spheres of education, work and marriage.

Many girls consider that the code of *izzat* restricts young people from asserting and expressing themselves openly, as this is held to militate against the primary virtues of respect and obedience to one's elders:

LUKBIR: It drowns your own sense of identity, you can't do what
you want, you always have to think of your family honour [. . .] you
are supposed to be modest, simple, reserved [. . .] you're not supposed to wear make-up and you should cover your legs and above all
you shouldn't talk back to older people.

In *Neighbours*, young people, especially girls, are seen to exercise considerably more freedom and control over their lives than do youngsters in
Southall. Therefore one of the most attractive features of *Neighbours*
to young people is watching how young people assert themselves,
especially verbally, to their parents and elders. The favourite characters
like Bronwyn and Henry, for example, are admired because they are good
'backchatters', or because they know how to stand up for themselves and
what they believe in. Watching how young people negotiate their family
relationships is a key attraction of *Neighbours*.

Gender roles within the family are of major concern to many girls and
although families vary considerably in the restrictions they impose on girls,
it is a widely held view that double standards exist:

AMRIT: You can see that families in *Neighbours* are more flexible,
they do things together as a family, they don't expect that girls should
stay at home and do housework and cooking, boys and girls
are allowed to mix much more freely [. . .]. Indian families do go out
together to eat and that but most of us can only get out with
the family, they can't go out with their mates like the boys do [. . .].
Boys live on the outside and girls on the inside.

In making judgements about soap families in their everyday interactions
at home and at school young people are giving indirect expressions to
norms associated with family life. For example, the Robinson family is seen
as ideal in the sense that they are loyal and supportive yet offer their
younger members independence, space and privacy:

PARAMJIT: They stick by each other as a family and always support
each other through bad moments [. . .]. They trust each other and
if they have a problem they don't try to avoid it, they sit down
and talk about it logically and reasonably and try to sort it out
together, they don't end up rowing [. . .]. There's a great family bond
between them all.

Paramjit's view of the Robinson family is typical. Above all, effective
communication in the family is valued and seen to ensure the bonds of
love and loyalty. The soap's matriarch and grandmother character,
Helen Robinson, is pivotal to the perceived success of this family's
relationships. She is seen to have a unique ability to listen to and understand people, including teenagers, and their problems. She is everyone's

ideal 'agony aunt'. She is caring and understanding and she offers realistic, sound advice. She is able to help young and old people sort out their problems.

Trust between parents and children is an area of key concern to many girls and poses a serious dilemma. Even a slight aberration in behaviour may, in some families, incur a breakdown of trust on the part of parents. Open and honest communication may also lead to a breakdown of trust or to parents becoming suspicious that their daughter or son is getting 'spoilt' (in the sense of 'tainted') and this may lead to even tighter control and regulation of their daughter's movements and communication with friends. But some girls claim that they, too, have reasons to lack trust in their parents. In some cases, the discovery of a romantic liaison may lead parents to quickly arrange a marriage without involving their daughter in the decision-making. The issue of open, truthful communication and trust between parents and children recurs frequently in talk about soaps and real life.

The Ramsay/Bishop household is admired for being a 'fun' family, mainly because of Henry, who is the key young comic character in the soap. He is seen to be given support and independence:

KAMALJIT: They have a nice open atmosphere in their house, they're funny, I like the way Henry picks on Harold [his stepfather] and the way Madge and Harold argue, they always stand by each other but they let their kids stand up on their own two feet, like when Henry has problems they let him discover for himself how hard it is to do certain things like get a good job [. . .]. I like how they all get on.

The Mangels are seen as less successful:

AMAR: It's a small family so it's not interesting, Joe is crafty and not that respectable, they're a rough-going family, they use a lot more slang, they don't have people round for dinner parties and that like the Robinsons, they treat each other as strangers, not as a family, they're not organised and they're hopeless with housework, they also interfere with others when no one wants them to get involved.

But Hilary's household is seen as the least successful of all, and she is also despised as the major gossip character:

FARZANA: I hate Hilary because she's always bossing Matt and Sharon, she never lets them do what they want, she rules their lives and expects them to take orders [. . .] she makes everyone lives hell [. . .] she's a really bitchy gossip [. . .] she spoils teenagers' fun [. . .]. Her way of being a mother is no good! She never listens and you can't tell her anything, she's not to be trusted.

It is clear from these comments that young people are using these families to articulate their own emergent norms and values and are indirectly commenting upon their own families. But while they use the families in *Neighbours* to judge their own, the reverse case is also true. Given the limited access to 'white' families, the viewing of soaps enables young people some, albeit fictional, insight into them. It is frequently commented upon that the Robinson household is an extended family consisting of three generations. It is also seen to share some similarities with Southall families, in that they have kinship links with two other households in the same street:

BALJIT: It's an extended family, they've got Helen living with them and then there's Paul who lives in the same road and Hilary, who's Jim's cousin's sister in the same road [. . .] it's a bit like our family.

However, this is as far as the perceived similarity goes.

Their sophisticated understanding of kinship ties draws their attention to what most regard as the highly unconventional constitution of many Ramsay Street households, which are 'reconstituted' families as a result either of death, divorce or remarriage.

BALJIT: We have bigger families than they do and our households aren't shared like theirs, ours are strictly for family [. . .], there isn't as much divorce and single-parent families [. . .], there's no swapping around of households like Bronwyn does, she's lived in nearly every household in the street [. . .], there's no lodgers or people being adopted who come to live with you.

Sharing one's house with people other than kin by blood or by marriage is considered most unusual. Taking in lodgers, especially those who have lived in the same street, would be considered highly risky, especially as regards safeguarding family honour and protecting the family from revelations about their private internal affairs.

Neighbours is seen to be 'white' rather than Australian. As Diljit points out, 'All families in *Neighbours* are white, I don't really see them as Australian'. Young people readily admit that they know little or nothing about white families:

ANOPAMA: We don't know nothing about white families [. . .] except the Robinsons [bursting into laughter] [. . .] they're not even real, they're only a soap family [. . .] we probably have very stereotyped ideas, it makes you realise what sheltered lives we lead.

Indeed many young people claim they get most of their ideas of 'white' family life from soaps like *Neighbours*:

PARAMJIT: We get more ideas about white families from TV than we do from our own experience, so its helpful to see how they live and relate to one another because you get to know the characters in their family situation.

Viewing the private life of 'white' families is seen to serve a useful function:

MOHINDERPAL: If we didn't see white families on TV, like in *Neighbours*, we'd probably be even more suspicious of white people even more cos we don't know what they're really like and we don't chat to them [. . .] and we'd think they were all racist to us but when you see families like the Robinsons you think, oh my God! they're just like us, they love one another and they look after their chldren and they're not as bad as, er . . . um . . . some Indian people think they are.

But *Neighbours* also encourages slightly overinflated ideas about the 'freedom' that young 'whites' have:

RASHPAL: They've got more freedom than us, they can go out and stay out until a reasonable time, families seem to care less about what others think of them [. . .] they don't have arranged marriages and it's like dating is the norm [. . .] it seems so strange to us that a girl could bring home her boyfriend and sit round the table and eat with her parents [. . .] and that her parents would approve!

Of course, these issues – of 'dating', or romance and courtship rituals, and marriage – are a prime area of young people's concern, consistently highlighted by their soap talk.

COURTSHIP AND MARRIAGE

Teenage romance is central to many of the narrative strands in *Neighbours* and to young people's talk, both 'soap talk' and 'real talk', yet it is taboo in the parental culture. Fifty-eight per cent of young people surveyed agreed with the statement that 'dating is normal at my age'; whilst 40 per cent agreed that 'It's not normal in my culture and I respect that'. Sixty-seven per cent agreed that if young people date 'Parents should know more about it but be more understanding', whilst 31 per cent agreed that 'It's all right as long as you keep it a secret'. Only 10 per cent confirmed that 'My parents think that 'it's normal at my age' (see Appendix 7a). Of course this raises the question of what is meant by 'dating' or 'going out'. Since 'dating' is conducted primarily within the limits of school life it may simply mean that there is a mutual acknowledgement of attraction which in fact never progresses much beyond fleeting but longing glances in the school corridors. But many 'couples' establish themselves as 'steady' boyfriend and girlfriend and, by doing so, acquire considerable status. And one of the major causes of friction in the peer culture are the romantic liaisons that are constantly breaking up and being remade. 'Steadies' take time off school to meet in the park, to go to the cinema or to attend an afternoon bhangra disco in London. Generally speaking, dating couples are extremely resourceful in subverting parental strictures. Increasingly, young people are 'dating' at an early stage (some as young as twelve) and it is gaining widespread acceptance in the peer culture.

Young people use soap operas like *Neighbours* to work through some of the tensions that arise from their 'illicit' relationships and from their attempts to keep them hidden from the family. They keenly observe how romantic relationships are conducted on screen and eagerly follow the ups and downs of courting couples and the associated rituals of gift exchange, holding hands, kissing, etc. They pay special attention to the language of romance and the conventions associated with declarations of feelings. The relationship between Henry and Bronwyn was a focal point of interest at the time of fieldwork. Henry is one of the most popular characters of the soap, due to his perceived attractiveness, comical nature and pop-star status. Familiarity with romantic narratives is evident in discussions of Henry and Bronwyn's relationship. Talk focused on the nature of the obstacles faced by the couple and speculations about how they would over-come their problems. Ongoing judgements on the courting couple were made and there was an overriding belief that they would overcome their problems and establish an enduring bond:

SAIRA: In spite of their ups and downs Henry and Bronwyn are made for one another, but with the Mike situation you learn from them that relationships are not easy and why sometimes sacrifices have to be made.

A successful relationship is equated with the notion of endurance, and this is attributed to skill in sorting out problems, the ability to communi-cate and compromise and to keep respect for one another rather than argue. One of the least successful relationships was seen to be that between Jane and Des, due primarily to their age difference:

GITA: He's well into his thirties and she's only just twenty and she wants to work and to share housework but he wants a wife who will stay at home and cook and look after his child but Jane can never be a proper mother to that child because it's not hers.

Work is also seen as another potential obstacle to relationships: 'Paul always puts his work before Gail [. . .] he's too ambitious and neglects Gail and makes her unhappy'. But the key problem remains that most girls in Southall are not permitted to have boyfriends:

PARAMJIT: Girls in *Neighbours* are allowed to have boyfriends and have a good time whereas us Asian girls aren't allowed to be this independent so we seek it out in someone else. It's an asset, you know, to go out with someone, it looks good, some girls like to pretend they are someone else but it doesn't really work [. . .] but we like the independence that girls [in *Neighbours*] have because they are free and can do what they want.

Diljit, a 16-year-old Sikh boy, like many of his peers, studies how romantic relationships are conducted by observing couples on the screen:

When I was going out with Ruby and I used to see someone like Charlene and Scott [on *Neighbours*], I used to daydream off, especially when they were talking about what they'd been doing and then I just used to look at them and think to myself, 'How can I improve?' [laughing] I used to do that [. . .] like when he's talking and turns round and says something like [laughing] 'I love you' and I'd just imagine saying it and think, what do we talk about when we're together? Is there any way of improving? and you just think that by looking you might be able to get better at it [. . .] and maybe you think what are these two doing wrong? [. . .]. In a way I think soaps are good for you [. . .] but it depends what you take from them.

Young people's observations of courting couples and courtship rituals are later included in intimate talk among close friends about their own relationships and their dating peers. Couples on and off screen are compared and contrasted for their suitability and success or lack of it.

But even in the peer context, it is the girls' behaviour which is most closely scrutinised. If a girl is seen to flirt 'excessively', wear 'too much' make-up or skirts which are 'too short', or if she deceives a boy by 'two-timing', then she will soon acquire the label 'slag'. There is no equivalent term available for boys, except perhaps 'stud' – which has more favourable connotations. Thus, despite the rising incidence of what is decribed as 'dating', double standards plague the peer culture. Amrita (quoted in Chapter 1) pointed out how these operate in brother–sister relationships, underlining how older brothers, whose protective role is dictated by family norms, 'would not let their sisters date a boy, but they would conveniently forget that they are also dating someone else's sister.'

Viewing *Neighbours* and talking about it in the peer group enables young people in Southall to compare and contrast their family lives and neighbourhood with 'white culture on the box'. This activity undoubtedly contributes to their consciousness of cultural difference and encourages them in their aspirations towards change. *Neighbours* often catalysed inter-generational debate and even conflict. However, its power to do so resides, in the last analysis, less in the substance of its representations than in the homology between the modes of narration which characterise it as a soap, and those which prevail in the dense kinship, social and communicative networks of Southall. In order to appreciate more fully the nature of young people's aspirations, it is necessary to consider the questions of taste and style addressed in my final chapter.

Chapter 6

Cool bodies: TV ad talk

It is now a common theoretical assumption among cultural theorists and anthropologists that social identities, differences and inequalities are shaped and legitimated through our material and cultural consumption (Appadurai, 1986; Douglas and Isherwood, 1979; McCracken, 1988; Miller, 1987). Bourdieu has given the now classic demonstration of the way in which distinctions of social class and status are expressed through distinctions in taste: 'taste classifies and it classifies the classifier' (1984: 6). This final chapter examines how ethnicity, as a form of cultural difference, shapes and in turn is shaped by material and symbolic consumption practices and aspirations. It investigates how young Punjabis identify and distinguish, critique and endorse particular hierarchies of taste and style in how they look, what they eat and drink, and in what they find beautiful or ugly, 'cool' or 'naff' (or '*pendu*'). It demonstrates how, from a position of generally limited consumer potential, young people articulate their preferences, distinctions and aspirations as consumers through talk about the TV ads which they consume, both literally and metaphorically.

The need to be and look 'cool' and 'safe' was repeatedly stressed in the survey returns (see Appendix 11). Dress and other aspects of personal appearance and style had to be 'cool' above all, according to 66 per cent of boys. Girls gave it rather less priority; indeed among girls, only 47 per cent considered 'to look cool' as the prime consideration, and it was narrowly overtaken by 'to be respectable' (49 per cent) or 'to stay OK with my parents' (48 per cent) – matters to which boys claimed to attach rather less importance. This of course reflects both boys' greater freedom from parental constraint, and the wider range of public contexts in which they are likely to appear; and the paramount importance attached, in the parental culture of *izzat*, to female modesty and therefore girls' dress codes (cf. Yates, 1990: 78). Girls' pragmatism is reflected in their responses to the survey, but it is clear from fieldwork that they are highly inventive when it comes to subverting parental demands, as well as the norms of school uniform, in order to create a 'cool look' for themselves.

Ads which target young people address them as consumers in an international teenage market and aim simultaneously to construct and satisfy a range of consumer needs and problems, tastes and desires focussed around the body in a physical, social and aesthetic sense. Youth cultures are increasingly transnational cultures of consumption which apparently transcend ethnic and other divisions. However, the hierarchies of taste and style which are endorsed among the youth of Southall are marked not only by ethnic, gender and generational differences but also by material and other cultural differences. In their ad talk young people discuss these differences; they clarify distinctions between American, British and Indian consumer lifestyles and aspirations; and they talk in a manner that would otherwise appear utopian – unrealistic aspirations and desires and fantasies acquire varying degrees of plausibility and credibility in ad talk. The discourses of advertising are reproduced and recreated in everyday discussions of ads as they fantasise about how easy life would be if one used this product; or how successful, popular or beautiful one could be if one bought this product.

Consuming an ad for a product often involves buying into an image, an identity, a fantasy, a feeling and even, as we shall see in the case of the Coca Cola advertisements, a myth – a mythical construction of an American teenage lifestyle and of America itself. Arguably, America, as experienced through the media has itself become the prime object of consumption and a symbol of pleasure (Webster, 1988). The ad talk of Southall teenagers highlights the way in which ads sell products through promoting a set of associated values or qualities which are 'magically' transferred to, or conferred upon, the consumer in the act of their consumption (Williams, 1980). TV advertisements function as myths and metaphors, providing people with simple stories and explanations through which certain ideals and values are communicated and through which people organise their thoughts and experiences and come to make sense of the world in which they live.

This chapter focuses on three key areas of teenage consumer culture, all of which revolve around the body: fashion and style; body-care and beauty products; and food and drink. Young people's greater awareness of ads in these areas is apparent in their TV talk and is also evident from data obtained through a small-scale survey of seventy 16- and 17-year-olds (involving equal numbers of boys and girls). Selected results of this survey will be used to give an overview of local teenage consumer culture and perceptions of TV advertising. The second section explores the cultural significance of clothes for Southall youth, highlighting the particular appeal of black American 'street culture' and its incorporation into local style and fashion, and presenting a hierarchy of style types gleaned from ad talk. The section on body-care and beauty products investigates young people's preoccupation with matters of physical appearance, their criteria of physical attractiveness, and their responses to the dominant ideology of beauty, purveyed by the mass media, which equates attractiveness with white skin colour. The fourth section addresses the reception of Coca Cola ads, and examines how young Punjabis' aspirations towards cultural change are articulated through talk about these ads, which are seen to represent a very desirable, though idealised, American teenage lifestyle. Finally, tastes in food, especially the appeal of fast foods from high-street outlets and pre-prepared microwavable foods, are examined in the context of local food culture and youth leisure activities.

TEENAGE CONSUMER CULTURE AND TV ADVERTISING

Consumer culture among the youth of Southall is marked by clear gender differences in spending power, most girls being at a material disadvantage as compared with boys when 'pocket money' is used as an index. According to survey data the majority of 16- and 17-year-old girls (56 per cent) receive between £1 and £5 pocket money per week, and 22 per cent do not receive pocket money on a regular basis at all. In contrast, just under 80 per cent of boys receive between £5 and £20 per week. Some boys (28 per cent) and fewer girls (18 per cent) are able to supplement the money that they receive from their parents through part-time employment. But such differences in material resources also derive from the greater participation of boys in public life and their higher status in most Punjabi families where they are treated preferentially when it comes to money and household duties.

It is customary that the eldest son in the family continues to live with his parents, brings his wife to live with them and provides for his ageing parents. Parents have a vested interest in treating their eldest son well, if not indulgently. By ensuring his material comfort while young they hope to secure their future comfort in old age. In contrast, daughters leave the family home – often at considerable expense, since a dowry is usually paid – and so are seen to represent a financial burden on families which is unlikely to produce a return. This is why the birth of a boy is usually celebrated while that of a girl is not. While some families do indeed adhere strictly to such traditional practices, especially the more religious families, many are re-inventing such traditions in the British context and finding new ways of organising themselves so as to ensure that the family continues to look after elderly parents and other relatives. But it is still commonly accepted that in most families boys receive preferential treatment.

Young people may at times influence their parents' consumer decisions, especially those who mediate between 'British' and 'Indian' consumer preferences. Females appear to be more vulnerable to the persuasive powers of ads than boys, but it is likely that girls are simply more willing to admit to this. Sixty per cent of girls and 46 per cent of boys claim to have bought a product because they had seen an ad and wanted to try it. Just under 80 per cent of girls report having bought a body-care or beauty product because of an ad, as compared with only 28 per cent of boys. Sixty-eight per cent of girls report that they usually spend most of their money on food and drink, followed by magazines (42 per cent), music (20 per cent), clothes and beauty products (17 per cent). Many girls regularly buy Indian magazines such as *Cineblitz*, which covers new Hindi films, gossip about the stars and the latest Indian fashions. They also select from the range of British magazines for teenage girls such as *Just Seventeen* which covers romance, beauty and fashion. Boys spend most of their money on food and drink (45 per cent), followed by video games arcades (26 per cent). This is clearly a male-specific, public activity. In contrast girls neither play nor spend money on video games. Boys also spend more money than girls on videos, though spending on music cassettes is roughly similar.

One of the most tangible examples of the way that the discourses of TV and everyday life are intermeshed is when jingles, catch-phrases and humorous storylines of favourite ads are incorporated into everyday speech. Ads provide a set of shared cultural reference points, images and metaphors which spice local speech. There are countless examples of this in the data on TV talk but to mention just one: a common refrain which accompanies a spectacular feat, such as a goal, is the slogan, 'I bet *he* drinks Carling Black Label!' The exceptional subtlety and humour of some British ads no doubt encourages most young people (86 per cent) to think of TV ads as a form of entertainment rather than as a means of persuasion or information, although they are well aware of the persuasive functions of advertising. Girls especially appear to enjoy discussing TV ads with their friends, perhaps as a recompense for their lack of consumer power. Yet just under half of all respondents claim that they find most ads boring and hardly ever discuss them, and just under 40 per cent claim that when the ads come on they usually go and get something to eat or drink – suggesting that they only pay attention to ads which they find entertaining. The majority of young people claim that they take most notice of ads with good music (78 per cent), a funny storyline (74 per cent) and attractive characters (58 per cent). Other criteria, identified by under 50 per cent of respondents, include: 'a good slogan', 'ads showing products I would like to have' and 'ads which show products which relate to my dreams'.

The most popular categories of ads among both boys and girls concern products which aim at satisfying the body in a physical, aesthetic or social sense. It is not surprising that ads for soft drinks and snack food feature prominently in their discussions of ads since these ads are specifically targeted at the youth market and most money is spent on these products. Thereafter, gender differences in preferences for ads appear. While boys go for humorous ads, girls tend to prefer ads which feature male characters whom they find attractive, appealing or, in local idiom, 'hunky'. At the time of the survey (Autumn 1990) beer ads were the most popular among boys (these are also the most heavily gender-stereotyped ads), followed by ads for the sale of Electricity Shares, British Satellite Broadcasting and Hamlet cigars, which all combine humorous stories and appealing jingles. The most popular ad among girls was for LA Gear trainers, which features Michael Jackson, followed by those for Gillette and Levi 501 jeans. According to girls, these all feature 'hunky' males.

Differences in educational and cultural competence also affect how ads are discussed. For example, low educational achievers tend to interpret TV ads more literally than their more academically orientated and successful counterparts. The latter prefer ads which challenge and flatter their intelligence by encouraging them to solve enigmas, to spot cultural references and to demonstrate their appreciation of more subtle and sophisticated forms of humour. They also pay much more attention to the formal and aesthetic features, as well as to the persuasive techniques, of an ad. The British advertising industry is in fact highly respectful of the visual literacy and critical sophistication of young consumers. Contrary to the widely held commonsense view that youth are particularly gullible and vulnerable to being persuaded to desire or buy useless items:

> No other group is considered as discriminating, cynical and resistant to the hard sell. Furthermore, no other group is as astute at decoding the complex messages, cross-references and visual jokes of current advertising (except perhaps the industry itself). These critical skills are untutored and seem to arise out of an unprecedented intimacy with the cultural form of the TV commercial. (Nava and Nava, 1992: 172)

Nava and Nava's industry-based research indicates that young people consume commercials independently of the products advertised. This is clearly often the case, though one should be wary of dismissing the economic effectiveness of advertising: ads do succeed in persuading. And, moreover, it is far from clear that young consumers' sophisticated literacy and critical scepticism regarding the artistic or cultural form of ads, which are more or less brazen about their persuasive intent, also extend to other forms.

THE HIERARCHY OF STYLES

Style is self-defining and culturally defining. Clothes are part of the social and symbolic construction of a self which can be seen, classified and judged. Stylistic change, innovation and re-invention are at the heart of the in-built obsolescence of the products of consumer culture, but they are also a tangible facet of the processes of cultural change. The cultural importance attached to clothes, and the social and symbolic meanings they articulate and express, raises important questions about social identity and the criteria of group membership. Clothes are markers of religious distinction: for example, Punjabi Hindu women tend to wear saris whereas Sikhs and Muslims wear *salwaar kameez* and *chunni* (baggy pyjama trousers, tunic and chiffon scarf). Sikh men are distinguished by their turban and Muslim men by a lace prayer-cap; and the size and shape of turbans distinguishes Sikhs of East African and Punjabi background, while other markers identify supporters of the Khalistan movement. However, some of these distinctions are tending to fade in Britain where, for example, many Sikh men and boys cut their hair and do not wear turbans, and young people increasingly experiment with both 'western' and 'Indian' styles and fashion.

So clothes are an important manifestation, often a conscious public statement, of one's cultural affinities. While all young people wear 'western' clothes to school, 'Indian' clothes may be worn at home always, often or never, variously by desire or constraint. At family and religious celebrations – weddings, coming-of-age parties, at Diwali or Eid – 'Indian' clothes are always worn. Style may symbolise revolt. For example, on the Broadway, a miniskirt, tight T-shirt, high-heeled shoes and make-up would very speedily earn a girl the reputation of a 'slag' and would encourage all manner of harassment. On the other hand a girl who does not keep up with 'Indian' fashions is quickly labelled a *pendu* ('peasant'). The variety of styles and fashions open to young people and the kind of cultural distinctions, borrowings and cross-overs that characterise their lives is made explicit in the following interview exchange between two 16-year-old girls:

HARJINDER: You see at home we're totally one thing, and at school we're totally a different thing, in our dress, our behaviour, language.

KAMLESH: Not all of us, like, I'm the same at school as I am at home except in the way I dress. I'm not totally Indian at home cos my mum understands English, so it's easier to communicate in English, but when you come to school you have to sort of act the way other English people do, dress like them [. . .].

HAJINDER: At school we're all mixed up, English, black, white, coloured, Sikhs, Muslims, Christians, Hindus, at home it's just one culture.

KAMLESH: But you can't really say there's such a thing as British culture because within that you've got other people, you've got coloureds, English, Asians and blacks and sometimes you find each of these in a group [of friends] and they all mix their cultures together so you could pick up the way a Rasta person dresses or talks or white people who learn the Indian lingo [. . .].

HARJINDER: And now Delhi is more westernised than Southall [. . .] they've got more variety there – more sari and suit [*salwaar kameez*] shops with brilliant and very modern styles. Lots of people in Southall are still living in the India they left behind them and they don't realise how fashions and other things have changed.

This paradox – the fact of greater conservatism in Southall than in modern India – is frequently commented upon (cf. Yates, 1990: 83f.). Compared with cosmopolitan, fashion-conscious, 'with-it' Bombay or other Indian cities which are open to change, Southall is seen by many as a *pendu* town dominated by village-bred, tradition-bound farmers. Certainly those with a rural background are slower to adopt new styles in 'Indian' clothing than those whose background is urban, whether Punjabi or East African.

The dynamism of cross-cultural interactions, cross-overs and borrowings among Southall youth is particularly apparent in the selective appropriation of black youth styles. Black American 'street culture' is a major force in popular youth cultures throughout Britain today, in terms of rap music and dance crazes as well as street fashion and style. Sportswear (trainers, shell suits and track suits) has become the popular 'street uniform' of local youngsters, and designer labels are of paramount importance. A new pair of trainers can cost some £80. Three months later they will be worn out, and this inbuilt obsolescence places considerable financial pressures on households, in some of which £80 may constitute the larger part of the family's weekly income. Cheaper labels are then often purchased and are frowned upon by those who can afford the more up-market products. The wrong label or shabby, dirty trainers can lead to mocking and bullying or to insults about a person's family being too poor to afford the 'right' label. Here the conspicuous consumerism and status competition between friends and rivals, endemic amongst 'western' youth, can become implicated in the more culturally specific patterns of status competition among families tied up with the notion of *izzat*. Cross-media advertising plays a crucial role in shaping teenage consumer culture and in making material values important. Opportunistic advertising, which extends across the worlds of sports, music and fashion, shapes consumer preferences and choices, exerting considerable financial pressure on parents and young people. Sportswear, jeans and leather or suede jackets are part of every fashion-conscious young person's wardrobe. 'Labels' are high-status consumer items. A 'puffy' Chipie jacket, for instance, can cost up to £300 in the UK (but many youths who can afford them have become reluctant to wear their jackets for fear of having them stolen).

Afro-Caribbeans have very high status among young Punjabis in Southall because, collectively, they are trend-setters in fashion, music and dance styles (cf. Gilroy, 1993b: 82). They are seen to be subject to less parental control and to enjoy greater mobility, enabling them to socialise 'outside' and 'bring fashion back into Southall'. They are considered to be 'honorary Americans': 'cool', 'streetwise, city kids', 'not easily put down', 'proud' and 'fit'. They are seen to have a tough, rebellious, assertive personal style which many Southall boys admire. Many Punjabi boys incorporate and appropriate elements of 'black culture' not only in their speech patterns, idioms and slang but also in their behaviour, dress and musical tastes. The sucking of teeth to express displeasure, and expressions such as 'yo man!', 'safe', 'bad' (meaning good), 'skank' (betray), 'vex' and 'y'know what I mean' are but a few examples of idioms appropriated from local black youth and popular black media and sports stars. Music is also a powerful focus of culturally convergent tastes, as evidenced in the example of ragga bhangra discussed earlier.

Sarita, a 15-year-old Hindu girl, claims she is drawn to 'black culture' but that this is discouraged by her parents. Attitudes to black people in the parental culture are often highly prejudiced. Most Punjabi parents do not wish their children to associate with black youth, citing a variety of reasons: their perceived rebelliousness, associations with crime and the police, and above all their 'otherness'. The pressures of endogamy are one of the most powerful forces affecting cross-cultural relations in Southall:

> I listen to reggae and soul music but my mum hates it if we start enthusing about black singers on *Top of the Pops*, you know saying he's gorgeous and that, so we play our feelings down, we don't show her how much we like the black guys cos she worries we'll get mixed up with them [. . .]. The parents think that to marry a black person is worse than marrying a *gore* [white person] and you know some Asians want to be white, I don't know why, but if I had the choice I'd be black.

The film *Mississippi Masala*, which centres on a romance between an Asian girl and a black boy, was, according to some informants, greeted with horror by parents, while young people enjoyed it greatly.

Black youth collectively set dress trends in Southall and are much admired for their 'personal style' as individuals. They are regarded as being fashionable 'outside' Southall, and this is one of the key criteria of style success among local youth. Such success is very much dependent upon where you shop, the labels you wear and your overall image. Departing from a discussion of the ads for Levi 501 jeans and LA Gear trainers, a group of 16- and 17-year-olds, one Friday afternoon in the sixth-form common room, drew up their own hierarchy of style types, identifying six categories of local style. They positioned themselves at the top among the 'classies' and their least stylish peers at the bottom with the *pendus*. Though the vagaries of fashion dictate that, by now, the content of this hierarchy will have changed, it is worth presenting in some detail because its structure tellingly reveals the key oppositions which underlie perceptions of style difference and which change less quickly. Being 'cool', it emerges, is a matter of detachment from specifically local, territorially-based styles. Thus the 'cool body' is 'cosmopolitan', in Hannerz's sense of a certain 'orientation' which he describes as:

a willingness to engage with others [. . .], an intellectual and aesthetic stance of openness toward divergent cultural experience, a search for contrasts rather than uniformity [. . .], a matter of competence [. . .   and] skill in manoeuvering more or less expertly within a particular system of meanings [. . .]. (1990: 239)

By contrast, *pendus*, at the bottom of the hierarchy, are caricaturally depicted as locked into a closed local style, one which is doubly bound to a certain symbolic space: that of Southall; and beyond Southall, that of the Punjabi village. In between these extremes come categories on an ascending scale of boundedness and uniformity, closely correlating with perceived expensiveness or cheapness, but signifying far more than the level of disposable income. And the sixth category denotes an alternative style to the *pendu*, more 'image-conscious' but yet more strongly, though in a different way, bound to a particular symbolic territory.

Classy

To be 'cool' is to be 'classy': it is to head the style hierarchy. For classy dressers, 'authentic' labels matter: labels conspicuously connote affluence, and their cachet obtains both within and outside Southall. But it is not one label or article of clothing that matters but the 'overall look'. Classies are into 'personal style': they flee uniformity and seek to distinguish themselves as individuals. They always shop in central London and buy expensive labels – such as 501 jeans and LA Gear trainers – but: 'Some people think that just by wearing LA Gear they look cool but they don't cos it's everything, their whole image that counts'. Classies always look 'cool' and 'safe'. They do not need to follow the latest fashion slavishly: 'If you go to the right shops it doesn't really matter what your idea of fashion is, you'll get the right gear, you don't have to follow the fashion in every detail'. Girls shop at the more up-market retail outlets such as Next, Miss Selfridge, Snob, River Island and Principles, and buy their shoes in Ravel, Dolcis and Lilley and Skinner. Boys shop at designer label shops like Pie Squared, Whack and Oaklands. The clothes they buy are always expensive and well-cut, and it is important to be 'trendy', but individual style is 'crucial': 'If someone else has got what you're wearing you don't want to wear it any more'. 'Classies' read fashion magazines: girls read *Just Seventeen* and *More*, boys read the very up-market glossies *GQ* and *Arena*. They get their ideas for fashionable ways of assembling a 'look' from watching what other people wear and from magazines, rather than from TV. There are accepted limits to their cosmopolitanism: most stick to styles which are within the bounds of locally acceptable clothing: 'I really like those Lycra hot pants and ski pants, but you could never wear those kinds of clingy clothes around Southall because you'd get leers and cut eyes [. . .] anyway they make my legs look too skinny'.

The 'classies' have individual style because they know how to mix and match their clothes. They are concerned to look original and wear their clothes well, and are very conscious of context. One example of a 'classy' combination would be: 'White massive jeans, BK Boots and a cropped jumper for everyday wear, or for a disco at the Hippodrome, a tight black velvet dress'. Although bhangra discos at the Hippodrome are for 'Asian' youth, 'Indian' clothes would not be worn to them by 'classies'. At one stage *patiala* or very baggy *salwar* (trousers), tight round the lower knee and ankle, were worn by classies on such occasions, but now they generally only wear *salwar kameez* at family occasions, where 'Indian' clothes would be 'in place'.

Style categories can never be rigid or exhaustive, but the 'classy' style category was felt to need particular differentiation. For example, classy clothes may be 'posh-smart' or 'casual-sporty':

ABJINDER (17):   I'd say I'm a casual-sporty type [. . .] that's all I can take cos I'm a bit overweight but look what I'm wearing – Levi's 501s, they cost around £30 and an Adidas top – the actual track-suit costs £90 – and my trainers are Condors, an American make, they're worth £60 [. . .]. I'm not dressed up cheaply but I don't really call that 'classy' fashion.

Hair-style – to which we will also return later in the context of body-care ads – is very important as part of the overall 'look' or 'image', as well as being a key 'ethnic signifier' (Mercer, 1987). Hair is an important symbol of Sikhism, a religion which prohibits the cutting of hair. Keeping long hair and wearing a turban may be read as sign of conformity to religious and cultural traditions. The turban may also be worn with pride and used to create a specifically Sikh youth style. Today, however, many young people are cutting their hair and discarding their turbans and long plaits. The pressures within the peer group to conform to the latest, shorter hair-styles are immense and a family crisis can ensue if a boy or girl cuts their hair. In some families cutting one's hair is seen as a major symbolic act of rebellion. But other parents accept that short hair is easier to manage and do not necessarily interpret it as an act of defiance. Many boys shave their hair along the sides above their ears in line with black street style. Girls wear their hair long and permed or in well-cut 'bobs', although the group agreed that 'perms are on their way out now.'

Hip-hop

Hip-hop is seen as a 'black/American' style, and its high position in the hierarchy reflects the high status of black and American youth cultures. Again, 'showing the label' is a way of creating a 'cool', fashionable, trendy and affluent image. These people wear 'smart', 'trendy' clothes with expensive labels: LA Gear or Fila trainers in suede, costing £60–£100, puffy

Chipie jackets, Levi 501s or baggy jeans. They buy their clothes 'up London' or at expensive 'classified' shops (those which sell expensive labels). Most importantly, they look good outside Southall. They are distinguished from 'classies' in that they are following fashion rather than creating 'their own look'.

Acid House

Acid House is seen as a 'white/English' style. It involves wearing colourful, hooded tops, baggy track-suit bottoms (tight at the ankle with buttons for girls) and massive, bulging trainers with the tongues hanging out. These people look fairly 'trendy' in Southall but not at all outside. They buy their clothes in markets and cheap shops in adjacent Ealing and Hounslow: 'Acid is just baggy clothes, it's not really caring what you look like, just feeling comfortable, it's sloppy, casual wear'. At the time of fieldwork this fashion was on the wane and those who continued to present themselves in this style were ridiculed by the classies as being 'behind' current trends:

> Like acid and hip-hop are two dance crazes so if they're dance crazes people wanna dance, be comfortable and look good at the same time, but in Southall people are into hip-hop more than acid, acid's like for kids, it's not that cool, you see a lot of little white kids running round acid-style but the cool dudes go for hip-hop.

Southallis

Southallis 'try to keep up with fashions' but they wear cheaper versions of the current styles, or what is referred to as 'normal fashion'. They buy clothes in cheap shops in Southall or adjacent towns: blouses with large lacy collars and double-breasted fronts and cheap 'imitation' baggy trousers for girls, and for boys, cheap versions of expensive clothes – 'but you can tell the difference' – from the 'down-market' department stores such as C & A. The girls have 'masses of permed or hennaed hair'. The Southallis – as some call them, using a rarely heard term with derogatory overtones – try to appear 'westernised' but display a lack of fashion awareness and consumer power which bind them to the culture of the local territory.

Pendus

The same is true for the *pendus*, but more so. *Pendu* derives from the Punjabi word *pind*, or village, and young people use it (both as noun and as adjective) to encompass a range of derisory connotations from 'peasant', 'backward', 'thick' and 'uncouth' to 'traditional', 'uncool' and 'lacking style'. *Pendus* are 'out of place' among young people and belong in the parental culture. Often child and teenage migrants are denigrated as *pendus*. The caricature of a male *pendu* is someone who has just stepped off the plane from the Punjab, wearing flairs, huge shirt collars hanging out over a shrunken acrylic jumper and platform boots. His female counterpart wears ankle bracelets above white stilettos and a shiny satin-look, frilly blouse *outside* a pencil-thin skirt.

The term is applied to young people who do not try or cannot afford to follow youth fashions. They are viewed disdainfully as 'modern versions' of their parents or as 'playing safe just to please parents': 'They wear what they can get away with in the eyes of parents without completely selling out to them, they try their best not to look out of it, they wear cheap jeans and lacy jumpers in horrible colours'. *Pendus* shop for cheap clothes in 'Indian' shops on the Southall Broadway, and wear track suits from cheap local markets; or stone-washed, bleached jeans and jackets, checked shirts and trainers from Woolworths; or cheap, straight Farah jeans (a local label). Girls wear *jutiya* (Indian sandals) from local shoe shops and boys wear trainers with trousers rather than jeans: 'Ugh! No one else would dream of doing that!' They wear 'nasty jumpers with patterns or shiny beads on them', bought from stalls on the Broadway or in the local market:

> GURINDER: The girls wear *goti* [cardigans] which are either really long or like the one in the ad that comes on Hindi films, you know where there's this fat woman waddling through Southall Park and there's this man chasing her and she's scared cos she thinks he's after her so she runs faster and hides behind a tree and eventually he catches up with her and says 'I love your *goti* where did you buy it?' and she takes him to the shop on the Broadway and it's the most disgusting cardigan, pink with beads and pearls on it everywhere.

The *pendu* wears strong, uncoordinated colours and inappropriate combinations of elements of traditional 'Indian' dress with a version of 'western' style which is itself associated with poorer 'Asians' attempting – and failing – to look 'westernised'. The hateful details of *pendu* style were elaborated with as much animation as were those of 'classy' style, in order to bring out the contrasts as fully as possible. *Pendus* are the antithesis of 'classies' in their alleged total ignorance of current fashion as well as lack of spending power – and as young people, in their more or less slavish adherence to the dress codes of the parental generation. Their clothes were referred to once as 'unclassy imports', implying cheap 'western'-style clothes manufactured abroad. This reference jars with the evidence in several of the above quotations that *pendu*s, and to a lesser extent 'Southallis', are more likely than any other category to be wearing garments not only sold but manufactured in Southall itself. It is rather the wearers of these clothes who appear as 'imports'; they might be in rural Punjab. Their style is seen as an emblem of Southall's much-bemoaned status as an enclosed territory with few links to wider British society, whose inhabitants' links with India, furthermore, are not with the cosmopolitan, modern India of the big cities, but with 'poor and backward' villages.

Hard

The last style category is exclusively for boys who wish to present a 'hard' image, associated with membership of one of the local gangs. They appropriate the symbols of Sikhism (see above, p. 122) to represent a special type of machismo:

> MANJIT (17):   We associate certain people with particular types of habits and particular styles, for example [. . .] you'll see guys with black leather jackets, several large gold earrings, tight Lois black jeans, Adidas 'Gazelle' trainers – and an attitude problem [. . .]. They are influenced by western culture but 'they're more strong in their Indian background cos they've got big *karas* [steel bracelets worn on the right wrist by Sikhs] [. . .]. Some still wear turbans [. . .]. They wear a lot of gold, Indian gold [. . .]. Often you'll see a large *khalsa* pendant around their necks [. . .]. They like to drive round in red Ford Capris or Cortinas [. . .]. They trade on their image as 'pure' in the Jat sense, tough and macho [. . .] but you'll rarely see one alone [. . .] they go round in groups of five or six and act tough but if you see them when they're alone they're like chickens some of them.

This style-type assembles different styles and symbols – combining Sikh emblems with 'western' garments connoting machismo – in order to convey locally specific meanings. This might be compared with what Hebdige refers to as 'bricolage' in subcultural styles, whereby a range of commodities are brought together in an ensemble which erases or subverts their 'straight' meanings (1988: 104). The 'transformation' of meaning involved here is in a sense more limited. For those unfamiliar with the Sikh religion and with the specific position of Jats in Southall, it would be difficult to read the signs. As explained earlier in my discussion of the 'Holy Smokes', this gang-member style was often associated with proclaimed support for the Khalistan movement. Again, the style is doubly linked with a territory but, in contrast to the *pendu* style, which merely signifies an unreflected connection with place in the form of a lack of any economic and cultural alternative, the 'hard' style announces a claim to territorial power both on the streets of Southall and in the Punjab.

The elaboration of this hierarchy of local styles began spontaneously, though it was completed with some prompting from me. Many informants subsequently confirmed it as an accurate depiction. It developed out of a discussion of the very popular TV ads for two highly sought-after labels. Clearly, TV advertising plays an important role in shaping youth fashions, notably in focusing desire on particular products and linking the wearing of 'cool' labels with certain desirable qualities of personal and group identity. But TV is only one channel among many and, in examining the impact of fashion advertisements, one should consider the power of the cross-media and intertextual circulation of images, music and narratives in ads targeted at the teenage consumer. But equally, as this data shows, it is essential to examine how the products of the global fashion industry, as well as other, national and local garment industries, are incorporated into local cultures in specific ways.

BODY BEAUTY

Ads for body-care and beauty products often figure in young people's conversations. Both hair and skin are important 'ethnic signifiers', each representing 'a highly sensitive surface on which competing definitions of "the beautiful" are played out in a racial struggle' (Mercer, 1987: 32):

> Classical ideologies of race established a classificatory symbolic system of colour with 'black' and 'white' as signifiers of a fundamental polarisation of human worth in terms of 'superiority/inferiority'. Distinctions of aesthetic value, in terms of 'beautiful/ugly', have always been central to the way racism divides the world into binary oppositions in its adjudications of human worth. (Mercer, 1987: 35)

Thus the politics of 'racial' appearance is inevitably implicated in Southall teenagers' talk about these topics, though there is seldom explicit reference to the dominant assumption, purveyed by the media, that 'whiteness' is the measure of 'true beauty', or to the ideological status ascription of 'races' according to a 'scale of whiteness' (Hall, 1977).

Many features of young people's talk about these ads are no doubt common to all teenagers who are exposed to them. Girls show a much greater awareness of ads for beauty products than do boys, an awareness which is not solely confined to ads targeted at females. One of the most popular series of ads among girls, at the time of the survey, was for Gillette's 'new' line of shaving products, which were enjoyed because of the 'hunky' male character. Boys claim not to be influenced by the ads but clearly, certain brands of products are seen to confer 'classiness'. Labels matter here too:

> ABDUL (17):   Which of the guys says I use Gillette to shave? They're not saying 'I use Gillette cos I like the ad' [. . .], they're just saying 'Oh God! Turn it over on the other side', whereas girls would think, 'Oh! he's all right' [. . .]. I use Gillette, it's nothing to do with the ad [. . .], I just picked up the gel quickly at the chemist [. . .]. I suppose I do go for the big name things [. . .]. At the end of the day, Gillette sounds much better [. . .]. See what I mean it gets to you, you have to

have a named product, it's a bit of class rubbed in as well, I suppose it rubs off on you as well cos people like to be seen using classy products.

There is no evidence in this domain that ad consumption and product consumption are independent, as suggested by the argument of Nava and Nava (1992), cited earlier. The products are easily within the spending reach of the great majority of young people and the TV ads influence their buying greatly.

Interview data suggests that boys are just as preoccupied with their physical appearance as girls. A key concern is body odour:

NIRMAL (18):   Yeah of course I buy my own deodorant, I have done for a while [. . .]. You need strong soaps and deodorants at this age cos your hormones are working overtime [. . .], you tend to sweat a hell of a lot [. . .], bloody hell you sweat! and then you get spots and you try to control them [. . .]. We all used to buy products like Biactol, Clearasil, oh yeah, and Oxy 10.

Ads for spot creams and lotions are seen to play upon the insecurities of teenagers regarding body odours, acne and personal appearance more generally, and though they display critical distance to such ads, this does not mean that the ads have no effect:

DILIP (17):   They're kind of psychological [. . .] cos they're showing a girl with a bucket over her head and how you feel when you go to a party with a face full of spots, and like when you use Oxy 10 they imply you won't need the bucket [. . .] and that girls will fall at your feet – that would be nice!

Such advertisements strike a raw or sensitive nerve in some teenagers, often defused in discussions (as the advertisers no doubt intend) by laughter. The ad for Clearasil works on the 'before–after' principle, suggesting that a young person's life can be transformed by using the product. Typically, it is claimed that it is not the speaker, but *other people*, who are affected by these ads:

BALBIR (16):   Have you seen the Clearasil ad? The girl's really spotty and she's a heavy-metal fan dancing to music, her hair is all over the place, her room's a mess and she holds a mirror to her face and it cracks. Her sister who's really pretty gives her Clearasil. The next scene is where her sister goes to her bedroom and she's transformed into this beauty and her room's tidy and she's playing soft, romantic Marvin Gaye music and she's dancing with her boyfriend and the camera focuses on her as she admires her face [. . .]. Some girls are likely to go out and buy Clearasil after seeing this [. . .], this is something a lot of girls think is real.

But the pressures upon teenagers in Southall to conform to conventional standards of beauty propagated by the media of 'western' culture can pose particular problems for those who are sensitive about their skin colour. It is, after all, skin colour which is the focus of much racist abuse. Furthermore, an important criterion of beauty in the parental and peer culture alike is 'fairness' of skin, which is considered to be a sign of beauty. Often a description of a person will begin with a reference to the shade of their skin – to whether they are 'fair' or 'dark'. Dark-skinned people are considered unattractive and, to compound the matter even further, dark skin is associated with low caste. Dark facial hair is also viewed as unattractive and bleaching products are often used, mainly by girls, to lighten the skin and to disguise dark hair on the upper lip or on the side of the face. Similarly, facial scrubs are used in the hope of obtaining a blemish-free, 'fair' complexion. Indian ads for beauty products play upon such prejudices by promoting bleach products. Such advertisements commonly interrupt Hindi videos and discussions of face products often highlight the importance, to girls, of being fair-skinned (as well as their low opinion of Indian advertisements):

JASBINDER: I hate those ones for moisturising cream, 'Fair and Lovely' and they say it makes you whiter and whiter and then I think how stupid I don't want to get like that.

GURINDER: Yeah it's true these Indian ads are always going on about how to be white and everything white skin, white teeth.

AMRITA: And there's this ad for Vico Ayureval, it stinks, my mum has got that but it doesn't work [. . .], it's meant to make your skin smooth and fair.

GURINDER: You know my sister bought that and you know what it is? it's bleach! Because she tried it on her face, she came out in a rash.

The use of such products does not imply a desire to 'become white', or to engage in what Mercer (1987) calls a 'deracialising sell-out'. But dominant western ideology and the beauty criteria of Indian culture both set standards which devalue darkness, even though the positive ideals are not identical.

Hair, as we saw earlier, is an important factor for 'coolness'. This concerns both styling and hair quality. Ads for hair products – shampoos and gels – are commonly referred to and are recognised as having a very direct impact on consumer purchases. More people freely admit to being more influenced to buy hair products because of ads than is the case with any other product, apart from chocolate. The appeal of the hair ads is usually related to the desired aims of achieving the qualities of shine and thickness:

DALVINDER: I like the Timotei and Silkience ads, it's the hair it's so lovely and soft and shiny [. . .]. I did buy Timotei after seeing the ad but now I like it.

TEJINDER: I bought it cos of the ads too but I don't like it so I stopped using it.

Many girls were wearing their hair permed into curls in imitation of Michael Jackson, a 'cool' look which entailed using lots of moisturising products. It contrasted strongly with the 'traditional' and 'uncool' look of girls who wear their uncut hair in long plaits.

Teenagers' preoccupation with all these elements of personal appearance make them an easy target for the advertisers of beauty products. Girls and boys compete to attain recognition and status as an attractive person. In the peer culture, attractive girls and boys acquire very high status and are admired, desired and envied. The message of advertising for young people is that to be happy, popular and liked you have to be, above all, attractive, especially to the opposite sex.. By consuming beauty products, young people hope to improve their image and attractiveness, and the ideologically loaded criteria of beauty propagated by the British media can sometimes cause problems of self-esteem. Exposure to popular Indian and Pakistani media provides young people in Southall with alternative models and standards of beauty, and some identify positively with, and emulate, images of beauty from the realm of Bombay fashion. But the widespread denigration of popular Indian culture more often leads young people to reject such models and to seek alternative role models in British, or most commonly in American culture. Indeed it is in relation to an idealised American teenage culture, represented in its most compelling form in Coca Cola ads, that young people express their aspirations towards cultural change.

YOU CAN'T BEAT THE FEELING: COCA COLA AND UTOPIA

Coca Cola ads have sustained an unparalleled popularity among the youth of Southall over the last decade or so. Over the years, the ads and their accompanying jingles and songs – which have repeatedly been major chart hits – have entered every young person's repertoire of media knowledge. Coca Cola songs and slogans are familiar to all, and few would be unable to recite them upon request. They are seen to convey a 'feeling' which is captured in the slogan:

DALVINDER: I love the Coca Cola ads, I don't know why, there's just something about them, they're just good, more lively, teenagers jumping around and having a laugh [. . .], I don't know [laughs] you just can't beat the feeling.

This slogan is a catch-phrase among local youth. Its very ambiguity (the reference to 'feeling' as both an emotional state and a physical experience), is the source of many a *double entendre*, especially in exchanges between boys and girls. The tensions inherent in that ambiguity seem to capture something of the nature of the emotional and sensual experience of adolescence.

Discussions of Coca Cola ads also refer to the 'feeling' that they convey in terms of the representation of a teenage world and lifestyle to which many young people aspire. It is an imagined or projected feeling of participating, albeit vicariously, in an idealised lifestyle where young people sing, dance, have fun, socialise, fall in love, and easily gain friends, status and popularity. The following exchange took place during a taped discussion between two 16-year-old vocational students about why they like their favourite advertisements. It captures the ads' utopian quality:

SAMEERA: My favourite ads are the Coca Cola ads, they're American ads, I prefer American ads, I don't know why but I could watch them over and over again without getting bored [. . .]. I like them cos I just love drinking Coca Cola [. . .]. I enjoy listening to the music [. . .]. I think the characters are fantastic. Every time I see the ad I always feel tempted to go out and buy it, even when I go out shopping, I always buy Coke cos, well, I love the ad [. . .].

SUKHI: Yeah, they're really happy and active cos they mix pop songs with kids in America, you know, the sun's always shining and everyone is smiling and it gives the impression of being free. The music and song puts more energy into it and like each line of the song is backed up with dancing, sports and fun [. . .]. 'You just can't beat the feeling!'

SAMEERA: Yeah, and all races seem to get on well, their roles aren't changed around because of the colour of their skin. There are no signs of people being angry [. . .].

SUKHI: They have a very tempting way of selling Coke [. . .], you know the one where the guy is sweating, he's thirsty as anything but he drinks it very slowly, taking his time as if it's something precious.

SAMEERA: Yeah, it's like after a hard day's work he's rewarded with a refreshing Coke. The little droplets of water on the bottle glisten and sort of add to the temptation.

SUKHI: After watching the ad you think, 'Oh yeah, next time I need a cool drink, I'll have a Coke'.

SAMEERA: [. . .] then there's a boy and girl about to kiss but then, just as their lips are about to meet another shot comes [. . .].

The preference for American advertisements is stated without any explicit reasons being offered, but the chain of associations in the exchange implies that it is based on the attractiveness of the American teenage lifestyle portrayed. The feelings ascribed to the young people are conflated with the advertisement and the product. Coke-drinkers are seen to be 'happy', 'active' 'kids in America' where 'the sun is always shining', everyone is 'happy' and 'free', 'all races get on' and there are 'no signs of anger'.

'TV ad talk' is clearly influenced by the discourse of advertising itself which relates products to myths and dreams, fantasies and emotions, rewards and promises in order to sell products. Advertisements are the most condensed of all TV narratives and viewers have to make symbolic associations in order to read them. These associations become evident in ad talk, which can take on some of the persuasive rhetoric of the ads themselves. The repeated use of the word 'temptation' in several different contexts highlights an awareness of the persuasive techniques used. Sameera claims that when she sees the ad she is tempted to go out and buy a Coke both because she loves the ad and because she loves drinking Coke. Sukhi adds that the way 'they' sell Coke is tempting. The glistening droplets on the bottle in the ad 'add to the temptation'. Then Sameera introduces the idea of being rewarded with a Coke after a hard day's work, making the connection with Coke-drinking and leisure. Finally, the temptation of a kiss appears, only to disappear at the very end of the advertisement. In this account, thirst and desire are connected: thirst is satisfied by a Coke but desire, as represented by the promise of a kiss, is left to the imaginative fulfilment. By placing the product within an idealised world of teenagers, free from parental and other constraints, a utopian vision of a teenage lifestyle is represented. The plausibility of the idyllic lifestyle and utopian relationships depicted by the ad is not questioned.

The following exchange between two 16-year-old vocational students further highlights the way in which the Coke ads lead some young people to engage in talk that would otherwise appear foolish or utopian:

GURVINDER: It makes you think that if you drink Coke that you will be popular and loved by people you didn't even know existed.

GITA: Innit, it's like everyone cares about each other, their relationships are simple, they all get on, life is peaceful and full of fun so enjoy it while you can.

GURVINDER: They all socialise together, boys and girls, everyone loves each other and if you buy Coke it makes you feel that you could be happy and free like them.

GITA: But I don't think the ads influence us to buy it, most of us buy it anyway.

GURVINDER: And old people won't be influenced because they think that soft drinks are bad for you anyway.

GITA: But I think you are supposed to value the feeling that you get after drinking it, you know [sings] 'you can't beat the feeling', and for such a small cost.

GURVINDER: The music is great as well and goes with the feeling.

Thus the consumption of Coke promises happiness, love, friendship, freedom and popularity. In the world promised by the ads, relationships are uncomplicated (unlike in real life); young people simply care for each other, everyone loves one another and socialises together (unlike in the peer culture where group boundaries are strong); life is fun and free (a teenage dream). If they do not feel themselves to be influenced by the ads, it is evidently only because they already have been: the girls buy Coke in any case. Finally, teenage tastes are distinguished from those of older people who think Coke is unhealthy.

Discussions of Coke ads invariably lead to a consideration of what it is like to be a teenager in America, articulated in contrast to what it is to be a teenager in Southall. The word most consistently used to describe American teenagers is 'free'. They are seen to have much greater freedom to do what they want, to participate in 'fun' activities; freedom from parental constraint; and especially, freedom to have boyfriends and girl-friends. The emphasis on freedom appears to be exaggerated, but when considered against the background of social constraints under which girls especially live, it becomes easier to appreciate.

Perceptions of American 'kids' obviously derive from a variety of media sources, but the Coke ads have undoubtedly played a formative influence in shaping perceptions of an idealised teenage lifestyle. The following exchange again highlights the rosy image of American 'kids' which is presented in the ads, as well as in the popular American 'college films' and 'vacation films' (such as *Dirty Dancing*), and TV series such as *Beverly Hills 90210* which revolves around the recreational pursuits of high-school teenagers:

GURINDER: American kids . . . they're ideal . . .

BALJIT: . . . they're really good-looking . . .

PERMINDER: . . . they all drink Coke and drive fast cars, like in *Beverley Hills 90210*, the girls are so pretty . . .

AMRITA: . . . Brandon is so cute . . .

GURINDER: . . . so's Dylan he's r-e-a-l-ly nice . . .

BALJIT: . . . they're free . . .

PERMINDER: . . . all rich, they've got massive huge houses and they all dress smart and they've got wicked cars . . .

GURINDER: . . . they've got more things to do as well . . .

AMRITA: . . . they're all sunbaked aren't they . . .

BALJIT: . . . they're always going to pool parties . . .

PERMINDER: . . . they're all healthy . . .

BALJIT: . . . like the Coke ads make you think they're free and have lots of fun and they have . . .

GURINDER: . . . boyfriends! [All laugh]

The idealisation of American youth in the Coke ads is recognised by Baljit to be a constructed image, but the others talk about the representation as if it were 'the real thing' (another Coke slogan). This representation of American kids as rich and above all free (to have boyfriends) contrasts sharply with the lives of these girls who consider themselves neither rich nor free to have boyfriends. Thus the Coke ads and other media sources encourage girls to fantasize about what life might feel like as an attractive teenager in Beverly Hills.

Whilst the ideal of teenage freedom is a recurrent theme when Coke ads are discussed, some young people are also aware of the darker side of the 'American way of life':

KARIM (19):   American kids have more freedom [. . .], freedom to rebel AND WIN, you know, like in films like *Dirty Dancing* [. . .] they rebel AND the family stays together but, over here, if you rebel against your family, you're out on your own, parents won't tolerate certain things [. . .]. They have more freedom, they also have more of a drug problem, more violence and there's more of a colour problem there as well [. . .], the Hispanics and blacks are stuck in ghettos and slums [. . .], even though they're American they're not integrated.

The impression of 'racial harmony' produced by the Coke ads is seen to be contradicted by other available images, of 'ghetto' life and 'racial conflict'. Nevertheless, Coke – and Pepsi – are favourite drinks among young people locally, strongly associated with a 'cool', 'safe' image. In one of the local Punjabi cafés, 'Rita's' in old Southall – a 'hang-out' for local youth in the lunch-hour – red cans of Coke stand on almost every table. Often, that is all there is on the table, because eating 'out' is expensive (compared to school dinners or home lunches) and most youngsters can only afford a kebab roll or a samosa and a can of Coke.

No other drink has quite the 'cool image' of Coke. The Pepsi ads are considered to be very attractive because they use famous stars like Michael Jackson, Tina Turner and Madonna, but most prefer the taste of Coke and claim to find Pepsi sweeter: 'I think they spend more money on the Pepsi ads but Coke ads are more for the common people and cos they're young people, you can sort of relate to them'. This idea that Coke is for the 'common people' relates to a perception of Coke being a drink consumed by young people in all parts of the world; it is testimony to the success of Coke's 'multi-local' global marketing strategy (Webster, 1989; Robins, 1989). The 'cool' image of Coke evidently 'rubs off' on its consumers; and this creates problems for other drinks manufacturers.

For example, a company called Rubicon, producing 'exotic', 'tropical' canned drinks, based on flavours such as mango juice or passion-fruit, organised a vigorous TV advertising campaign specifically targeting ethnic-minority consumers, broadcasting on Channel 4 over several months during the period of fieldwork. In discussions of this campaign, the consensus seemed to be that the major problem was that the can lacked style: 'I've tried it and I like the taste of the mango juice but the can is so awful you wouldn't be seen dead with it, it's so badly designed [. . .]. I hate it, it's so uncool'. And not only is the can 'uncool', but the ad itself is seen by many to portray 'Asian' families as 'stupid':

> GURINDER: I hate that Rubicon ad, you know the one where there's this Indian family, the mum, dad and the two kids – the kids are so cute! I think they're *gore* [whites] – and they're all in the kitchen watching a Hindi film and the husband goes to his wife, 'Have you got any mango juice dear?' and they're all really engrossed in the film so they ignore him. Then he goes dancing round the kitchen to the fridge and gets out the mango juice and starts singing [. . .]. They're watching the bit in the film where Rajesh Kanna takes her to a hut [. . .] and the tune to the ad is the same as in the actual film, you know, it goes 'Rubicon must have some' [all laugh and sing it]. They're so stupid though, I hate the way they do that, it makes Indian people look really stupid.

However good it tastes, if a drink does not have the right kind of 'cool' image, the terms of which are pre-established by the dominant advertising media, many will not buy it. And such attempts to construct an 'ethnic' image are particularly unlikely to find favour among Southall youth. No 'Indian' ads were mentioned in the survey, but they were brought up in every group discussion and interview and critically or humorously juxtaposed to 'more sophisticated' British or American ads. The consistent denigration of 'Indian' ads – including both those for 'Indian' products appearing in 'Indian' media, and those targeting 'British Asians' in 'western' media – stands in sharp contrast to the high regard for 'western' ads targeted at teenagers.

In their ad talk about soft drinks young people establish hierarchies of consumer taste and style in sharp contrast to those which exist in the parental culture. The stylistic qualities and persuasive techniques of ads targeted at the parental generation are seen to be 'unsophisticated'. The representation of the 'Asian' family in the above example is considered to be demeaning. The father, dancing and singing around the kitchen, is perceived as 'stupid'. Many young people who discussed this ad showed concern that it would just reinforce negative stereotypes of 'Asians'. They argue that, because there are so few representations of 'Asian' families on British TV, those that do appear have greater representational power. Yet implicit in this ad talk are a series of unanswered questions: How should an Indian father behave and act? What should an 'Asian'family look like? Why are the children found to be cute because *gore* ('white')? Gurinder's detailed and accurate recall of an ad she hates – including recognition of the intertextual reference to a Hindi movie – may be likened to the detail in which *pendu* style was elaborated, as a means of underlining the contrast between 'classy', 'cool' style and its antithesis.

In juxtaposing Rubicon and Coke in discussions about soft drinks advertisements young people are drawing connections between texts which are incomparable in certain crucial ways; they seem to be unaware that the Rubicon advertisements are targeted at 'British Asian' families, and mothers as shoppers, whereas those for Coca Cola are aimed specifically at teenagers. However, they feel themselves to be implicated in these ads as young 'British Asians', and are highly critical of the way adult 'Asians' are invariably portrayed as having Indian accents. As young people born and brought up in Britain, without Indian accents for the most part, they often express aspirations toward a greater participation in mainstream British society, from which they feel cut off by Southall's 'island' status. Representations which emphasise the 'foreignness' of 'Asians' are seen to further alienate them from society. Such concerns override the fact that the depiction of a family watching a popular Hindi movie and the playful behaviour of the father are features of the ad which make it attractive to many local adults. For young people, it is a further unwelcome marker of their difference.

Their comments reveal a sense of the excessive 'burden of representation' which affects those few images of 'Asians' which appear in mainstream media, especially on British TV. As Williamson points out, this is a question of collective cultural power: 'the more power any group has to create and wield representations, the less [any one image] is required to be representative' (1993: 116). Young people are faced with what they believe are inappropriate representations of 'Asians' in the very few British TV ads in which they are portrayed. Ads in 'Indian' media fare no better, but are treated as objects of ridicule in the peer group. In criticising both so vociferously, they are demarcating distinctions in taste and style between the parental and peer cultures, and also, at least implicitly and sometimes explicitly, expressing a desire for alternative images. Again, the politics of ethnicity are involved: Who represents us? Who speaks for us, or to us? Since the spaces available for public representation of what they see as their generational culture are so limited, and since neither British nor Indian media offer representations which they view as acceptable or appropriate, it is perhaps no wonder that they turn to a third, alternative space of fantasy identification: they draw on utopian images of America to construct a position of 'world teenagers' which transcends those available in British or Indian cultures.

FAST FOOD AND FASTING: EATING, AUTONOMY AND THE BIG MAC

A similar process can be observed in talk about food ads. Food is not only a basic human requirement but a fundamental aspect of material culture. Taste in food is the archetype of all tastes (Bourdieu, 1984: 79). It is also one of the most significant markers of ethnicity in plural societies. One of the legacies of British imperialism is the presence of 'Asian' restaurants and take-aways in virtually every high street: 'Indian' (and other 'ethnic') settlers have redefined 'white' British food culture over the past decades. Southall is the major 'Indian' wholesale and retail centre in Britain. The majority of local retail outlets are owned and managed by 'Indians' who sell 'Indian' food products. There is also a plethora of cafés and restaurants which service the local population. However, at the time of fieldwork, there were no national supermarket chains or franchised fast-food outlets in Southall, and the availability of certain types of 'English' food products was very limited. Pizzas and beefburgers were very popular foods among young people, but only available in adjacent towns and suburbs. It was a frequent source of complaint that one could 'only' eat 'Indian' food in Southall: an index that living in Southall means not 'really' living in Britain. But on the other hand this also meant opportunities for 'escape' from Southall to the 'outside': going to the cinema in Ealing or Hounslow and having a pizza or a McDonald's was very much a feature of the teenage leisure scene, an occasion to participate in peer-group activities away from the surveillance of parents and elders.

The public and private consumption of 'English' or 'American' food is perceived not simply as feature of the teenage scene but also as a way of feeling or appearing part of the wider society and culture. Above all perhaps, it is a means of distinguishing oneself from those who are seen to eat 'only' Indian food. TV ads are the main source of information about 'new' food products on the market, which are often not locally available. Through their discussions of food ads, young people provide an account of their tastes and preferences in food and consider a range of factors affecting their food consumption: parental control over their diet; religious restrictions on foods; health and beauty concerns; financial constraints; and the impact of domestic technologies, such as the microwave oven and the fridge freezer, on their food consumption, and the way in which these have stimulated the purchase of pre-packaged foods.

The majority of the young people in this study eat Indian food in their homes on a daily basis. Local schools are required to provide food for Hindu, Sikh and Muslim pupils, in line with religious prohibitions on beef and pork. Ironically, it is the teachers who avidly consume this food, much to the amusement of the young people who consider it to be tasteless by comparison with home cooking and with the food available in local restaurants. Students who eat in the canteen prefer 'English' fast foods such as chips and beans, pizzas, sausages or fritters. Some go to the local shops and buy a can of Coke and a packet of crisps, some go to one of the local Punjabi cafés, and others get fish and chips, whilst a small number of boys spend their dinner money in the games arcades. Approximately £1–£2 is spent per day on lunch by those who do not receive free school meals or return home for lunch. The arrangements made for lunch not only act as a means of organising peer-group relations during the lunch-hour but also provide an indication of one's consumer power or lack of it, as well as being a way of distinguishing cultural tastes in food. The idea of 'English' food (other than the school canteen variety) is found to be very appealing, though the experience may not live up to the anticipation:

> NIRMAL: When I was younger it was like a delicacy having English food, you just never had it and you didn't really know what it was and you felt you were missing out on something [. . .]. Then I went on a school trip [. . .]. I was glad to get home for some home cooking.

But 'English', in this kind of context, usually means 'fast', 'convenience', 'frozen' or 'junk food'.

There is a tendency in the peer context for young people to express a dislike of 'Indian' food. This may be a way of appearing 'westernised', a way of expressing resistance to parental attempts to control their diet, or a way of complaining about the lack of variety in their day-to-day food consumption, rather than a genuine distaste for 'Indian' food *per se*. In the following exchange, a group of 16-year-old girls discuss the special appeal of McDonald's ads and express resentment at their parents' attempts to control their diet:

> AMRITA: The thing is Mum and Dad only cook Indian food.
> DALVINDER: I don't like Indian food very much . . .
> TEJINDER: . . . especially not 365 days a year . . ..
> DALVINDER: . . . then it gets disgusting, it's like we have to have Indian food, we have it every lunchtime and again in the evening, but we have to have it in the family.
> TEJINDER: With your mum and dad you have to sit down and eat chapatis, you have to, if you don't you get into trouble and they start giving you a lecture, 'Oh! you're turning English, you're not Indian' and stuff like that.
> DALVINDER: And if you don't eat your *dal* [lentils] they give you a lecture on the poor, starving people in Ethiopia [. . .] but you can parcel my food to them, give me a McDonald's any day, I don't know cos 'it makes your day', it's just a feeling you get, 'it makes your day'.
> TEJINDER: It makes your mouth water.

Clearly the appeal of McDonald's and Coca Cola ads and slogans succeeds on a very similar level; and burgers connote freedom because they represent a food which you don't *have to have*.

The negotiation of what one eats is but another facet of the way young people negotiate their relationship to the parental culture, and parental attempts to control their behaviour more generally. The desire to consume 'English' food regularly is seen by parents as one further index of 'westernisation', and most parents try to retain some control over how far their children become 'westernised'. 'Indian' food is an important and distinctive aspect of Punjabi culture, and to show a dislike or distaste for Indian food is perceived to be a rebellion against 'the culture'.

The solution to the 'problem' of eating Indian food every day is, for some, provided by fast foods such as burgers. When asked why McDonald's beefburgers are so appealing, the response was formulated in terms of the slogan, 'Well, it makes your day', and 'it's just a feeling you get'. The nature of the 'feeling' becomes apparent when notions of 'freedom', 'choice' and financial independence are related to the ability to eat what you want. But the 'feeling' is also associated with a trip to McDonald's capturing a moment of 'freedom' outside Southall: freedom from the watchful eye of the parental culture and freedom to participate on the 'teenage scene'. McDonald's and Pizza Hut are considered to be both the cheapest and the 'best' of fast foods. The McDonald's outlets in the Hounslow and Ealing are places where boys and girls can safely meet and where courting rituals are conducted discretely. In a market survey of 240 'Asian' school students in west London (40 per cent of whom were from Southall), conducted in 1991 by an 'Asian' advertising company, Channel A, 'burger bars' (46 per cent) were the most regularly frequented of places after the cinema (69 per cent). On several occasions I accompanied informants to McDonald's only to find that large groups of Southall 'escapees' had occupied the entire upstairs section:

DALVINDER: It's good to get out of Southall, go down Hounslow with me mates and sit in McDonald's, get a Big Mac and a Coke . . .
AMRIT: . . . yeah, and have a good gossip. . .
DALVINDER: . . . and check out the guys [giggling]. . .
AMRIT: . . . and get checked out by the guys.

The apparent rejection of Indian food by many young people in the peer culture can be seen as a gesture expressing the desire to establish some degree of independence from the family culture and at the same time to exert some control over one's own body. Teenagers experience their bodies as, in many respects, beyond their control. Rapid and often sudden physical and hormonal changes can be quite difficult to deal with and some young people respond by trying to gain more control over what they eat. Unlike hair and skin colour, 'ethnic signifiers' which are more or less completely beyond personal control, body-shape can, to some extent, be controlled by means of dieting. Body-shape ideals are strongly influenced by the media, and may also have a 'racial', ideological dimension. 'Indian' food is regarded as being fattening, due to the amount of *ghee* (purified butter) added to curries. It may be referred to as 'village' or *pendu* food, and its 'filling' and 'fattening' qualities, when it is contrasted with 'healthy' 'western' food, mark it as low status, in a hierarchy similar to that described by Bourdieu, who found that French working-class or rural peasant food, similarly, was seen as 'fattening' (1984: 190). Girls in particular, but by no means exclusively, are under considerable peer and media pressure to look slim and 'fit' in accordance with 'western' norms. Many girls diet and cases of anorexia nervosa are not uncommon in this age group. Punjabi culture provides legitimating opportunities for·extreme dieting practices: fasting for religious reasons is common among women and girls, who may fast up to two days a week, especially when they are 'petitioning God' for a special request. But 'fasting' is sometimes the excuse girls give to parents for dieting in pursuit of a slim body.

It is not difficult to see the appeal of certain low-fat, 'fast' foods among girls, and in some cases also among their mothers:

INDERJEET: I tell my mum not to put so much *ghee* in the food but my dad likes it like that [. . .]. My mum's been influenced by some of the fast food ads and so have I – like the one for Bird's Eye Healthy Options, it's low-calorie food, when you see that you just wanna run round to your local shop to buy it – you can just stuff it in the microwave when you can't be bothered to cook.

Parents try to discourage their children from eating 'English' food – that is 'fast', 'convenience', 'frozen' or 'junk' food – as it is considered to be unhealthy and unwholesome. They too have their hierarchy of values attached to different foods, which they try to foster in, or impose upon, their children:

BALJIT: My mum goes [Indian accent], 'It's good for you, *dal*, go on eat up,' and when you go to the doctor he says, 'Eat *dal*, *saag* [spinach], *subji* [vegetable curry] and *roti* [unleavened wheat bread] like a good girl' [. . .]. My mum's always on about *saag* and how good it is for you, they think if you don't eat Indian food that you'll fall into bad health.

There are even more compelling, financial reasons why some parents encourage their children to eat Indian food:

PERMINDER: Indian food works out much cheaper, you just buy a big bag of *dal*, some vegetables [. . .]. We only have meat at the weekends [. . .]. You can't have English food, like pizzas and frozen foods every day cos that works out too expensive compared to Indian food.

Financial constraints will obviously affect the diet that young people have and this acts as a marker of social difference. In low-income households it is not unusual for *dal*, *subji* and *roti* to be the staple daily diet. Thus, many households are vegetarian less for religious reasons (vegetarianism is associated with religiosity and spiritual purity among Sikhs and Hindus) and more because meat is simply too expensive and considered to be a luxury for special occasions. Low-income households are extremely unlikely to buy 'convenience' foods. But, where income will permit, young vegetarians are easily persuaded to buy frozen vegetarian foods by TV food ads.

Religious prohibitions on pork for Muslims and beef for Hindus and Sikhs means that neither of these meats can be bought locally. Yet many youngsters transgress religious taboos in consuming 'fast' foods, Hindus by eating beefburgers and Muslims by select the 'Spicy Sausage' pizza at Pizza Hut (spicy and 'hot' foods are well-liked by most young people). Thus participation in a 'fast-food teenage scene', in some cases, threatens parental religious rules. Young people sometimes breach these taboos in an act of defiance against their parents. Moreover, peer pressures may be exerted in order to encourage transgression, which poses a serious moral dilemma for some; while conversely, some young people's refusal to consume these foods becomes a strong statement of allegiance to their religious and cultural identity.

Take-away pizzas, fish and chips and Kentucky Fried Chicken are enjoyed as a 'treat' by some families to accompany a video at the weekend. Many interviewees reported that they had some form of take-away 'English' food at least once a week at home to 'break with habit': 'Yeah, we like to do that too at the weekend, you know, get fish and chips or something and watch a video'. However, probably the most significant changes in eating habits, routines and arrangements have occurred as a result of the widespread take-up of the microwave oven and deep-freeze among Southall families. Microwave ovens are very popular and became common in high-income households in Southall in the early 1980s. For those households which have a deep-freeze and a microwave oven and can afford fast food, the ads for convenience foods have a great attraction: 'You don't have to have Indian food [. . .], your freezer's full with whatever you want'.

These technologies open up further possibilities, which young people find very appealing, for exercising a degree of control not only over what one eats but also, in some cases, over when and with whom one eats in the home. It can mean the opportunity to avoid parents at meal-times and establish independent eating habits. There is also some evidence to suggest that it encourages boys to cater for themselves:

PERMINDER: I'm going to try Napolena, you can make your own pizza, it's just a pizza base and then you add your own topping.

NIRMAL: [. . .] I don't eat with my parents any more, I eat later, especially now that I'm studying for exams, like sometimes I'll sit with them, but I eat when I like now.

PARAMJIT: Yeah, I think the microwave is a real advantage, you don't have to spend much time cooking, you can eat when you want [. . .] and best of all it means that my lazy brother even manages to throw something in and sort his own food out and that's saying something.

The changes in family food rituals enabled by these technologies are likely to have far-reaching implications, given the symbolic and material centrality of food and eating arrangements in the transmission of cultural traditions.

Frozen 'Indian' foods however are not generally appreciated, partly because the standards of home cooking are so much better: 'Have you seen the one for English-made Indian food, we've tried the *dal* but there's a weird taste to it, I think it could be the preservatives'. These products usually meet with particular resistance on the part of mothers, who consider home cooking to be of better quality and taste and more healthy: 'When these ads come on my mum always goes "I can make it better anyway" [. . .]. Mum's answer to everything: "Home-made's best!" '. Moreover, as with 'ethnic' canned drinks, there is also a high degree of sensitivity towards the stereotypical portrayal of 'Indian' people in ads for 'Indian' fast foods. These have become more prevalent on British TV, and are widely perceived as an attempt by the advertisers to sell 'frozen Indian culture'. But such sensitivity is not shared or recognised by all, as is evident in the following discussion between two 16-year-old boys:

NIRMAL: Have you seen the Indian couple doing a British ad you know, these fast foods.
RANJIT: Oh, you mean English-made Indian food.
NIRMAL: Yeah.
RANJIT: But they're really westernised, they're not like traditional Indians.
NIRMAL: They are, I think it's quite patronising in fact, they, like sell a different culture and say, 'Ah . . . it's so sweet!', it's like frozen Indian culture.
RANJIT: [laughs] What do you mean patronising?
NIRMAL: The ad is patronising cos they only use Indian people for these types of product.
RANJIT: But in one way they're just trying to get their point across that, hey! this is Indian food.
NIRMAL: But they stereotype them [. . .] they all have accents.
RANJIT: But most of them do speak with accents.
NIRMAL: Not all of them, you don't speak with an accent do you? But you were born here.
RANJIT: Yeah but what about the Findus punch-line? [laughing].
NIRMAL: Oh yeah.

RANJIT: When the wife brings the pudding to her husband and he goes, [Indian accent] 'What's that dear?' and she says, [Indian accent] 'Oh! it's spotted Dick' [laughs].

NIRMAL: But it's taking the piss, it shows that Indians don't know the English language or their food!

Thus quite different readings can be made of the same ad. Ranjit finds the couple both 'westernised' and amusing and is little concerned about stereotypical portrayals. He quite readily accepts that many 'Indian' people speak with ('Indian') accents and it does not bother him that they should be represented as such. Nirmal on the other hand shows concern about the 'burden of representation' (Mercer, 1988) carried by such TV ads. 'Indians' only appear on British TV to advertise the stereotypical 'Indianness' of ('western') products, and are portrayed as stereotypically ignorant of the English language and English foods. As with the Rubicon ads, such representations are seen as an indication of 'foreign' status: 'They make us out to be more foreign than we actually are – as if we are not part of their culture, but we are!'

There is a marked lack of images on British TV, but also on on 'Asian' or 'Indian' TV and video, which young people in Southall feel able to identify with or which confirm a recognition of their identity by others. McDonald's in the sphere of food, and Coca Cola in the sphere of drink, are seen to represent an alternative. These brands connote, both through the suggestions conveyed by the imagery, songs and slogans of their ads, and through the particular place assumed by their consumption in local life, an ideal 'freedom' which transcends boundaries. Not only the numerous boundaries which divide Southall internally – boundaries of religion and caste, gender and generation – and those which divide Southall from the wider British society 'outside'; but also the global boundaries of ethnicity and nationality are portrayed in the Coke ads as transcended through a sense of easy participation in a global youth culture modelled on an American teenage dream. This idealised global youth culture is shaped by consumption practices: it expresses the utopian desire for a world in which everybody is equally 'cool', 'safe', affluent and free to consume at will. Yet even though the expression of this desire is to a great extent constrained by the logic and imagery of consumerism, the talk about Coke ads consistently highlights the style of open, expansive sociability which they represent; and this suggests that the desire at stake here may be understood as the desire for full integration into a pluralistic society where the social implications of cultural differences are minimal. Thus in talking of Coke ads – and elsewhere in their ad talk – young people in Southall articulate, negatively and positively, aspirations for cultural change which deserve to be taken seriously as the potential matrix of a future, genuinely pluralist culture.

Conclusion

This book has explored the microprocesses of the construction of a British Asian identity among young people in Southall, against the backdrop of the emergence of 'new ethnicities' in the context of post-colonial migration and the globalisation of communications. It has brought together the study of TV reception and the study of diaspora cultures: audience research has delivered insights into the lives of young Punjabi Londoners, while intensive and extended fieldwork has allowed the integration of TV experiences in a local culture to be studied in depth. And in presenting the voices of participants in the collective process of cultural change, voices normally absent from academic discourse, this study tries to enable readers to understand that process as its subjects experience it, and contribute to shaping it, in their everyday lives.

The central methodological argument of this book is that, in order to understand how TV is implicated in the remaking of ethnicity, or indeed in any process of cultural change, we must submit to the rigours of ethnographic enquiry. TV talk, though it may often seem esoteric and trivial, is an important form of self-narration and a major collective resource through which identities are negotiated. Ethnographic fieldwork makes it possible to document and analyse the forms, contents and implications of such talk as a ritualistic form of everyday interaction, whether in front of the TV set or elsewhere. Both anthropologists and media reception researchers have much to gain from combining their efforts in this field. It is certainly to be hoped that academic TV research will in future produce more empirical studies, and perhaps not so many theoretically oriented summaries of the few pieces of research which already exist.

The type of questions addressed in this study resist easy answers; nor does the ethnographic approach lend itself to unambiguous conclusions. I have tried to present the data, and my analyses, in such a way that readers can arrive at their own assessment. Here I will just summarise some of my key findings, and suggest possible directions for further research.

In Southall, the redefinition of ethnicity is enacted in young people's collective reception and appropriation of TV. Transnational and diasporic media representing several cultures are available in Southall homes, offering a range of choices of symbolic identification. This range is sometimes felt to be too wide, as when, in situations of international conflict such as the Gulf War, young people find themselves facing difficult or even painful dilemmas. On the other hand, in key respects the range is not wide enough: young people complain, for example, that too few images of 'Asian' style and beauty are available which they feel able to take as role models. Yet the very coexistence of culturally diverse media is a cultural resource. It engenders a developed consciousness of difference and a cosmopolitan stance. It encourages young people to compare, contrast and criticise the cultural and social forms represented to them by their parents, by significant others present in their daily lives and by significant others on screen. This is the kind of context in which the construction of new ethnic identities becomes both an inevitable consequence and a necessary task.

We have just seen how the aspiration towards cultural change among Southall teenagers takes its most emphatically positive form from images (and sounds) designed to market the products of US-based transnational corporations such as Coca Cola and McDonald's. This utopian 'teen dream' might easily be dismissed as gullibility. But when the responses to these ads invoke a hoped-for transcendence of ethnic – and other – difference, in a setting of consumerist freedom, they define an ideal arena, an imaginative space, within which the construction of new identities becomes possible as a real project. The relatively humdrum, material corollary of their utopian ad talk, discussed in the previous chapter – the visit with friends to McDonald's in Hounslow – is an entirely real 'escape' into a new social and communicative space, in which young people can actively re-define their culture.

The position of young British Asians – and other minorities – has long been described in the metaphor of 'culture clash', with its implicit notion of 'culture' as a bounded, impermeable, monolithic entity. Such thinking in terms of binary oppositions is not only characteristic of academic and media accounts of cross-cultural encounters and flows, but also structures everyday perceptions of cultural interaction and change among people of all ages in Southall. The oppositions of 'east' and 'west', tradition and modernity, religious and secular, poverty and wealth are rooted in the history of imperialism and colonialism, and continue to shape people's understanding of the cultural changes in which they participate. Images of cultural 'purity', fears of cultural 'contamination' and 'weakening' abound. Young people in Southall tend to claim that, while their parents are concerned with maintaining 'the culture', they themselves are open to change. Yet in the face of news events which represent a challenge to their sense of identity, they become acutely aware of the range of options open to them and trapped in binary thinking themselves.

Responses to the Gulf War, an event mediated primarily by TV, provided a paradigmatic example of this.

In this book I have used the term 'ethnicity' in the sense of an array of strategic positionings in a field of differences, and adopted a dynamic concept of culture, in the hope of challenging in some small way the limiting, paralysing or destructive effects of such binary thinking. It remains to be seen whether the collective identity which is still in the process of being developed by young British Asians will succeed in avoiding its snares.

Young Punjabi Londoners' media consumption is characterised by a reflective awareness of cultural difference even when, as in the case of *Neighbours*, they are drawn to a programme because (though they would express this differently) they perceive it to offer a complex metaphor for their own social world. A valuable parallel to my analysis of *Neighbours* in Southall is the work of Miller (1992) on the reception of the American soap *The Young and Restless* in Trinidad: it proves that ethnographic studies can indeed produce potentially generalisable results. Many of his informants offered the term *bacchanal* (scandal, confusion, disorder, exposure of truth) as a one-word characterisation of Trinidad society, and referred to the soap – an imported media product – in order to exemplify what the term meant. Underlying and linking the various meanings of *bacchanal*, Miller argues, is a notion close to that of 'gossip': thus his study provides a close comparative parallel to mine. In Southall too, 'gossip' is the term which young people use to characterise the essence of their local society, as well as the essence of the soap, and of the talk which embeds the TV representation in their everyday life. Thus in Trinidad as in Southall, according to a very similar pattern, a transnational media product is locally appropriated in ways which encourage people to refine their conceptions of their own local culture, and at the same time redefine their collective identity in relation to representations of 'others'.

Such 'indigenisation' as an effect of globalisation involves enhanced cultural consciousness; but further ethnographic studies are needed to discover why particular local societies appropriate particular 'imported' media products – are they always melodramatic soaps? – in particular ways. And our conceptual vocabulary will also need revising, if we are to find better ways of describing and analysing the processes vaguely called 'hybridisation', 'syncretism', 'crossover' and the like.

'Cultural translation' offers one very useful addition to our vocabulary. Growing up in Southall involves learning to translate both literally – as young people translate British TV news to their elders – and, at the same, metaphorically, as they must acquire skills in negotiating from context to context between various cultures and various positions within each. As many commentators have pointed out, the contemporary development of global communications increasingly brings together cultures which might once have been clearly distinct, calling forth a range of ambivalent responses, sometimes hardening and sometimes dissolving boundaries. The apparently marginal experience of Punjabi Londoners can thus be seen to be, in fact, central to so-called postmodern culture, in which 'translation' is becoming a common global experience. But the uneven effects of globalisation, of the communicative linkage of diaspora cultures and of the emergence of the politics of identity as an apparent successor to class politics in contemporary societies, stand in need of further empirical research. This study at least suggests that class politics and the nation state continue to play an overriding role in structuring identities.

Most, though not all, of my informants would agree with this. Students from Southall's three high schools came together in the summer of 1992 to debate the issue of identity in a public, formal context, in a local community centre. The motion was: 'This house is British', and the alternative offered was initially 'Asian'. As the debate progressed, it became clear that this alternative was false. Most speakers affirmed a 'British Asian' identity. But the relative weighting of the two components, 'British' and 'Asian', and the objective or subjective, individual or collective, qualities of identity were much questioned. How does one 'show' one is 'Asian', it was asked, if one speaks no Asian language, and how does one 'show' one is 'British' if one has brown skin? Cultural, 'racial' and legal identity (citizenship) were invoked by turns. Some speakers proposed 'British Asian' as a political identity, a matter of choice – as one said: 'The next generation are looking for another category to put ourselves in [. . .]. Politically, I want a stake in this country, not under the banner "black" but as a British Asian'. But many felt they had no power to choose, either as individuals or collectively. While 'being British' is about citizenship and civic rights, it is also about 'racial' categorisation: 'No matter what we feel ourselves to be, others will always look on us as outsiders'.

Though much of this book may be read as an affirmation of media consumers' resourcefulness in constructing their own identities, we should not lose sight of the very real constraints upon their freedom to do so: the nation state continues to define its ethnic minorities as internal others; and class, gender, religion, locality, generation and other factors, which are not freely chosen, continue to set limits on self-invention. To believe that the market or consumption is the key arena of identity formation is to fall prey to the ideology of free marketeers. Yet, as the globalisation of communications and cultures articulates new kinds of temporal and spatial relations, it transforms the modes of identification available within societies. Media are being used by productive consumers to maintain and strengthen boundaries, but also to create new, shared spaces in which syncretic cultural forms, such as 'new ethnicities', can emerge. These processes are uneven and their consequences unforeseeable, though likely to be weighty. But they cannot be examined in the abstract or at a distance: in order for researchers to understand culture as a becoming, not a being, we have to participate too.

Appendix: Southall Youth Survey (1989–1990)

Note: Selected results only are given here. Percentage figures have been rounded to the nearest whole number. There were wide variations in the numbers of valid responses to individual questions (N). Percentages are calculated from absolute numbers. For further details, see Gillespie (1992); West (1991).

1 SAMPLE PROFILE

1a Age and gender

Age	Male	Female	Total
12	22	18	40
13	33	32	65
14	32	35	67
15	22	24	46
16	18	33	51
17	28	19	47
18	13	4	17
Total	168	165	333

1b Religion

The following figures give the religious composition of the sample as reported in this survey, compared with those of a survey of all 771 pupils in one local secondary school at the same time (April 1989).

	% survey (N = 333)	% school (N = 771)
Sikh	51	56
Hindu	16	20
Muslim	15	14
Christian	8	10
Other	5	0
Mixed	5	n/a

1c Parental occupation

Father's job	% (N = 306)	Mother's job	% (N = 263)
Manual	37	Manual	38
Semi-skilled	26	Housewife	28
Skilled	20	Skilled	17
Managerial/technical	8	Semi-skilled	10
Professional	6	Managerial/technical	4
Unemployed	2	Retired	3
Deceased	1	Professional	1
Retired	0.3	Deceased	0.3

2 KINSHIP NETWORKS

2a Grandparent(s) living 'in or near Southall'

Religion	% (N = 312)
Sikh	36
Hindu	29
Muslim	19
Christian	35
Overall average	34

2b Cousins living 'in or near Southall'

Number of cousins	% (N = 333)
0	19
1–5	30
5–10	17
More than 10	34

3 PERCEPTIONS OF CULTURAL DIVERSITY

'Southall has many different cultures. Please write down some cultures that you know are around.'

This open-ended question aimed to elicit the criteria used by youth to delineate what they understand by different 'cultures'.

Criteria mentioned in responses	% (N = 313)
Religion	75
Religious ritual (e.g. Diwali, Christmas)	8

Nationality (e.g. Indian, British)	31
Region/language (e.g. Punjab, Gujarati)	11
Named subculture (e.g. Rasta)	9
'Caribbean'	15
'Asian'	14
'Indian'	12
'Black'	7
'British'	6
'White'	5

4 PERCEPTIONS OF SOUTHALL

'Here are some things that young people have said to us. Please tick the ones that you agree with.'

Statement	% in agreement (N = 183)
Nothing in Southall can be kept secret	74
Everybody watches what everybody is doing here	69
Southall is too isolated, it's like an island	45
Not all communities are getting a fair deal	38
My community is like an island in Southall	17
Every community in Southall is like an island	13

5 DIVISIONS IN SOUTHALL

5a Youth

'What divides youth in Southall is mainly this: Please tick the more important ones.'

Factor	% ticked (N = 186)
Religion	55
Culture	55
Racism	47
Class	39
Race	37
Competition	36
School	36
Parents	35
Money	33
Fear	29
Politics	16
Media	11

5b Adults

'What divides adults in Southall is mainly this: Please tick the more important ones.'

Factor	% ticked (N = 185)
Religion	65
Culture	54
Class	38
Race	38
Money	34
Racism	30
Fear	23
Competition	21
Politics	20
Media	14
School	12

6 PARENTAL RULES

'In your family, do you have set rules about these things: Please tick'.

	% males	% females
	(N = 315)	
Times for going out in the day	27	37
Times for going out at night	37	35
I don't go out at night	23	47
Any school friends you can't bring home	15	19
Helping father	49	44
Helping mother	49	73
Praying at home	31	32
Going to worship	38	33
Time to start watching TV	20	22
Time to stop watching TV	20	23
Not watching sex on TV	24	28
Not watching violence on TV	10	8
Time for watching videos	17	24
Videos you can't watch	21	24
Recording programmes for yourself	17	18

7 COURTSHIP AND MARRIAGE

'Here are some statements that young people have made to us. Please tick the ones that you agree with.'

7a Going out

Statement	% ticked (N = 186)
Parents should know more about it but be more understanding	67
Going out with a boy or a girl is normal at my age	58
Going out does not have to lead to marriage	57
Parents should know about it so they can give advice	47
It's not normal in my culture and I respect that	40
If young people go out it's none of their parents' business	31
It's all right as long as you keep it a secret	31
If I go out, it's none of my parents' business	24
Going out should not lead to marriage	23
It is wrong for anyone unless they want to marry	17
My parents think it is normal at my age	10

7b Marriage

Statement	% ticked (N = 186)
People should be free to marry whom they like	75
I personally would prefer a marriage within my own culture	49
I would only enter a mixed marriage if my parents agreed	45
People who marry should be of the same culture	35
If I wanted a mixed marriage I would do it against my family	26
People should marry in their own caste	18

8 LEISURE

'In the last month have you been to any of these places?'

	% females (N = 154)	% males
Friends' parties	53	55
Place of worship	53	37
Disco	39	42
Leisure centre	26	52
Cinema	26	34
Sports club	22	45
Youth club	15	40
Games arcade	12	51

9 DOMESTIC MEDIA TECHNOLOGIES

9a Equipment

	% (N = 217)
1 fixed colour TV set	90
Video recorder	89
Remote control	86
2 fixed colour TV sets	52
Teletext	48
Portable colour TV set	42
3 fixed colour TV sets	22
Cable television	22
Portable black and white TV set	16
Fixed black and white TV set	14
Prestel	12
Satellite dish	9

9b Location of TV sets

	% (N = 217)
Main living-room	91
Main bedroom	48
Children's bedroom	43
Other living-room	26
Dining room	15
Kitchen	11

10 TV AND VIDEO USE

10a Family viewing patterns

(A) 'Which types of programme do you often watch with the family?'
(B) 'Which types of programme do you talk about with your parents?'
(C) 'Which types of programme did you actually watch in the last week?'
(D) 'Which types of programme do you prefer to watch without older people?'

For the results to all four questions (shown in 10a–e below), N = 217, of which 104 males, 113 females.

	% (A)	% (B)	% (C)	% (D)
News	76	43	64	0
Comedy	74	19	78	43
Crime	56	17	64	34
Soaps	54	13	59	37
Cartoons	51	7	72	36

Game show	51	10	65	0
Quiz	48	10	61	0
Pop	38	5	71	63
Children's	38	5	69	0
Nature	33	13	37	0
Documentary	25	9	39	0
Science	22	4	30	0
Sci-fi	20	3	36	0
Current affairs 20	4	28	28	0

10b Gender breakdown: (A)

'Which types of programme do you often watch with the family?'

	% males	% females
News	74	78
Comedy	72	75
Crime	57	55
Soaps	48	58
Cartoons	47	55
Quiz	42	54
Game show	51	44
Pop	31	45
Children's	33	42
Nature	35	39
Documentary	28	22
Science	28	16
Sci-fi	29	12
Current affairs	21	18

10c Gender breakdown: (B)

'Which types of programme do you talk about with your parents?'

	% males	% females
News	34	50
Comedy	17	20
Crime	13	21
Soaps	7	20
Nature	12	13
Game show	10	11
Quiz	7	13
Documentary	10	8
Cartoons	4	10
Pop	3	7
Children's	5	4
Science	4	4
Sci-fi	3	3

10d Gender breakdown: (C)

'Which types of programme did you actually watch in the last week?'

	% males	% females
Comedy	78	79
Cartoons	66	79
Pop	66	76
Children's	59	78
Crime	67	63
Game show	63	67
News	61	66
Quiz	57	66
Soaps	56	62
Documentary	42	36
Nature	49	26
Sci-fi	51	22
Science	41	21

10e Gender breakdown: (D)

'Which types of programme do you prefer to watch without older people?'

	% males	% females
Pop	54	70
Cartoons	72	36
Comedy	47	40
Soaps	32	40
Crime	43	25
All others	0	0

10f Favourite programmes

'Which programmes do you try to watch every week?'

	% total (N = 118)
Neighbours	67
The Bill	28
The Cosby Show	27
EastEnders	24
Dallas	22
Home and Away	20
Dynasty	20
Top of the Pops	18
Miami Vice	7
Grange Hill	6
Brookside	6
Prisoner Cell Block H	3

10g Preferred TV channel

	% family	% self
	(N = 188)	
BBC1	82	64
ITV	76	45
Channel 4	16	21
BBC2	7	13

10h Preferred video type

(A) 'often watch with whole family'.
(B) 'often talk about with father or mother'.

	% (A)	% (B)
	(N = 217)	
Indian video	66	32
English video	55	15
American video	51	10

10j Judgements about Indian films

	% females	% males
	(N = 213)	
I enjoy them	48	24
They bring the family together	33	33
They help me with the language	39	23
They tell me something about Asia	37	25
They tell me about my religion	19	28
My parents like me to watch them	21	24
They teach me about Asian culture	26	15
I can watch them with friends	18	4
I like watching the stars	64	22
I like the songs and dance most	61	21
I like the action most	18	31
I like the dialogue most	25	17
They do not show the real Asia	30	24
I find them too slow	18	26
I don't like any of it	14	30

11 PERSONAL STYLE

'In your own dress and style, what are the most important things to you?'

	% males	% females
	(N = 272)	
To look cool	66	47
To be respectable	43	49

To show a bit of class	48	44
To stay OK with my parents	34	48
To look elegant or sophisticated	26	36
To show guts	31	26
To look totally personal	25	31
To respect my culture	13	35
To be like my friends	21	26
To show modesty	13	20
To rebel against rules	17	12
To show self-esteem	9	10

12 COUNTRIES YOUNG PEOPLE WOULD MOST LIKE TO VISIT

	% (N = 184)
USA	46
Australia	14
Canada	7
Europe	5
India	5
Other Asian	5
East Africa	4
Pakistan	2
Others not listed	16

Bibliography

Alibhai, Y., 1987, 'A White Christmas', in *New Society*, 18 December 1987: 15–17

Allen, I., 1982, 'Talking about Media Experiences: Everyday Life as Popular Culture', in *Journal of Popular Culture* 16/3: 106–115

Allen, R., 1985, *Speaking of Soap Operas*, Chapel Hill and London: University of North Carolina Press

——, ed., 1987, *Channels of Discourse*, Chapel Hill and London: University of North Carolina Press

——, ed., 1994, *To Be Continued. Soap Operas Around the World*, New York and London: Routledge

Allport, G., 1959, *The Nature of Prejudice*, New York: Doubleday, Anchor

Anderson, B., 1983, *Imagined Communities: Reflections on the Origins and Spread of Nationalism*, London: Verso

Ang, I., 1985, *Dallas: Soap Opera and the Melodramatic Imagination*, London and New York: Methuen

——, 1990, 'Culture and Communication: Towards an Ethnographic Critique of Media Consumption in the Transnational Media System', in *European Journal of Communications* 5/2–3: 239–261

——, 1991, *Desperately Seeking the Audience*, London: Routledge

Appadurai, A., ed., 1986, *The Social Life of Things: Commodities in Cultural Perspective*, Cambridge: Cambridge University Press

Appadurai, A., 1990, 'Disjuncture and Difference in the Global Cultural Economy', in M. Featherstone, ed., *Global Culture: Nationalism, Globalisation, Modernity,* London: Sage, pp. 295–311

Appadurai, A. and C. A. Breckenridge, 1992, 'Museums are Good to Think: Heritage on View in India', in I. Karp and S. D. Lavine, eds, *Museums and Communities: The Politics of Public Culture*, Washington: Smithsonian Institute

Arnold, A., 1988, 'Popular Film Song in India: A Case of Mass Market Musical Eclecticism', in *Popular Music*, 7/2

Asad, T., ed., 1973, *Anthropology and the Colonial Encounter*, New York: Humanities Press

Aurora, G. S., 1967, *The New Frontiersmen*, Bombay: Popular Prakashan

Bains, H. S., 1988, 'Southall Youth: An Old-fashioned Story', in P. Cohen and H. S. Bains, eds, *Multi-racist Britain*, London: Macmillan

Balibar, E., 1991, '*Es gibt keinen Staat in Europa*: Racism and Politics in Europe Today', in *New Left Review* 186: 1–19

Ballard, C., 1979, 'Conflict, Continuity and Change: Second Generation Asians', in V. Saifullah Khan, ed., *Minority Families in Britain*, London: Macmillan, pp. 109–129

Ballard, R., 1982, 'South Asian Families in Britain', in R. Rappoport, ed., *Families in Britain*, London: Routledge & Kegan Paul, pp. 179–205

Barnes, D., 1975, *Language, the Learner and the School*, Harmondsworth: Penguin

Barthes, R., 1975, *The Pleasure of the Text*, trans. R. Miller, New York: Hill & Wang

——, 1977a, *Image, Music, Text*, London: Fontana

——, 1977b, *Writing Degree Zero*, New York: Hill & Wang

Baudrillard, J., 1988, *Selected Writings*, Cambridge: Polity

Bauman, Z., 1990, 'Modernity and Ambivalence', in M. Featherstone, ed., *Global Culture: Nationalism, Globalisation, Modernity*, London: Sage, pp. 160–168

Baumann, G., 1990, 'The Re-invention of Bhangra: Social Change and Aesthetic Shifts in a Punjabi Music in Britain', in *Journal of the International Institute for Comparative Music Studies and Documentation*, Berlin, 32/2: 81–97

——, 1991, 'Village Fieldwork Overseas versus Urban Research at Home? Textbook Dichotomies in the Light of Second Fieldwork', in *Journal of the Anthropological Society of Oxford*, 19/3

——, 1992, 'Ritual Implicates 'Others': Re-reading Durkheim in a Plural Society', in D. De Coppet, ed., *Understanding Ritual*, London: Routledge, pp. 97–117

——, forthcoming, *Contesting Culture: Two Discourses of 'Culture' and 'Community' in a multi-ethnic London*, Cambridge: Cambridge University Press

Bausinger, H., 1984, 'Media, Technology and Everyday Life', in *Media, Culture & Society* 6: 343–351

Bennett, T. *et al.*, eds, 1987, *Bond and Beyond: The Political Career of a Popular Hero*, London: Macmillan

Bernstein, B., 1971–5, *Class, Codes and Control*, 3 vols, London: Routledge

Bhabha, H., ed., 1990, *Nation and Narration*, London: Routledge

Bhachu, P., 1985, *Twice Migrants*, London: Tavistock

Bharucha, R., 1991, 'A View From India', in D. Williams, ed., *Peter Brook and the 'Mahabharata': Critical Perspectives*, London: Routledge

Bloor, M., 1983, 'Notes on Member Validation', in R. M. Emerson, ed., *Contemporary Field Research: A Collection of Readings*, Boston: Little, Brown

Blumenthal, A., 1932, *Small Town Stuff*, Chicago: Chicago University Press

——, 1937, 'The Nature of Gossip', in *Sociology and Social Research*, 22: 31–37

Blumler, H., 1969, *Symbolic Interactionism*, Englewood Cliffs, NJ: Prentice–Hall

Bordwell, D., 1985, *Narration in the Fiction Film*, London: Methuen

Boskoff, A., 1970, *The Sociology of Urban Regions*, New York: Appleton-Century-Crofts

Bott, E., 1957, *Family and Social Network*, London: Tavistock

Bourdieu, P., 1977, *Reproduction in Education, Society and Culture*, London: Sage

——, 1980, 'The Aristocracy of Culture', in *Media, Culture & Society* 2/3

——, 1984, *Distinction: A Social Critique of the Judgement of Taste*, London and New York: Routledge & Kegan Paul

Brah, A., 1978, 'South Asian Teenagers in Southall: Their Perceptions of Marriage, Family and Ethnic Identity', in *New Community* 6: 197–206

——, 1979, 'Inter-generational and Inter-ethnic Perceptions: A Comparative Study of South Asian and English Adolescents and Their Parents in Southall', unpublished Ph.D. dissertation, University of Bristol

——, 1982, 'The South Asians', in *Minority Experience*, Milton Keynes: Open University Coursebook (E354, Ethnic Minorities and Community Relations) pp. 1–26

——, 1987, 'Women of South Asian Origin in Britain', in *South Asia Research* 7/1

Brass, P., 1991, *Ethnicity and Nationalism: Theory and Comparison*, New Delhi and London: Sage

Brown, M., 1987, 'The Politics of Soaps: Pleasure and Feminine Empowerment', in *Australian Journal of Cultural Studies* 4

Bryce, J. and H. Leichter, 1983, 'The Family and TV: Forms of Mediation', in *Journal of Family Issues* 4/2: 309–328

Buckingham, D., 1987, *Public Secrets: EastEnders and its Audience*, London: British Film Institute

——, 1990, 'Seeing Through TV: Children Talking About TV', in J. Willis and T. Wollen, eds, *The Neglected Audience*, London: British Film Institute

——, 1991, 'What are Words Worth? Children's Talk about TV', in *Cultural Studies* 5/2: 228–244

——, 1993, *Children Talking TV: The Making of TV Literacies*, London: Falmer Press

Cardiff, D. and P. Scannel, 1987, 'Broadcasting and National Unity', in J. Curran, A. Smith and P. Wingate, eds, *Impacts and Influences*, London: Methuen

CCCS (Centre for Contemporary Cultural Studies), 1982, *The Empire Strikes Back: Race and Racism in 70s Britain*, London: Hutchinson

Chambers, I., 1986, *Popular Culture: The Metropolitan Experience*, London: Methuen

Chaney, D., 1983, 'A Symbolic Mirror of Ourselves: Civic Ritual in Mass Communication', *Media, Culture and Society* 5(2)

——, 1986, 'The Symbolic Form of Ritual in Mass Communications', in P. Golding, ed., *Communicating Politics*, Leicester: Leicester University Press

Chatterji, A. P., 1989, 'The *Ramayana* and Indian Secularism', in *Intermedia* 17/5

Cheesman, T., 1994, *The Shocking Ballad Picture Show: German Popular Literature and Cultural History*, Oxford and Rhode Island: Berg

Cicourel, A., 1973, *Cognitive Sociology*, Harmondsworth: Penguin

Clifford, J., 1980, 'Fieldwork, Reciprocity, and the Making of Ethnographic Texts: the Example of Maurice Leenhardt', in *Man* 15: 518–532

——, 1983, 'On Ethnographic Authority', in *Representations* 1: 118–146

——, 1986, 'On Ethnographic Allegory', in J. Clifford and G. E. Marcus, eds, *Writing Culture: The Poetics and Politics of Ethnography*, Berkeley: University of California Press, pp. 98–121

Clifford, J. and G. E. Marcus, eds, 1986, *Writing Culture: The Poetics and Politics of Ethnography*, Berkeley: University of California Press

Cohen, A., 1980, 'Drama and Politics in the Development of a London Carnival', in *Man* 15: 65–87

——, 1982, 'A Polyethnic London Carnival as a Contested Cultural Performance', in *Ethnic and Racial Studies* 5: 23–41

Curran, J., 1990, 'The New Revisionism in Mass Communications Research', in *European Journal of Communications* 5/2–3: 131–135

Dahlgren, P., 1988, 'What's the Meaning of This? Viewers' Plural Sense-making of TV News', in *Media, Culture & Society* 10: 285–301

Dayan, D. and E. Katz, 1983, 'Performing Media Events', in J. Curran *et al.*, eds, *Impacts and Influences*, London: Methuen

De Certeau, M., 1984, *The Practice of Everyday Life*, trans. S. Rendall, Berkeley: University of California Press

Diamond, N., 1970, 'Fieldwork in a Complex Society: Taiwan', in G. Spindler, ed., *Being an Anthropologist*, New York: Holt, Rinehart and Winston

Dissanayeke, W., 1988, 'Cultural Identity and Asian Cinema', in W. Dissanayeke, ed., *Cinema and Cultural Identity*, Maryland: University Press of America

Donald, J. and A. Rattansi, eds, 1992, *'Race', Culture and Difference*, London: Sage/Open University

Douglas, M. and B. Isherwood, 1979, *The World of Goods*, New York: Basic Books

Du Bois, W. E. B., 1986, *The Souls of Black Folk*, New York: Bantam Books

Evans, W., 1990, 'The Interpretive Turn in Media Research: Innovation, Iteration or Illusion?', in *Critical Studies in Mass Communications* 7/2: 147–168

Evans-Pritchard, E., 1937, *Witchcraft, Oracles and Magic among the Azande*, Oxford: Clarendon

Featherstone, M., ed., 1990, *Global Culture: Nationalism, Globalisation, Modernity*, London: Sage

Festinger, L., *et al.*, 1948, 'A Study of Rumour: Its Origins and Spread', in *Human Relations* 1: 464–486

Feuer, J., 1986, '*Dynasty*', paper presented to International Television Studies Conference, London, July 1986

Firth, R., 1956, 'Rumour in Primitive Society', in *Journal of Abnormal and Social Psychology* 53: 122–132

Fischer, M., 1986, 'Ethnicity and the Postmodern Arts of Memory', in J. Clifford and G. E. Marcus, eds, *Writing Culture: the Poetics and Politics of Ethnography*, Berkeley: University of California Press, pp. 194–233

Fish, S., 1980, *Is There a Text in This Class? The Authority of Interpretive Communities*, Cambridge, MA.: Harvard University Press

Fiske, J., 1985, 'TV and Popular Culture', paper presented at the Iowa Symposium on TV Criticism

——, *Television Culture*, London: Methuen

——, 1989a, 'Moments of TV: Neither the Text nor the Audience', in E. Seiter, *et al.*, eds, *Remote Control*, London and New York: Routledge

——, 1989b, *Understanding Popular Culture*, Boston, MA.: Unwin Hyman

——, 1990, 'Ethnosemiotics: Some Personal and Theoretical Reflections', in *Cultural Studies* 4/1

Fitzgerald, T. K., 1992, 'Media, Ethnicity and Identity', in P. Scannel, P. Schlesinger and C. Sparks, eds, *Culture and Power. A 'Media, Culture and Society' Reader*, London etc.: Sage, pp. 112–136

Freeman, D., 1984, *Margaret Mead and Samoa*, Harmondsworth: Penguin

Gans, H. J., 1979, 'Symbolic Ethnicity: the Future of Ethnic Groups and Cultures in America', in *Ethnic and Racial Studies* 2

Garfinkle, H., 1967, *Studies in Ethnomethodology*, Englewood Cliffs, NJ. : Prentice-Hall

Geertz, C., 1966, 'Religion as a Cultural System' in M. Banton, ed., *Anthropological Approaches to the Study of Religion*, London: Tavistock

——, 1973, *The Interpretation of Cultures*, New York: Basic Books

——, 1979, 'Deep Play: Notes on a Balinese Cockfight', in P. Rabinow and W. Sullivan, eds, *Interpretive Social Science: A Reader*, Berkeley: University of California Press

Geraghty, C., 1990 *Women and Soap Operas,* London: Polity

Giddens, A., 1990, *The Consequences of Modernity*, Cambridge: Polity

——, 1991, *Modernity and Self-identity*, Cambridge: Polity

Gigliol, P., 1975, *Language and Social Context*, Harmondsworth: Penguin

Gillespie, M., 1981, 'A Study of Young Asians' Perceptions of the Interaction of Home and School Cultures', unpublished PGCE dissertation, St Mary's College, University of London

——, 1989, 'Technology and Tradition: Audio–visual Culture among South Asian Families in West London', in *Cultural Studies* 3/2: 226–239

——, 1992, 'The Role of TV in the Negotiation of Cultural Identities and Differences Among Punjabi Londoners', in A. Millwood-Hargreave, ed., *The Portrayal of Ethnic Minorities on Television*, London: Broadcasting Standards Council, Research Working Paper VII

——, 1993a, 'From Sanskrit to Sacred Soap: A Case-study in the Reception of two Contemporary TV versions of the *Mahabharata*', in D. Buckingham, ed., *Reading Audiences*, Manchester: Manchester University Press, pp. 48–74

——, 1993b, 'Soap Opera, Gossip and Rumour in a Punjabi Town in West London', in *National Identity and Europe: The TV Revolution*, London: British Film Institute, pp. 25–43

——, 1994a, 'The Gulf Between Us: Young Punjabi Londoners, Television and the Gulf War', forthcoming in *Indo-British Review*

——, 1994b, 'Sacred Serials, Devotional Viewing and Domestic Worship', in R. Allen, ed., *To Be Continued. Soap Operas Around the World*, New York and London: Routledge

Gilroy, P., 1987, *There Ain't No Black in the Union Jack*, London: Hutchinson

——, 1993a, *The Black Atlantic: Modernity and Double Consciousness*, London and New York: Verso

——, 1993b, *Small Acts: Thoughts on the Politics of Black Cultures*, London: Serpent's Tail

Glaser, B. G. and A. L. Strauss, 1967, *The Discovery of Grounded Theory*, Chicago: Aldine

Goffmann, E., 1959, *The Presentation of Self in Everyday Life*, Garden City, New York: Doubleday

——, 1967, *Interaction Ritual: Essays on Face to Face Behaviour*, Garden City, New York: Anchor Books

——, 1969, *Strategic Interaction*, Philadelphia: University of Pennsylvania Press

Golde, P., ed., 1970, *Women in the Field*, Chicago: Aldine

Gott, R. 1986, 'Modernism and Post-modernism: The Crisis of Contemporary Culture', in *Guardian*, 1 December 1986, p. 10

Gray, A., 1986, 'Reading the Readings', paper presented at the International Television Studies Conference, University of London Institute of Education, July 1986

——, 1987, 'Behind Closed Doors: Video Recorders in the Home', in G. Baer, ed., *Boxed in: Women and TV*, New York and London: Pandora Press

——, 1992, *Video Playtime: The Gendering of a Leisure Technology*, London: Routledge

Guha-Thakurta, T., 1986, 'Artisans, Artists and Mass Picture Production in Late 19th and Early 20th Century in Calcutta', paper presented at the South Asia Research Conference, School of Oriental and African Studies, University of London, May 1986

Gumperz, J. J. and D. H. Hymes, 1972, *Directions in Sociolinguistics: The Ethnography of Communication*, New York: Holt, Rinehart and Winston

Gundara, J., 1986, 'Education in a Multicultural Society', in J. Gundara, C. Jones and K. Kimberley, eds, *Racism, Diversity and Education*, London: Hodder and Stoughton

Habermas, J., 1989, *The Structural Transformation of the Public Sphere*, Cambridge: Polity

Hall, S., 1977, 'Pluralism, Race and Class in Caribbean Society', in *Race and Class in Post-colonial Society*, Paris and London: UNESCO

——, 1987, 'Minimal Selves', in *Identity: The Real Me*, ICA Document 6, London: Institute for Contemporary Arts, pp. 45–46

——, 1988, 'New Ethnicities', in K. Mercer, ed., *Black Film, British Cinema*, London: Institute for Contemporary Arts, pp. 27–31

——, 1990, 'Cultural Identity and Diaspora', in J. Rutherford, ed., *Identity: Community, Culture, Difference*, London: Lawrence and Wishart, pp. 222–238

——, 1992, 'The Question of Cultural Identity', in S. Hall, D. Held and T. McGrew, eds, *Modernity and Its Futures*, Cambridge : Polity, pp. 273–326

——, 1993, 'Rethinking Ethnicities: Three Blind Mice (One Black, One White, One Hybrid)', inaugural lecture at the University of East London, New Ethnicities Unit (videotape), March 1993

Hammersley, M. and P. Atkinson, 1983, *Ethnography: Principles and Practice*, London: Tavistock

Hannerz, U., 1990, 'Cosmopolitans and Locals in World Culture', in M. Feather-stone, ed., *Global Culture: Nationalism, Globalisation, Modernity,* London: Sage, pp. 237–253

Hargreaves, D., 1967, *Social Relations in a Secondary School*, London: Routledge & Kegan Paul

Hartley, J., 1987, 'Television Audiences, Paedocracy and Pleasure', in *Textual Practice* 1/2

Harvey, D., 1989, *The Condition of Postmodernity*, Oxford: Blackwell

Hebdige, D., 1988, *Subculture: the Meaning of Style*, London: Routledge

——, 1989, 'After the Masses', in S. Hall and M. Jacques, eds, *New Times,* London: Lawrence and Wishart

——, 1992, 'Digging for Britain: An Excavation in Seven Parts' in D. Strinati and S. Wagg, eds, *Come on Down: Popular Media Culture in Post-war Britain*, London: Routledge

Hechter, M., 1975, *Internal Colonialisms: The Celtic Fringe in British National Development 1536–1966,* London: Routledge & Kegan Paul

Hobsbawm, E. and T. Ranger, eds, 1983, *The Invention of Tradition*, Cambridge: Cambridge University Press

Hobson, D., 1980, 'Housewives and the Mass Media', in S. Hall *et al.*, eds, *Culture, Media, Language: Working Papers in Cultural Studies 1972–79*, London: Hutchinson

——, 1982, *"Crossroads": The Drama of a Soap Opera*, London: Methuen

——, 1989, 'Soap Operas at Work', in E. Seiter, H. Borchers, G. Kreutzner and E. M. Warth, eds, *Remote Control*, London and New York: Routledge

Horton, D., *et al.*, 1986, 'Mass Communications and Para-social Interaction: Observations of Intimacy at a Distance', in G. Gumpert *et al.*, eds, *Inter/Media*, New York: Oxford University Press

Hymes, D., 1964, 'Toward Ethnographies of Communication', in *American Anthropologist* 66/6: 274–284

Jameson, F., 1991, *Postmodernism or the Cultural Logic of Late Capitalism*, London: Verso

Jordin, M. and R. Brunt, 1986, 'Constituting the TV Audience: A Problem of Method', paper presented to the International Television Studies Conference, University of London Institute of Education, July 1986

Julien, I. and K. Mercer, 1988, 'Introduction: De Margin and De Centre', in *Screen* 29/4 (*The Last 'Special Issue' on Race?*): 2–11

Katz, E. and P. Lazarsfeld, 1955, *Personal Influence: The Part Played by People in the Flow of Mass Communications*, New York: The Free Press

Katz, E. and T. Liebes, 1985, 'Mutual Aid in the Decoding of *Dallas*: Preliminary Notes from a Cross-cultural Study', in P. Drummond and R. Paterson, eds, *Television in Transition*, London: British Film Institute, pp. 183–198

Knight, J., 1986, 'Confinement and Isolation: Video in West Germany's Turkish Community', in *Independent Media* 60: 24

Lakoff, G. and M. Johnson, 1980, *Metaphors We Live By*, Chicago: Chicago University Press

Lazarsfeld, P., 1940, *Radio and the Printed Page*, New York: Duell, Sloane and Pearce

Leichter, H., 1979, *Families and Communities as Educators*, New York: Teachers College Press

Levitt, T., 1983, *The Marketing Imagination*, London: Macmillan

Lienhardt, P., 1975, 'The Interpretation of Rumour', in J. Beattie, E. E. Evans-Pritchard and G. Lienhardt *et al.*, *Studies in Social Anthropology*, Oxford: Clarendon

Livingstone, S. M., 1990, *Making Sense of Television: The Psychology of Audience Interpretation*, London: Pergamon Press

Lodziac, C., 1986, *The Power of TV*, London: Frances Pinter

Lull, J., 1988, *World Families Watching TV*, London: Sage

——, 1990, *Inside Family Viewing: Ethnographic Research on Television Audiences*, London: Routledge

McCracken, G., 1988, *Culture and Consumption: New Approaches to the Symbolic Character of Consumer Goods and Activities*, Bloomington: Indiana University Press

McGrew, A., 1992, 'A Global Society?', in S. Hall, D. Held and A. McGrew, eds, *Modernity and Its Futures*, Cambridge: Polity, pp. 61–116

Malinowski, B., 1964, *Argonauts of the Western Pacific*, London: Routledge & Kegan Paul (1922)

Mannheim, K., 1982, 'The Problem of Generations' (1929), in C. Jenks, ed., *The Sociology of Childhood: Essential Readings,* London: Batsford Academic and Educational Press, pp. 256–269

Manuel, P., 1988, 'Popular Music in India 1901–1986', in *Popular Music* 17/2

Maquet, J., 1964, 'Objectivity in Anthropology', in *Current Anthropology* 5: 47–55

Marcus, G. and M. Fisher, 1986, *Anthropology as Cultural Critique*, Chicago and London: University of Chicago Press

Marsh, C., 1982, *The Survey Method: The Contribution of Surveys to Sociological Explanation*, London: George Allen & Unwin

Mattelart, A., X. Delcourt and M. Mattelart, 1984, *International Image Markets: In Search of an Alternative Perspective*, London: Comedia

Mendelsohn, H., 1965, 'Listening to Radio', in L. A. Dexter and D. Manning White, eds, *People, Society and Mass Communications*, New York: Free Press, pp. 239–249

Mercer, K., 1987, 'Black Hair/Style Politics', in *New Formations* 3: 32–55

——, 1988, 'Recoding Narratives of Race and Nation', K. Mercer, ed., *Black Film, British Cinema*, London: Institute for Contemporary Arts, pp. 4–15

——, 1990, 'Welcome to the Jungle', in J. Rutherford, ed., *Identity: Community, Culture, Difference*, London: Lawrence and Wishart, pp. 43–71

Messaris, P., 1983, 'Family Conversations about TV', in *Journal of Family Issues* 4/2: 293–309

Meyrowitz, J., 1986, *No Sense of Place: The Impact of Electronic Media on Social Behaviour*, New York: Oxford University Press

Miller, D., 1987, *Material Culture and Mass Consumption*, Oxford: Blackwell

——, 1992, '*The Young and Restless* in Trinidad: A Case of the Local and Global in Mass Consumption', in R. Silverstone and E. Hirsch, eds, *Consuming Technologies*, London: Routledge, pp. 162–182

Mishra, V., 1985, 'Toward a Theoretical Critique of Bombay Cinema' in *Screen* 26/3–4: 133–149

——, 1991, 'The Great Indian Epic and Peter Brook', in D. Williams, ed., *Peter Brook and the 'Mahabharata': Critical Perspectives*, London: Routledge, pp. 195–206

Moores, S., 1993, *Interpreting Audiences: the Ethnography of Media Consumption*, London: Sage

Morley, D., 1975, 'Reconceptualising the Media Audience: Towards an

Ethnography of Audiences', Centre for Contemporary Cultural Studies, Occasional Paper
——, 1980, *The Nationwide Audience*, London: British Film Institute (1st edn 1978)
——, 1981, 'The Nationwide Audience: A Critical Post-script', in *Screen Education* 39: 3–14
——, 1986, *Family Television. Cultural Power and Domestic Leisure*, London: Comedia
——, 1989, 'Changing Paradigms in Audience Studies', in E. Seiter, H. Borchers, G. Kreutzner and E.-M. Warth, eds, *Remote Control: TV Audiences and Cultural Power*, London: Routledge
——, 1992, 'Where the Global Meets the Local: Notes from the Sitting Room', in *Screen* 32/1: 1–15
Morley, D. and K. Robins, 1989, 'Spaces of Identity', in *Screen* 20/4: 3–15
Morris, H. S., 1968, *The Indians in Uganda: Caste and Sect in a Plural Society*, London: Weidenfeld and Nicolson
Moser, C. and G. Kalton, 1971, *Survey Methods in Social Investigation*, London: Heinemann
Murdock, G., 1989, 'Critical Inquiry and Audience Activity', in B. Dervin *et al.*, eds, *Rethinking Communications*, London: Sage
——, 1990, 'Television and Citizenship', in A. Tomlinson, ed., *Consumption, Identity and Style*, London: Comedia
Nava, M. and O. Nava, 1992, 'Discriminating or Duped? Young People as Consumers of Advertising/Art', in M. Nava, ed., *Changing Cultures: Feminism, Youth and Consumerism*, London: Sage
Neale, S., 1981, *Genre*, London: British Film Institute
——, 1986, 'Melodrama and Tears', in *Screen* 27/61: 3–16
Nightingale, V., 1989, 'What's Ethnographic about Ethnographic Audience Research?', in *Australian Journal of Communications* 16: 50–63
Paine, R., 1967, 'What is Gossip About: An Alternative Hypothesis', in *Man* 2: 278–285
——, 1968, 'Gossip and Transaction', in *Man* 3: 305–308
Parmar, P., 1981, 'Young Asian Women: A Critique of the Pathological Approach', in *Multi-Racial Education* 10/1
Paterson, R., 1980, 'Planning the Family: The Art of the TV Schedule', in *Screen Education* 35
Perlmutter, H. V., 1991, 'On the Rocky Road to the First Global Civilisation', in *Human Relations* 44/9: 897–1010
Pettigrew, J., 1981, 'Reminiscences of Fieldwork among the Sikhs', in H. Roberts, ed., *Doing Feminist Research*, London: Routledge & Kegan Paul
Pfleiderer, B. and L. Lutze, eds, 1985, *The Hindi Film: Agent and Re-agent of Cultural Change*, New Delhi: Manohar Publications
Pike, K., 1966, 'Etic and Emic Standpoints for the Description of Behaviour', in A. Smith, ed., *Communication and Culture*, New York: Holt, Rinehart & Winston, pp. 152–163
Rabinow, P., 1977, *Reflections on Fieldwork in Morocco*, Berkeley: University of California Press
Roberts, H., 1981, *Doing Feminist Research*, London: Routledge & Kegan Paul
Robins, K., 1989, 'Reimagined Communities', in *Cultural Studies* 3/2: 10–36
——, 1991, 'Tradition and Translation: National Culture in its Global Context', in J. Corner and S. Harvey, eds, *Enterprise and Heritage: Crosscurrents of National Culture*, London: Routledge, pp. 28–41
Rosaldo, R., 1984, 'Grief and a Head-hunter's Rage: On the Cultural Forces of Emotions', in E. M. Bruner, ed., *Text, Play and Story: The Construction and*

Reconstruction of Self and Society, Washington DC: American Ethnological Society, pp. 178–195

——, 1989, *Culture and Truth: The Remaking of Social Analysis*, Boston: Beacon Press

Roth, P., 1989, 'Ethnography without Tears', in *Current Anthropology* 30/5: 555–570

Rushdie, S., 1991, *Imaginary Homelands*, London: Granta Books

Saari, A., 1985, 'Concepts of Aesthetics and Anti-aesthetics in the Contemporary Hindi Film', in B. Pfleiderer and L. Lutze, eds, *The Hindi Film: Agent and Re-agent of Cultural Change*, New Delhi: Manohar Publications, pp. 16–28

Said, E. W., 1978, *Orientalism: Western Conceptions of the Orient*, London: Routledge & Kegan Paul

——, 1990, 'Narrative and Geography', in *New Left Review*, 180: 81–100

Samani, S., 1993, 'Sunrise Radio: When the Local Goes Global. A Study into the Institutional Perceptions of "the Audience"', B.Sc. dissertation (Combined Social Sciences), Department of Human Sciences, Brunel University, London

Scannel, P., 1988, 'The Communicative Ethos of Broadcasting', unpublished paper given at the the 'Domestic Technologies' Conference at the Centre for Research into Innovation, Culture and Technology (CRICT) at Brunel University, May 1988

——, 1989, 'Public Service Broadcasting and Modern Public Life', in *Media, Culture & Society* 10/1

——, ed., 1991, *Broadcast Talk*, London: Sage

Schiller, H.I., 1969, *Mass Communications and American Empire*, New York: A. M. Kelly

——, 1973, *The Mind Managers*, Boston: Beacon Press

Schlesinger, P., 1987, 'On National Identity: Some Conceptions and Misconceptions Criticised', in *Social Science Information* 26/2: 219–264

Schutz, A., 1964, *Collected Papers*, ed. M. Natanson, The Hague: Nijhoff

Seiter, E., 1990, 'Making Distinctions in TV Audience Research: A Case Study of a Troubling Interview', in *Cultural Studies* 4/1

Seiter, E., H. Borchers, G. Kreutzner and E.-M. Warth, eds, 1989, *Remote Control: TV Audiences and Cultural Power*, London: Routledge

Shibutani, T., 1966, *Improvised News: A Sociological Study of Rumour*, Indiana-polis: Bobbs-Merrill

Silverstone, R., 1989, 'Let Us Then Return to the Murmuring of Everyday Practices: A Note on Michael de Certeau, Television and Everyday Life', in *Theory, Culture and Society* 6: 77–94

——, 1990, 'TV and Everyday Life: Towards an Anthropology of the TV Audience', in M. Ferguson, ed., *Public Communication*, London: Sage, pp. 173–190

——, E. Hirsch and D. Morley, 1991, 'Listening to a Long Conversation: An Ethnographic Approach to the Study of Information and Communication Technologies in the Home', in *Cultural Studies* 5/2

Singh, P., 1985, 'The Role of the Media', in A. Singh, ed., *Punjab in Indian Politics*, Delhi: Ajanta Publications, pp. 155–184

Smith, A., 1981, *The Ethnic Revival*, Cambridge: Cambridge University Press

Smith, S., 1985, 'News and the Dissemination of Fear', in J. Burgess and J. R. Gold, eds, *Geography, the Media and Popular Culture*, London: Croom Helm, pp. 229–253

Smooha, S., 1989, 'Ethnic Groups' and 'Ethnic Relations', in A. Kuper and J. Kuper, eds, *The Social Science Encyclopaedia*, London: Routledge, pp. 267–272

Smythe, D., 1977, 'Communications: Blindspots of Western Marxism', in *Canadian Journal of Political and Social Theory* 1

Sollors, W., 1986, *Beyond Ethnicity: Consent and Descent in American Culture*, New York and Oxford: Oxford University Press

Spencer, J., 1989, 'Anthropology as a Kind of Writing', in *Man* 23

Spivak, G., 1988, 'Can the Subaltern Speak?', in C. Nelson and L. Grossberg, eds, *Marxism and the Interpretation of Cultures*, Urbana: University of Illinois Press

Sreberny-Mohammedi, A., 1991, 'The Global and the Local in International Communications', in J. Curran and M. Gurevitch, eds, *Mass Media and Society*, London, New York and Melbourne: Edward Arnold

Stenhouse, L., ed., 1980, *Curriculum Research and Development in Action*, London: Heinemann Education

Thomas, R., 1985, 'Indian Cinema: Pleasures and Popularity', in *Screen* 26/3–4: 116–132

Thompson, J., 1990, *Ideology and Modern Culture*, Cambridge: Polity

Thompson, K., 1992, *Social Pluralism and Post-modernity*, in S. Hall, D. Held and T. McGrew, eds, *Modernity and Its Futures*, Cambridge: Polity: 221–272

Thorne, B., 1983, 'Language, Gender and Society: A Second Decade of Research', in B. Thorne, C. Kramarae and N. Henley, eds, *Language, Gender and Society*, Rowley, MA.: Newbury

Turner, V., 1966, 'Colour Classification in Ndembu Ritual', in M. Banton, ed., *Anthropological Approaches to the Study of Religion*, London: Tavistock, pp. 47–83

Wallman, S., 1984, *Eight London Households*, London and New York: Tavistock

Warren, C. A. B. and P. K. Ramussen, 1977, 'Sex and Gender in Field Research', in *Urban Life* 6/3: 349–369

Webster, D., 1988, *Looka Yonder: The Imaginary America of Populist Culture*, London: Comedia/Routledge

——, 1989, 'Cocacolonisation and National Cultures', in *Over Here* 9/2

West, R., 1991, 'The Same or Different? Cultural Patterns in an "Asian" Peer Culture: A Quantitative Analysis of a Survey of Southall Youth', unpublished B.Sc. dissertation, Department of Human Sciences, Brunel University

Williams, R., 1965, *The Long Revolution*, Harmondsworth: Penguin

——, 1971, *Culture and Society*, Harmondsworth: Penguin

——, 1975, *Television: Technology and Cultural Form*, London: Fontana

——, 1980, 'Advertising: the Magic System', in R. Williams, ed., *Problems in Materialism and Culture: Selected Essays*, London: Routledge

——, 1981, *Culture*, London: Fontana

——, 1989, *Raymond Williams On TV: Selected Writings*, ed. A. O'Connor, London and New York: Routledge

Williamson, J., 1988, 'Two Kinds of Otherness', in K. Mercer, ed., *Black Film, British Cinema*, London: BFI

——, 1993, 'A World of Difference: The Passion of Remembrance' [1986], in *Deadline at Dawn: Film Criticism 1980–90*, London: Marion Boyars, pp. 116–118

Willis, P., 1977, *Learning to Labour: How Working Class Kids Get Working Class Jobs*, London: Saxon House

——, 1980, 'Notes on Method', in S. Hall *et al.*, eds, *Culture, Media, Language*, London: Hutchinson

——, 1990, *Common Culture*, Oxford: Oxford University Press

Wilson, C. and F. Gutierrez, 1985, *Minorities and Media: Diversity and the End of Mass Communications*, Newbury Park, CA: Sage

Woods, P., 1979, *The Divided School*, London: Routledge & Kegan Paul

Woolgar, S., 1988, *Knowledge and Reflexivity*, London: Sage

Wright, R., 1965, *The Outsider*, New York: Harper and Row

Wright-Mills, C., 1959, *The Sociological Imagination*, Oxford: Oxford University Press

Yates, M., 1990, 'Interpreting Life Texts and Negotiating Life Courses: Youth, Ethnicity and Culture', in P. Spencer, ed., *Anthropology and the Riddle of the Sphinx*, London: Routledge, pp. 76–89

Index

The South East Essex
College of Arts & Technology
Carnarvon Road Southend on Sea Essex SS2 6LS
Tel: Southend (0702) 220400   Fax: Southend (0702) 432320